THE GREAT ROGUE

Also by PAUL LEWIS

QUEEN OF THE PLAZA

LADY OF FRANCE

QUEEN OF CAPRICE

THE GENTLE FURY

THE NELSON TOUCH

THE GREAT ROGUE

A Biography of Captain John Smith

by PAUL LEWIS

Noel B. Gerson

DAVID McKAY COMPANY, INC.

New York

THE GREAT ROGUE

Library of Congress Catalog Card Number: 66-19261

MANUFACTURED IN THE UNITED STATES OF AMERICA

VAN REES PRESS • NEW YORK

For

Charles N. Heckelmann

So vast are the forests of the New World, so broad and swift her mighty rivers, so towering her mountains and so great her riches that one who has cast anchor in her bays and lived in her wilderness is tempted to exaggerate her glories. But man is dwarfed by this virgin land, and the mind of the explorer is numbed; so one speaks the truth, as best one is able.

—Captain John Smith
(1630)

Contents

THE GREAT ROGUE

I

Hero, Scoundrel — or Both?

CAPTAIN JOHN SMITH HAD NO need of his sometimes military, sometimes naval, title to make him stand apart from all other bearers of the most common of English names. He was extraordinary, if not unique, and although he appreciated his own talents and achievements, it was his curse to be haunted by a lifelong fear that others failed to recognize his worth. This quirk of character was shared, oddly enough, by others who changed the maps of the earth in the fifteenth to seventeenth centuries, among them Columbus and Cabot, Raleigh and Smith's good friend, Henry Hudson.

A thirst for fame, apparently, was essential in the makeup of those men who sailed unknown seas and trudged through uncharted wilderness. Never in the field of human exploration was so much owed by so many to so few, to paraphrase a renowned Englishman of a later age, and rarely has any group been more eager to win the world's applause. John Smith's yearning for glory was greater than that of his colleagues in the select band; in fact, it was insatiable, and clouded the very image he tried so desperately to create.

The most charming and romantic myth in American history conceals and distorts the figure of a great man who may have been an even greater rogue. Behind the legend of Pocahontas, the twelve-year-old Indian maiden who allegedly braved the terrible wrath of her powerful father to save the life of an intrepid adventurer, is hidden the genius whose accomplishments would have spoken for themselves if he hadn't been tempted to tamper with the record.

Rarely have the ironies of poetic injustice been more cruel, for John Smith had already won a well-deserved, permanent niche in history as an explorer, cartographer, author, and warrior when his imagination and facile pen made him his own worst enemy.

John Smith was one of those remarkable Renaissance men who did most things well and some superbly. Perhaps his greatest gift was his insatiable curiosity, which led him to discover parts of Virginia and Chesapeake Bay previously unknown, New England and its Cape Cod, both of which he named, and took him on travels through Europe to Russia, the Ottoman Empire, and the interior of North Africa, parts of the world as far removed from his native England as the virgin forests of North America.

He was an author of distinction who wrote eight books about his many journeys, all of them popular, successful, and for many years regarded as authoritative in the English-speaking nations. Thousands crossed the Atlantic to settle in the New World after reading his books, and few men, if any, of his own or any other period contributed as much to the colonization of North America. He directly influenced the Pilgrims who set up their experiment in democracy at Plymouth, and translations of his work were responsible for an increase in transatlantic travel from France, the German principalities, and Holland.

Smith was a talented cartographer, and although he had no formal training as a map maker, his charts and maps of the American coastline from Newfoundland and Nova Scotia to the Carolinas were astonishingly accurate. Himself helped by the unlucky admiral, Sir Walter Raleigh, Smith passed on his knowledge of America to Henry Hudson, who relied on the maps when he discovered the great river to which a later generation would give his name.

Above all, John Smith was a tireless and enthusiastic propagandist whose unceasing labors over a quarter of a century ensured that Englishmen would inhabit the wilderness he had been so instrumental in discovering, exploring, and settling. First he proved through his own efforts at Jamestown, in Virginia, that permanent colonization of the wilderness was feasible. Then he spent the rest of his life persuading others to expand the boundaries of his conquests.

But he was the victim of his own weaknesses, and even in an age when men erred with gusto, he had too great a zest for life, too overpowering an ambition. He was too successful for his own good as a leader of men, a soldier, sailor, navigator—and lover. Two self-portraits, pen-and-ink sketches that decorated his maps of Chesapeake Bay and New England, indicate that he was an exceptionally handsome man with dark, magnetic eyes, a neatly trimmed, Satanic beard, and ruggedly attractive features. He may not have been quite as appealing as he saw himself, but he couldn't have missed the mark by much. Men of every station were drawn to him, and scores of women, from princesses to commoners, relished his practice of the arts of seduction.

John Smith's greatest fault was his inability to write about himself with the honesty and candor he employed in his discussions of others. He was so anxious to create a good impression of himself that he couldn't help embellishing, embroidering, and polishing his own exploits. At times he merely exaggerated. When it suited his purposes, he lied magnificently, with a straight face. So indefatigable was he in painting a larger-than-life self-portrait that he destroyed his credit with his fellow countrymen.

Had Smith been satisfied to let the facts of his adventures speak for themselves, he might have won a larger share of the immortality he craved. The real achievement of a young man fighting his way across Europe and Islam already guaranteed him an illustrious reputation, but his own accounts of his career were so glowing they became literary concoctions his compatriots were unable to digest.

Even his title, "Captain," caused people to doubt his word, in part because he had never held such a rank in the service of his own King, James I. But his versatility was also responsible for the lifted eyebrows, because he referred to himself sometimes as a ship's master and sometimes as the head of a military company. His claims happened to be true, but it was difficult for people to believe that one man could have been a successful professional soldier and the captain of his own seagoing vessel.

Oddly enough, there were far grander titles Smith could have used without causing even a ripple of skepticism. He could have called himself President of Virginia, a post to which he had been elected. He also held a warrant, personally signed by King James, naming him Grand Admiral of New England and the Fishing Banks. Why he continued to refer to himself as Captain John Smith to the end of his days is an inexplicable mystery.

The supreme irony of Smith's desire for fame is that his name has become permanently intertwined with that of Pocahontas, and his other, more important, deeds have been partially obscured. But, as will be seen in a later chapter, the fault was his own. His mistresses, including the woman with whom he was living when he died at the age of fifty-two after spending his whole life as a bachelor, were, without exception, blondes. Pocahontas, eighteen years his junior, was a full-blooded Chickahominy Indian, and therefore, of course, a brunette. She and Smith were known to have met on only one occasion after she reached adulthood, and at that time she was a respectable married woman, very much in love with her husband.

There is reason to question whether they ever actually came face to face during her childhood, and the romantic legend that links their names together may have been a legend created by Smith himself for a specific purpose. He would have been humiliated and angry, had he known that future generations would forget his accomplishments and remember him chiefly as the man whose life was supposedly saved by a charming and courageous little Indian girl.

It is true, of course, that during Smith's sojourn in Virginia he had many dealings with Pocahontas' father, Powhatan, sachem of the Chickahominy tribe and leader of a loose confederation of Indian nations. But it was the custom of the savages to conceal their squaws and squaw-children when visited by strangers they didn't trust. It may be that Smith caught his first real glimpse of Pocahontas when, as Mrs. John Rolfe, she made a journey to England in 1616–17, and created a sensation at the court of King James as well as in intellectual and religious circles.

Such a paradoxical situation would be typical of John Smith's life, which was filled with contradictions. He liked to portray himself as benign, but was actually one of the most ferocious, hot-tempered men of his time, and was always involved in one or more protracted feuds. He boasted of his diplomatic discretion, but recklessly and unnecessarily jeopardized his own life and fortune, as well as the future of the colonizing company that meant so much to him, when he blatantly advertised his loyalty to Sir Walter Raleigh during the great Admiral's confinement in the Tower of London on charges of treason.

The settlement of the Pilgrims at Plymouth, whose story has overshadowed that of the Jamestown colony through the centuries, was a direct outgrowth of Smith's own explorations and the accounts he subsequently wrote. Only a few students of seventeenth-century Americana realize that Smith came close to doubling his renown. He had planned to sail on the *Mayflower,* but "missed the boat" at the last minute. His personality was so overwhelming and his habit of assuming absolute command so deeply ingrained that the leaders of the Separatist brethren, among them John Carver, William Brewster, and William Bradford, broke off negotiations with him a short time before they set sail for the New World and instead hired Captain Miles Standish.

Perhaps it is as well that Smith did not take part in the Pilgrim experiment. Their ways were not his. They liked an occasional mug of small beer to wash down their meat, but he preferred stronger spirits. His colorful language made pious men shudder, and in his relations with women he was, more often than not, a cad, even in his dealings with the two young ladies he professed to love in a lifetime devoted to the pursuit of romance.

It is paradoxical, too, that Smith whetted the appetites of thousands by writing of the gold and silver, diamonds and emeralds, to be found in the New World. But such talk, as he well realized, was just propaganda. In his negotiations with prospective financial supporters of overseas settlements, he clearly and repeatedly indicated that he knew the real wealth of America to be her rich soil, her vast forests, the pelts of fur-bearing animals, and seas teeming with fish.

It may be that money, as such, meant little to him, for his

own financial situation became increasingly precarious as he grew more famous. The more he contributed to other men's knowledge of America, the less he himself earned from investments in colonizing companies. Hardheaded and unscrupulous as an adventurer, he allowed himself to be cheated and fooled by men who, as a result of his efforts, became enormously wealthy. At the time of his death, he was a near-bankrupt.

As he once confessed to Prince Henry, who died before he could succeed his father on the throne, "I did not take up the habit of smoking a pipe until long after I had sold at a loss the acres on whose soil grows the finest tobacco to be found in this world."

Many of his contemporaries wrongly believed him wealthy. His enemies worked ceaselessly during his lifetime and for years thereafter to blacken his reputation, claiming he spent money prodigally on women. Yet the fragments of records that have survived the centuries indicate the contrary. Great ladies were pleased to support him in style for the duration of their fleeting affairs with him, and his other blondes were content to live frugally with him. Apparently they were drawn to him by love alone.

One of the most perplexing twists of fate is that John Smith should have been all but forgotten, even while he still lived, by virtually everyone except those who hated him. Men who did far less for England were knighted, and some were given lucrative estates and seats in the House of Lords. Only once was Smith recognized by the Crown. It was his misfortune that the rank of Admiral of New England was honorary. Had his one royal friend lived to become Henry IX, he might have reaped a more rewarding harvest.

But lugubrious, lantern-jawed James I, the "wisest fool in Christendom," preferred men who conducted their affairs discreetly to those who were indifferent to their moral reputations.

And it was Smith's further misfortune to become an intimate of Henry's at a time when the Prince was in disfavor with his father. James had a long memory, as did the equally complex Charles I. In the last decade of Smith's life, at a time when the Treasury was beginning to enjoy the revenues of colonial expansion, the explorer was rarely seen at Whitehall and never invited to the King's summer residence, Hampton Court.

Everyone interested in the New World owned well-thumbed copies of all John Smith's books, yet he was never accepted by the academicians at Oxford and Cambridge, where men of far fewer accomplishments were entertained and invited to deliver lectures. Smith was condemned because he tried too hard to simulate the role of a gentleman, and the snobbish dons, who were far more careful of the company they kept than were the nobility, closed their doors to him. Only Richard Hakluyt, the greatest geographer of the age and Smith's close associate in the formation of the London Company, the organization that promoted the Jamestown colony, appreciated his worth. In this relationship, too, Smith's luck was bad. Hakluyt, who may have helped him learn the science of map making, died in 1616, just at the period when his protégé's troubles were beginning. Had Smith's mentor lived a few years longer, he might have had a restraining influence on the flamboyant books that, in spite of their fascinating wealth of accurate detail, were so self-laudatory that readers snickered at the author.

Hakluyt was buried with great ceremony at Westminster Abbey. Sir Walter Raleigh was executed—an act that outraged a nation, made him a martyr, and guaranteed his reputation. Henry Hudson was abandoned by his mutinous crew on the shore of the great bay that bears his name, and the sensation that was created when the surviving mutineers returned to England assured Hudson's immortality, forced the Crown to give his widow a government post, and drew the attention of even the most ignorant to the great explorer's exploits.

When John Smith's days on earth were ended, only a small handful of people, among them his mistress of the moment, attended his funeral in his parish church, St. Sepulchre, in London, where he was buried in a modest tomb beneath the choir stall. Even that inconspicuous resting place was only temporary, however, as the church was destroyed in the Great Fire that burned so much of the city to the ground thirty-five years later.

It was John Smith's unhappy fate, after living an almost incredibly adventurous life, to die an ordinary death in a rumpled bed he shared with the buxom young blonde who happened to be living in his cheap lodgings with him. So many others expired under similar circumstances that the event passed unnoticed, and he had no champions to draw attention to his achievements.

Worst of all, the public had stopped reading his books. Other articulate men were traveling to the New World now, and were publishing their versions of living conditions there, so people were no longer interested in the adventures of someone who had spent more than ten years at home.

Royalties continued to accumulate at a modest rate for another fifteen years, however, and eventually John Smith's name was in the news again, briefly, when his sister and brother, his only survivors, battled vituperatively in court over his earnings. Each claimed to be the sole beneficiary named in his will, but no such document was produced for the edification of the court, and the presiding magistrate solved the dilemma by adding insult to injury and assigning the royalties to the Crown. Charles I was fighting for his throne and life in the Civil War, and London was in the hands of his enemies at the time, so Oliver Cromwell put the finishing touches of irony on John Smith's story by appropriating the money for the use of his Roundheads.

Smith's ghost must have shuddered as he watched sober Puritans spend his royalties. That ghost must have been pained, too, to see the Captain's reputation decline and almost vanish. But Smith always had a sense of humor, so it is reasonable to assume that the ghost was also capable of enjoying a hearty laugh.

If so, the astral shade has been chuckling merrily for three and one-third centuries. Smith's most enduring monument was the tale he invented about the little Indian princess who had saved the life of a doughty warrior by risking her own. The story has had a self-perpetuating appeal, which is a tribute to John Smith's creative powers of imagination. And there was nothing the dashing Captain enjoyed as much as hoodwinking people eager to be deceived.

The influences that made this extraordinary man a combination hero and rogue were unusual, although for the better part of his life no one suspected he was made of uncommon clay. Certainly it never occurred to his ambitious father or sweet mother that their eldest son and heir was a genius who would spend years trying, by fair means and questionable, to win the world's recognition and approval of his unique accomplishments.

II

Great Armadas and Small Boys

STATUS WAS IMPORTANT TO George Smith of Willoughby, Lincolnshire. Lord Willoughby de Eresby had a half-dozen tenant farmers, and George Smith alone was different. For one thing, he owned several large parcels of pastureland and orchards adjoining the property he rented from his lordship, which made him a freeholder of consequence. He was also a member of the gentry, with a coat of arms passed down to him through at least five generations by the Smiths of Crudley, in Lancashire.

He and his wife, Alice, were the only tenants invited regularly to the Willoughby manor for Sunday suppers, and the Willoughbys condescended to break bread with no one in the neighborhood but the Smiths. This, George believed, was as it should be. Ambitious and hard-working, he was ever eager to improve his family's place in a caste-conscious world.

No one knows what, if anything, Alice may have thought. Fifteen years younger than her husband, she was a blonde from Yorkshire, where most women were brunettes. Fair-skinned and lovely, she was spoiled by her husband and worshipped by her two sons. "Francis and I," wrote her elder son, John, in his own middle age, "thought her the most gloriously beautiful of all God's creatures. I think so still."

John Smith was born on the second day of January, 1579, in his parents' comfortable house, and according to the parish register, was baptized seven days later, with Lord Willoughby standing up as his godfather.

By the age of four, the boy was being assigned chores of his own on the farm and had already been taught his alphabet by his father, from whom he inherited a boundless ambition and the conviction, unusual in an era when middle-class beliefs had not yet been articulated, that success and happiness had to be earned. Farm life and his own pets, including three dogs, a cat, and two goats, taught him fearlessness. His heritage from his mother was more subtle, and he spent the whole of his adult life seeking a woman in her image. Lord and Lady Willoughby were fond of John, and his lordship, impressed by the boy's quick mind, opened his library to him.

At the age of six or seven, John was sent to the grammar school at nearby Alford, a few miles to the north, commuting on a pony his father bought him. He was taught English reading and grammar, Latin and arithmetic and Greek, and failure to respond correctly to the schoolmaster's questions was punished by caning. There was no reward for accuracy.

Lord Willoughby's second son was his close friend and classmate, and together they pored over the books in the library of the manor house. The boys had been born into a world changing more rapidly in a few years than it had in centuries, and it was an exciting time to be alive. Sir Francis Drake had sailed around the world, changing man's concepts of geography and arousing exciting though still dimly perceived visions of the future. Francis Bacon and other great scholars were extending intellectual frontiers, and everywhere the old philosophies, religions, and sciences were being questioned, tested, and discarded.

England was in a ferment of nationalistic fervor under Queen Elizabeth I, who shared her subjects' determination to make the nation a great and respected power. Poets and playwrights flourished, among them one William Shakespeare, and although everyone still paid lip service to the old codes of chivalry and honor, a new creed was emerging: the world belonged to the strong.

John was closer to the Willoughbys than to his own kin, and was encouraged in his associations by his father. In later years John observed that his brother Francis was "an honest fellow, but a dullard." He thought his sister, Alice, "pretty enough, but dark of hair." He remained dutifully fond of her until the day of his death, but they were never close; even within the family circle, brunettes did not appeal to him.

When John was nine years old, two events of supreme importance influenced his life. He and the younger Willoughby boy were transferred to a grammar school at the town of Louth, where the curriculum was more difficult than that at Alford. The class was small, the discipline unusually strict—and John Smith was the only commoner enrolled there. All the other pupils were the sons of nobles, and he not only had to fight for social acceptance, but was forced to prove himself their intellectual peer.

In that same year, King Philip II of Spain, increasingly annoyed by England's growing power, decided to put the upstart island nation in its place. He began to gather a mighty fleet, but three times his plans were interrupted by Drake, who made lightning raids on Spanish cities and destroyed heavily armed squadrons of ships at sea. At last, in midsummer, a vast armada appeared in the English Channel, and the strongest naval power on earth was poised for a fatal blow.

The English defended themselves with a courage and skill

that became legendary even in their own time. The ramshackle fleet commanded by Lord Howard inflicted severe punishment on the foe, and if Drake and Sir John Hawkins performed only a fraction of the feats attributed to them, they won immortality. Even the weather turned against the Spaniards. A great storm blew up, the English vessels took shelter in their native harbors, and the remnants of Philip's armada were scattered.

England rejoiced, and no one went wilder than fiercely patriotic, highly imaginative boys of nine. "It became my urgent desire," Smith wrote in later life, "to make myself like Sir Francis Drake in all things, great and small."

In the same climactic summer of 1588 he had his first experience as a seaman. He and the Willoughby boys went to the North Sea, about six miles from their homes, and there built themselves a "boat." Inasmuch as they spent only a short time at their task, completing the project within a few hours of the time they started, their craft could have been little more than a crude raft.

Eager to emulate their heroes, they cast off. It is significant that John was the "master" of the raft, even though outranked by his companions, the elder of whom, heir to the Willoughby title, was two years his senior. The future history of America was in the balance at that moment, but fortunately a fishing boat happened to put into the cove from which the boys were launching their untrustworthy vessel.

They were hauled onto the boat, recognized, and delivered to their parents. Smith, in writing of the incident, made no mention of the punishment that was meted out, but did observe, casually, that neither he nor the Willoughby boys could swim.

Apparently Lord Willoughby succeeded in beating romantic notions out of his boys' minds, but John Smith continued to dream of great adventure. His imagination was fired anew in 1595 when word reached England that a dashing trio of admirals, Howard, Raleigh, and Essex, had successfully conducted the most daring raid in English history, sailing into the harbor of Cadiz and sinking or burning more than fifty new galleons that were to have been the nucleus of a new Spanish armada. What they had accomplished, the adolescent John Smith decided, he could do, too.

He was now sixteen, and his formal education had come to an end, since only real scholars with a thirst for learning went on to Oxford or Cambridge. He was ready to apply for a commission in the new, permanent Royal Navy that Queen Elizabeth had established, and apparently it did not occur to him that he had no training for an officer's rank.

He made the mistake of mentioning his dream at the family supper table, and his father promptly apprenticed him to Thomas Sendall, "the greatest merchant of all those parts." Young John, duly chastised, meekly went off to the town of Lynn, where he was given a room in Sendall's comfortable home.

His future was assured, and his parents had reason to feel proud of him. Thanks to his own school record and Lord Willoughby's influence, he had been given a rare opportunity. Sendall had no sons of his own, and in time John could expect to rise to a partnership. He could look forward to a life of prosperity, comfort, and dignity—but there was nothing he wanted less.

He accepted the apprenticeship for private reasons that he kept to himself. Merchants, including Sendall, were engaged in a thriving foreign trade, and the travel-hungry boy imagined himself being sent abroad to act as Sendall's agent in buying French silks, Dutch leather, and German ironware, all popular in England. He was quickly disillusioned. Sendall dealt with agents in Paris, Amsterdam, and the German principalities, and an apprentice was expected to sit on a stool all day, writing letters and adding columns of figures.

John thought of running away, but his father's unexpected death early in 1596 abruptly changed his plans. John inherited seven acres of pastureland, three fine orchards, and the bulk of his father's livestock. Francis, as the younger son, had to be content with the rent-producing houses in Louth. The bulk of George Smith's property went to his widow for her lifetime, after which it was to pass into John's hands. Daughter Alice received bequests of cash and personal mementos.

Lord Willoughby was named executor of the estate and guardian of the Smith children until they came of age, so John now came under Willoughby's authority as well as Sendall's, but believed he could handle both men more easily than he had been able to sway his father. He sold his livestock to his lordship, giving half the proceeds to his mother as a gift and secretly putting aside the rest as a nest egg.

The elder of the Willoughby boys was at Orléans, France, completing his education, and the younger planned to visit him for six weeks in the spring. The persuasive John obtained permission from Lord Willoughby and Sendall to go, too, and talked his guardian into giving him an additional ten pounds in silver out of his inheritance.

The two boys went to London and were so fascinated by the brawling, bustling city they remained for a week, instead of sailing for Boulogne on a packet boat within twenty-four hours of their arrival, as they had been instructed. Their week in London was hectic—and educational.

The English capital, just beginning to emerge from the provincial isolation that had blanketed the nation itself for generations, was no glamorous world capital. In no way could it compete with Paris, where magnificent new palaces and public buildings were dazzling natives and foreigners alike. Nor was London in a class with Madrid, the seat of a mighty empire. It lacked the fabled ruins of Rome and Athens, the worldliness of Amsterdam, and the cozy, almost intimate grandeur of Vienna.

Queen Elizabeth still entertained a distrust of the Scots that she had felt all her life, and although her heir was James of Scotland, virtually no one ever crossed the border separating the two countries. At most, there were seventy-five uncomfortable Scotsmen in London. The Welsh didn't feel at home there, either, and preferred to remain in their own hills. Continental merchants had not yet begun to visit England in appreciable numbers, so few foreign languages were heard on the streets.

Several decades would pass before Inigo Jones would enlarge and beautify Whitehall Palace and build Covent Garden. And it would be another century before Sir Christopher Wren erected St. Paul's Cathedral.

But country bumpkins from Yorkshire were stunned by what they thought to be the magnificence of the city. They were awed by Westminster Abbey and spent a half-day gaping at the grim and ancient castle, the Tower. St. James's Palace, which had been rebuilt by Henry VIII, was the most impressive residence they had ever seen.

Most streets were cobbled, in itself a wonder. The boys were young enough and nimble enough to walk over and around the mounds of garbage that householders habitually threw into the gutters. There were theaters everywhere, and the citizens stomped, cheered, and made their likes and dislikes known in no uncertain terms. Londoners enjoyed eating and drinking well, and scores of taverns were scattered through the city, catering to every purse.

Traffic, of course, was a hazard. Young gallants rode their mounts at full tilt through the narrow streets, scattering pedestrians and upsetting the carts of wine sellers, chestnut vendors, and old women who offered passersby chunks of hot, savory stewed meat for a farthing.

Ladies and gentlemen often went about their business in sedan chairs carried on the shoulders of liveried servants, and, because the danger of assault by footpads and other ruffians was ever-present, most of them were also attended by burly guards who carried stout staffs with weighted metal ends.

John drank in more than the sights. For the first and last time in his life, he consumed strong spirits to excess. He became deathly ill, and found his face, arms, and torso covered with an ugly rash. A poultice of flour and beef blood restored his appearance to normal. However, he had learned that liquor was not for him. Cautious experiments quickly taught him that the more he drank, he more severe became his rash. What another age would call an allergy kept him relatively sober for life.

But other delights of the flesh had a less harmful effect on him. He lost five shillings on a wager throwing dice, but found the experience exhilarating. It was his first gaming venture, but he felt at home immediately, his instincts being those of the born gambler. For the next three and one-half decades, he cheerfully and repeatedly risked his life, vast sums of money belonging to others, and his own small fortune, in adventures that were, in the ultimate sense, games of chance played with men and ships on the high seas and a new continent.

Before the evening ended, John formed another lifelong habit, too. Somewhere in London's bawdy maze of bear pits, taverns, and theaters he found a female companion; in all justice to both of them, it might be more accurate to say that she found him. There were few opportunities in Lincolnshire for a budding gentleman to roister, and he was remarkably innocent, a condition which the lady of the evening quickly remedied.

"I was initiated into Aphrodite's mysteries that night," he wrote in his fiftieth year, "and my memories of the lass are still fresh. She was very fair, and I thought her dewy-sweet, a notion which I would needs hasten to rectify were I now to meet her like again." It is scarcely surprising that he was initiated in the rites of manhood by a blonde and for the next thirty-five years seldom looked at any other type.

He would have lingered in the city indefinitely, but young Willoughby finally persuaded him to leave, and they took passage on a small Channel packet boat of four tons that was supposed to discharge them at Boulogne but, for unexplained reasons, carried them farther down the French coast to St.-Valéry-sur-Somme. John, who had dreamed of emulating Sir Francis Drake, became violently seasick and spent most of the two-and-one-half-day voyage in his hammock below deck.

When the vessel dropped anchor, however, the knowledge that he was about to stand on foreign soil revived him, and he raced ashore, leaving his saddlebags behind in his haste. Henry Willoughby brought them to him, and took charge of the expedition, renting two post-horses in the village.

Because they were already a week late for their meeting with nineteen-year-old Sir Thomas Willoughby, they avoided temptation and made a detour around Paris. But, when they arrived at Orléans, Sir Thomas's weary tutor told them the heir to the Willoughby title had grown tired of waiting and had gone off to Paris. They followed.

Sixteenth-century Paris was the most cosmopolitan city in Europe. It boasted more cobbled streets than any other great population center, and only in the sprawling slum districts was garbage thrown into the gutters. The packs of wild dogs that lived on this refuse had been reduced in recent years, thanks to King Henry's constabulary. The King, mindful of his country's glory—and his own—was adding a new wing to the Louvre, expanding the Tuileries and building the Palais Royal and Hôtel de Ville. There were countless inns where the food was excellent, and taverns for every purse.

The city boasted even more theaters than London, and almost as many highborn clergymen as Rome. There were large private parks within the town walls, some stocked with game and protected by watchmen, and a few were actually thrown open to the public on special occasions. The smells of garlic, cheap wines, and onions were omnipresent in the poorer sections; bread bakers were as highly regarded as nobles; and bishops walked unattended—but carried loaded pistols to frighten away footpads.

Beauty was a mania, and the women, the architecture, the marble statues displayed in the open, and the artful arrangement of food served in the inns, reflected the city's tastes. The cathedral of Notre Dame was dazzling, but the art treasures in a dozen other churches were even more impressive.

The impact of Paris dazed John Smith, confusing and delighting him as much as it has overcome countless thousands of other Anglo-Saxons by its charms in succeeding centuries. In writing of the experience, he could only say that one day melted into the next, and soon his holiday of six weeks was drawing to an end.

Young and energetic, his pockets heavy with more money than he had ever before carried, John spent his mornings seeing the sights of the city, his afternoons with Sir Thomas's sophisticated friends, dining and settling the world's problems, and his evenings with an endless succession of blondes.

Among those he met in Paris was an ingratiating Scotsman named David Hume, who was short of funds but, he intimated, well-connected at the royal court in Edinburgh. At Hume's sly suggestion, they struck a "bargain," and many years later John was still rueful when he recalled how he had been cheated.

He gave Hume the better part of his funds, and in return received letters of introduction to Hume's friends in Edinburgh, who, the Scotsman assured him, would obtain a commission for him in the Royal Highland Guards regiment. These gentlemen were so influential, Hume declared, that it would be no problem to obtain a position for the young Englishman in the honor company assigned to guard the person of King James VI, son of the late Mary, Queen of Scots—the man who would eventually succeed Elizabeth, his mother's executioner, as James I of England.

Hume stressed the urgent need for secrecy, however. There was keen competition for important posts, he said, and his friends could work effectively only if no one knew their intentions. The eager John Smith, seeing himself launched on a quick and easy path to glory and power, faithfully promised to say nothing to anyone.

When he and Henry Willoughby started out on their return journey to England, however, he found the temptation to break his word irresistible. Finally, at Rouen, he told his childhood friend he was not going back to Lincolnshire and his apprenticeship.

The incredulous Henry listened to his story, read the letters, and saw through the flimsy scheme. The communications, he told the humiliated and heartbroken John, were addressed to fictitious persons in Edinburgh. Even had they been real people, Hume's promises were worthless. King James lived in constant dread of assassination at the hands of killers hired by Elizabeth, and was surrounded day and night by Scottish clan chieftains he and his advisers knew to be fanatically devoted to his person. Under no circumstances would any Englishman be admitted to his court, much less commissioned in his Guards regiment and assigned to a post of responsibility in the honor company.

Not only had John been swindled, but his purse was almost empty, and his dream had become a nightmare. He tried to take stock of his situation, and one hard fact stood out above all others. If he went back to Lynn and resumed his apprenticeship with Sendall, it would be virtually impossible for him to obtain another leave of absence before his apprenticeship ended. His father's death had created unique circumstances, but even the most kindhearted of employers would not grant him another holiday. Therefore, by the time he ended his term of service and was given a journeyman's status in Sendall's firm, he would be too old, too settled in his ways, to seek the adventure he craved.

That night, while Henry Willoughby slept, John Smith paced the empty streets of Rouen. He had a decision to make and knew there could be no turning back if he made up his mind to go ahead with a wild plan that had occurred to him in his desperate attempt to gain his goal. A short time before dawn, he returned to his lodgings and wrote letters to his mother, Lord Willoughby, and Sendall.

At breakfast he broke his startling news to Henry. He was not returning to Lincolnshire, he said, but intended to enlist in the French army as a volunteer. Henry tried to dissuade him, but John wouldn't listen to a voice of reason, and his friend was forced to resume the journey alone, carrying the three letters.

John told his mother that he had no choice and begged her for understanding and love. He asked Lord Willoughby to think well of him and look after his inheritance. The note to Sendall was brief, almost curt. "My mind and body," he declared, "are not suited for the life you offer, and the humours in my blood cry out for a more active life, so I crave your indulgence in relieving me of the obligations undertaken with you on my behalf."

Alone in a strange land, John recklessly spent most of his remaining funds on a rented post-horse and set out for the headquarters of the French army in the hilly countryside a few miles from Le Havre. An adult counselor would have told the youth that his idea was mad. The army of King Henry IV, which had fought on his behalf for ten years as he slowly unified his nation, was the best in Christendom. Already called Henry the Great by his foes as well as by his followers, the brilliant ruler was a perfectionist who had built an élite corps of professional soldiers that was unique in Europe. Henry's troops had proved themselves repeatedly in battle against Spaniards, fellow Frenchmen and German mercenaries.

Certainly there was no opening in the ranks of this hard-bitten corps for an amateur, and John Smith knew literally nothing of war. He had taken fencing lessons with the Willoughby boys, but knew only the routine fundamentals of swordplay. He could not qualify as a cavalryman, although he had been familiar with horses since early childhood, and it is doubtful that he had ever seen, much less fired, a cannon.

He had no special skills in the arts of war that Henry and his generals appreciated—siege breaking, storming castles, or planting charges of explosives beneath the walls of enemy towns. The troops of Henry's arch-foe, Philip II of Spain, were also professionals, and the French had learned that it was costly to send recruits into the field against men who knew every trick of war.

Worst of all, John knew only a few words of French, which he had picked up in the month he had spent in the country. He was totally lacking in experience, with nothing to offer but his body.

A recruiting sergeant in leather breeches and rusty armor turned him away, but John stubbornly pretended to misunderstand the man's orders to leave, and insisted on an interview with an officer. Soldiers, shabby in worn, patched clothing and chain mail with broken links, lounging in the vicinity of the sergeant's tent, were amused by the youngster's aggressive manner and teased him, hoping to egg him into starting a fight. But John was cautious as well as courageous, a quality he would demonstrate throughout his life. He realized that one youth, still in his teens and armed only with a light sword and an unloaded pistol, would not be able to defend himself adequately against a dozen or more armored ruffians who carried pikes and halberds, vicious weapons that were combination spears and battle-axes.

He refused to rise to the bait. The scene was witnessed by an English-speaking French captain, who was impressed by the lad's coolness under pressure and took pity on him. There was no place in the French army for a recruit, the officer told John, but suggested that he try one of the mercenary companies at the opposite side of the bivouac.

John accepted the suggestion because he had no choice. The mercenary soldier was considered a rogue, a thief, and a scoundrel by gentlemen, but a youth whose purse was almost empty was in no position to pick and choose. If he failed to find employment immediately, he would be reduced to begging in the streets or stowing away on a ship bound for England—and admitting complete defeat.

III

The Apprentice Rogue

CAPTAIN JOSEPH DUXBURY was a renegade Englishman who had spent five years in the service of Henry IV and had little to show for his efforts except a magnificent stallion, a formidable arsenal of personal weapons, and a silver suit of armor he had stolen from the body of a dead foe on the battlefield. His face and body were scarred, and he had learned that a mercenary commander, seldom paid in cash by the kings and great nobles who hired him, earned his living and paid his troops in loot taken from conquered enemies and helpless civilians.

The youngest son of a baron, thirty-year-old blond Duxbury had lost his inheritance at gaming tables in London, and had been forced to flee England in order to escape the almost certain fate of death by starvation and disease in a debtors' prison. His company, which numbered one hundred men when at full strength, was made up of kindred spirits from many lands. Fellow Englishmen made up the hard core of his band, and others in the ranks included Scotsmen and discredited Irish gentry, Danes, a few sullen Germans, and several Spanish deserters. His second-in-command, a dark, taciturn man with a smashed nose who called himself Luis de Toledo, had risen from this dishonorable group.

Duxbury was always glad to welcome another English-speaking recruit, but the company had its own standards, and applicants were submitted to a test administered by Lieutenant de Toledo. John Smith was asked to strip to the waist and fight the grizzled Luis with his bare hands. John accepted the challenge because he had no alternative and quickly discovered that there were no rules in such combat.

Luis de Toledo was a scoundrel among scoundrels, and a sketch John drew of him, many years later, indicated that he must have presented a fearsome appearance to his young opponent. His nose spread across his lean face, and a long scar that extended from his temple to one corner of his mouth twisted his lips, giving him a permanent, ugly leer. He dressed exquisitely, as did many mercenary officers, who had first choice in plundering the attire of battlefield corpses.

He wore a corselet of fine silver links, a compromise between chain mail and plate, and beneath it a shirt with a huge collar of lace, probably Belgian, that spilled over his armor. He, too, stripped to the waist for the fight, and John, in recalling the experience, remembered that there were many scars made by swords, knives, and pikes on his torso.

Luis's eyes were commanding, the cold eyes of a professional killer, a man totally lacking in patriotism who had abandoned his country for cash and booty. He was not the type to waste sympathy on an inexperienced boy or treat such a foe gently.

His first blow was a kick in the groin that doubled John over, and then he leaped on the boy, biting his ear as he bore him to the ground. John literally didn't know what had hit him as the veteran went to work in earnest, using every trick of the gutter criminal. Schoolboys in rural England had been taught the importance of sportsmanship, but in combat of this sort there were no rules.

The experience was significant, because it made John realize that there were values in the world other than his own and that it was frequently necessary to abandon principle in order to achieve victory. It was a lesson he never forgot.

The youth fought bravely, but in vain, and Luis knocked him senseless after a fight that lasted only a few minutes. When John regained consciousness and, dazed and bleeding, tried to sit up, he thought he had failed and would be sent on his way. But he found that Luis was splashing *calvados,* a cheap and potent Norman brandy, on his cuts, and suddenly Duxbury appeared to inform him he had passed the test.

John was given a plumed helmet of steel, the only item of attire that served as a uniform. In addition to his own weapons, which he was allowed to keep, he was issued a harquebus, a clumsy, unreliable musket with a recoil so vicious that it knocked down the man firing it if he failed to brace himself with his feet planted wide apart. Members of the company were given food each morning, usually meat and bread, and were allowed to eat it whenever they pleased.

The company hadn't been paid in several months, and the newcomer soon learned that his chances of obtaining even token wages were slim. He had no blanket, and therefore would have to do without until he took one from a dead or wounded Spaniard in battle. He was forced to deliver his rented horse to an inn in Le Havre, and Duxbury sent Luis de Toledo with him to make certain he didn't try to keep the animal. Henry IV, John was told, insisted that all troops in his service refrain from intimidating or cheating his civilian subjects. Violators were punished swiftly and severely: a soldier who stole a horse would be beheaded, and his immediate commanders would be lashed with a whip.

There was no honor among mercenaries, John soon discovered. His pistol vanished one night while he was sleeping, and when he found it in the possession of another member of the company the following day, the man blandly told him he was mistaken. Thereafter, John slept with his sword strapped to his leg, but had no need to protect his harquebus. All soldiers hated the cumbersome weapon, and shed it as quickly as possible by capturing others in battle.

Most members of the company owned their own horses, and the few who did not were expected to follow the others into battle on foot. Duxbury hoped that all of his men would manage to provide themselves with mounts after the next clash with the Spaniards. Recruits were not trained, and were expected to know what to do in combat. John gleaned that he would avoid difficulty if he stayed in the rear, waited until a hot fight developed with an enemy cavalry unit, and watched for an apportunity to snatch a horse.

The newcomer's first weeks of military service were miserable. He slept under a coarse tent that protected him from the elements, and he had enough to eat, but the last of his money had been spent on some cakes sold by an itinerant peddler, and his purse was empty. Worst of all, he had literally nothing to do, and he found inactivity galling. The men were expected to spend their mornings at the bivouac, where they usually passed the time gambling with dice. At noon they were allowed to go where they pleased, and most went to the taverns of Le Havre for drinking and wenching. All these pleasures required funds.

In his boredom, John began to roam through the countryside, and in the village of Harfleur, scarcely more than a stone's throw east of Le Havre, he finally stumbled into part-time employment that was profitable. A butcher in the village who sold beef, mutton, and ox-meat to the army's quartermasters was hard pressed for assistants, in part because of his booming business, in part because both his sons were in the army and stationed elsewhere, unable to help him. He advertised his need on a small sign tacked to the front of his slaughterhouse, and John saw the notice while wandering aimlessly through the village.

Opportunity beckoned, and the youth who had closed the door on an apprenticeship to a wealthy merchant snatched it. Having been reared on a farm, he was no stranger to a butcher's trade, although he could scarcely claim to be an expert. But he could not afford to lose the chance to earn some money, so he applied for the position. The butcher accepted him.

What John didn't already know, necessity forced him to learn quickly, and he spent his afternoons hacking at the carcasses of animals that were then sold to the quartermasters. The work was unpleasant, and the pay was small, but a tiny sum of money was better than none, and there were other benefits to be enjoyed, too.

Chief among them was a crude but hearty dinner served every night by the butcher's wife to her husband and his helpers. There was always meat on the table, of course, and John ate his fill of bread, cheese, and butter, too. He could now consume his company ration at breakfast and noon, instead of spreading it out over three meals, and then dine every evening as well.

In later years he wrote that he became acquainted with a young female cousin of the butcher who sometimes aided in the preparation of the food. This girl, "not comely, but fair-haired and withal endowed with a primitive charm," soon became his mistress. He had no need for the trollops of Le Havre whom the other members of his company patronized.

One detail of his romance is suspect. The lower classes of the Le Havre region were dark-haired and dark-skinned, almost without exception. So it is possible that, in his gentlemanly preference for blondes, his imagination, combined with a faulty memory, led him to recall her as a blonde when she was really a brunette. It would be unkind to Smith to suggest that she may have existed only in his mind, and that, wanting a pinch of spice to make his brief career as a butcher more palatable to his readers, he invented the girl out of whole cloth. In any event, she was not important to him and played no significant role in his life.

At least he was keeping out of serious trouble, which was more than could be said for his colleagues. Idle soldiers were mischief-makers, and the peace of Le Havre was broken daily by brawls in which French troops were usually pitted against men from one or more of the seven mercenary companies. Taverns were sometimes wrecked, and shop owners dreaded visits from rowdy bullies who could not be made to pay for damages they caused.

Unfortunately for the good citizens of Le Havre, the war was at a temporary standstill. King Henry was busy consolidating the appreciable gains he had made in the preceding two and one-half years. The Vatican was no longer opposed to him, and Pope Clement VIII had quietly stopped giving his financial and moral support to Henry's enemies. The French nobles who had held out for so long against the "upstart monarch from Navarre" had been defeated, one by one, and Henry had not only forgiven them, but had given the more important of them positions in his regime.

One of the King's former foes, Charles, Duc de Mayenne, had been assigned nominal command of the Army of the North, although the reins of real power remained in the hands of long-faithful generals whom the King could trust. Mayenne, who loved good food so much that he weighed more than three hundred pounds, was paying a visit to the Governor of Le Havre when the peace of the town was disrupted by quarrels between French troops and their mercenary allies.

Henry, Duc de Montmorency, the King's deputy and one of the great military leaders of the age, made a journey to Le Havre from Rouen and conducted a personal investigation of the unpleasant situation. He had ample authority to take any steps he deemed necessary, but preferred not to act in his own name. None of the units had been paid their wages in six months, but their commanders remained loyal to him, and he wanted to do nothing that would disturb their relationship. Montmorency believed, as did the King, that the tentative negotiations being conducted with Philip of Spain would fail, and if the war was resumed in earnest, he would need the support of every officer and soldier in a campaign to the death.

So he concocted a neat scheme to make Mayenne a scapegoat. During the course of a long banquet at the Governor's castle, Montmorency made a "suggestion" to Mayenne, whose mind was on his meal rather than on military discipline. Spanish cavalry from Philip's headquarters at Brussels were making reconnaissance sorties in strength, and as many as five hundred enemy horsemen had been seen in the vicinity of Amiens. That city, currently occupied by the French, had changed hands several times within the past decade, and its citizens, understandably, were apprehensive.

Montmorency thought Mayenne could kill several birds with one stone by dispatching the seven mercenary companies to the Amiens region under orders to seek the Spaniards and defeat them. Philip would be taught a lesson, and Le Havre would enjoy a respite when the mercenaries departed. Montmorency refrained from saying that, since the assignment to seek and destroy an elusive cavalry force would be unpopular with the men given the task, the mercenary officers and their troops would blame Mayenne. Montmorency himself would not be involved.

Mayenne, who was anxious to demonstrate his willingness to serve King Henry, not only endorsed the idea, but decided to lead the expedition in person. Three days later, on a fine, hot summer morning, he rode out of Le Havre in a litter, surrounded by the men of a French cavalry troop to whom he had given the dubious honor of acting as his personal escort.

The seven companies of mercenaries followed, the horsemen at the head of the line, the infantry behind them. Bringing up the rear was recruit John Smith, his heavy harquebus making his shoulders ache, his nostrils thick with the dust kicked up by those who preceded him in the line. His boots, the only footgear he owned, were wearing thin, and he must have wished himself comfortably ensconced in the Lynn house of Thomas Sendall. There was little glory to be found on the rutted dirt roads of northern France.

The troops marched aimlessly for eleven days, the men becoming increasingly short-tempered. Food rations were meager, and the soldiers' dispositions were not improved by the tantalizing odors that drifted across their nightly bivouac from the headquarters pavilion, where Mayenne and the gentlemen of his suite dined in splendor, eating multicourse dinners from tables laid with expensive linens.

By sheer accident, on the twelfth day of its meandering, the column passed within a few miles of the small town of Grandvilliers, southwest of Amiens, and learned that the Spaniards were encamped near the town. Their commanders were being entertained by the lord of the town, Sieur Guy de Beauchamp, who had been one of Mayenne's own subordinates when the Duke had been Philip's ally. It appeared obvious that de Beauchamp had not abandoned his former associations.

The mercenaries, eager for loot, needed no urging as they started toward Grandvilliers. Someone notified the enemy of their approach, and the Spaniards retreated into the walled town, accompanied by de Beauchamp, his two younger brothers, and their families. Peasants told Mayenne of their flight, and he promptly ordered his units to surround Grandvilliers and lay siege to it.

But Captain Joseph Duxbury had a mission of his own to accomplish first, and led his company to the abandoned manor house. His mercenaries, ruthless scavengers all, sacked the place, stripping it of everything valuable. John Smith did not accompany his comrades into the house, but headed straight for the stables. His luck was good. The de Beauchamp family had gone off in such great haste that they had taken only those horses they needed for their ride into town.

Several frightened grooms were in the stables when John and two other infantrymen from Duxbury's company burst in. The servants were duly terrified by the soldiers' ferocious weapons, and John seized a bay gelding, "a spirited beast about four years old, and the most handsome creature I had ever seen." He also took two saddles, a cloak of thick wool, and an old double-edged sword, sheathless, that he found propped in the corner of a stall.

His raid lasted no more than a quarter of an hour, and in that time he was graduated from the infantry and promoted himself to the cavalry. The sword he had found was at least fifty years old, and was a heavy, unwieldy weapon, but was far superior to his harquebus, which he threw into a supply wagon.

In the meantime, the other members of the company went through the manor house like a swarm of locusts attacking a wheat field. They found the de Beauchamp wine cellar, and only threats of immediate decapitation made by Duxbury and Luis de Toledo prevented them from sampling their loot on the spot. They emptied the storage bins behind the kitchen, too, and resumed their march with wagons overflowing. For the next few days, even Mayenne would envy them as they ate wine-cured hams, smoked trout, wildfowl, and bread made from flour so white that only the wealthiest of nobles could afford to buy it.

John was learning his trade in a hard school, and was making rapid progress. He asked for barter bids on the spare saddle he had taken, and finally made a deal he found eminently satisfactory, obtaining a new pair of knee-high boots that fitted "tolerably well," and a poniard with a pewter handle.

Members of the other companies had good reason to envy Duxbury's men, and Luis de Toledo mounted a guard over the booty when the unit reached the walls of Grandvilliers. Guy de Beauchamp and the Spanish commander were already conferring with the Duc de Mayenne in a tent outside the walls, so it was fast becoming evident to the mercenaries that there would be no siege of Grandvilliers and, consequently, no wild orgy of pillaging and rape when the town surrendered.

De Beauchamp was a fast, convincing talker, and he persuaded Mayenne that the Spanish colonel, an old friend, was paying him a courtesy call. Under the rules of chivalry that still prevailed, Mayenne was forced to give the Spaniard and his officers and men their parole, in return for which they promised to return to the Belgian plains.

The agreement was signed that evening at a gala dinner given by the Mayor of Grandvilliers. The Spanish squadrons rode out into the open, encamping on one side of the town, and the fuming, disappointed mercenaries established their bivouac on the far side. Only Duxbury's company enjoyed the evening, eating and drinking to their hearts' and stomachs' content. The Captain and Luis de Toledo diplomatically entertained the officers of the other companies, and armed sentries guarded the loot from the manor house all night.

John was one of the sentries, volunteering for the duty because he had no interest in drinking strong spirits. He and the other guards had a busy night, beating off four attempts of men from other units to steal the loot.

In the morning the Spaniards rode off toward the east, and Mayenne announced that his column would return to Le Havre.

The members of six mercenary companies were bitterly disappointed, but could find no valid excuse to attack a French town whose inhabitants had shown no disloyalty to King Henry.

There was a last-minute delay when Sieur Guy de Beauchamp recognized some of his furniture and other belongings in the supply carts of Duxbury's company. He protested to Mayenne, who agreed that the looting had been unreasonable, and Duxbury was ordered to return de Beauchamp's property.

Duxbury refused, knowing his men would mutiny. He argued that the booty was legitimate, that it had been seized before the agreement had been signed at sundown. De Beauchamp replied that, inasmuch as he had not rebelled against the authority of King Henry, his liege lord, there had not been a state of war and, therefore, the taking of his property had been outright stealing.

Mayenne, aware that Duxbury's men would resist violently if he tried to force their compliance with his original order, reversed himself and ruled against de Beauchamp. The company cheered, the men toasting each other with drinks from upturned jugs of de Beauchamp wine, and the column started out toward Le Havre.

Inevitably, the other mercenaries, who were still envious, made several further attempts to take some of the loot. Their attacks were repulsed, and Smith, writing about the affair years later, laconically noted that "a halfscore heads were cracked." Apparently he didn't think the mayhem committed was worthy of more detailed comment.

His status was now vastly improved. He had a horse and saddle, a cloak that served as a blanket, and two new weapons. Soon he had money in his purse, too, for the furniture, bric-a-brac, and other items of booty that were of no use to soldiers were sold to a Le Havre pawnbroker who already had a client eager to purchase the merchandise. The unfortunate Guy de

Beauchamp, anxious to recover as much of his property as possible, was offering an excellent price.

The proceeds were divided in the usual way, Duxbury receiving fifteen shares, Luis de Toledo taking ten, and veterans who had been with the company for more than a year getting two. John received one share, which was considerable, and three gold florins clinked pleasantly in his purse. There was no need for him to return to his part-time employment in the butcher's abattoir; he had enough money now for food that would augment the rations of meat and bread issued to him. And he could, when he chose, find amusement in the brothels of Le Havre.

The abortive expedition had transformed him into a professional soldier, even though he had fought no one but other mercenaries trying to steal his loot. He was a cavalryman now, capable of attacking in battle, and was truly launched on his extraordinary career.

IV

The Soldier

JOHN SMITH CAME OF AGE AS a fighting man at the siege of Amiens, the protracted battle that marked the climax of the long war between Henry of France and Philip of Spain. The skill, endurance, and courage of men on both sides were put to the ultimate test in the long, bitter contest that began in early March, 1597, when the Spaniards broke the truce and captured the fortress town of Amiens, the key to the Low Countries.

Henry IV immediately mobilized all his available forces to meet the threat, and himself took command of his army, which consisted of six regiments of horse and eight of infantry, two battalions of artillery, and seven companies of mercenaries. His Constable, Montmorency, accompanied him into the field as his second-in-command, and the two great generals waged war in earnest.

The investment began on March 18th, and the foot soldiers began the weary, almost endless task of digging siege trenches, concentrating their efforts on the south and west sides of the walled town. The professional troops were placed under the command of Charles, Duc de Biron, one of the most talented and emotionally unstable of all Henry's generals. Biron, who was also Admiral of the French Navy and Governor of Burgundy, was a small-boned, almost effeminate man with delicate features, exquisite manners, and an insatiable appetite for combat. Long Montmorency's rival, he saw an opportunity to impress the King with his competence, and gave the mercenaries the most difficult of tasks.

The siege could succeed only if the defenders were starved into submission, which meant that under no circumstances could relief supply columns from the Netherlands and Brussels be allowed to slip through the French lines. The professional companies were assigned to patrol duty on the north and east sides of the town, heavily wooded, rolling country that made life miserable for cavalrymen. Guards were ordered to remain in the saddle day and night. Each man was expected to stand duty for eighteen hours out of twenty-four. No leaves of absence were granted for any purpose.

The work was grueling. The men rode in groups of three to five, ate all their meals except one in the saddle every day, and maintained their patrols regardless of weather or other conditions. Frequently they were harassed by parties of Spanish cavalrymen who made sudden, unexpected sorties from the north and east gates of Amiens; sharpshooters fired arrows and musket balls at them when they ventured too close to the walls; and occasionally the artillery gunners inside the town relieved their boredom by training their cannon on the mercenaries and practicing their marksmanship.

But there were compensations that few armies of the period enjoyed. Henry, who understood men-at-arms, made certain that the troops were paid their full wages each month, and sometimes surprised the mercenaries by giving them a bonus. The men slept under snug canvas tents, quartermasters issued extra blankets of heavy wool free of charge, and the food was both plentiful and good. Beef, venison, and lamb were served at the one hot meal of the day, supplies of bread were ample, and the King issued rations of beer and wine to all, paying for the spirits out of his own purse.

John Smith soon lost count of the skirmishes in which he participated. Only the initial engagement in which he took part, an incident typical of action throughout the siege, later remained distinct in his mind. The affair took place only three days after his arrival at the camp outside Amiens.

He and three companions were given the task of patrolling a small sector between the wall of the city and a patch of deep woods, at the near edge of which stood a deep, rock-strewn ravine. The corridor was approximately two hundred yards wide, and the assignment seemed simple to the four young men who rode out into the field.

A rattle of musket fire aimed at them by hidden sentries stationed on the parapet quickly taught them the fundamental principle of caution. Unable to see their foes or return the fire, John and his companions prudently moved as far from the wall as they could, and rode near the lip of the ravine. The enemy fire continued, but the marksmanship of the defenders on the wall was poor, and the quartet soon assured themselves they were in no real danger.

While riding back and forth, three hundred yards in one direction, then three hundred in the other, they became bored. So, like soldiers everywhere, in all wars, their minds turned to more pleasant matters, and they began to discuss two of their favorite subjects—women and food.

They became so preoccupied that they failed to preserve the vigilance their situation demanded. Accordingly, John was startled when he saw a platoon of Spaniards in light armor charging toward him and the other members of his squad from the direction of the town.

The Spanish cavalryman, later experience taught him, was courageous to the point of foolhardiness, as ferocious as a savage, and as deft as an artist. King Philip's horsemen were superbly trained, the pride of Castile and the terror of their foes.

All John knew at the time was that he and the other mercenaries appeared to be caught in a trap. If they retreated into the gully, where footing was hazardous, their horses might stumble and fall, and they themselves would be easy marks for the onrushing Spaniards. The only sensible alternative was to beat a hasty, undignified retreat and try to reach a point too close to the French camp for the Spaniards to follow them.

John's companions needed no urging and no orders. They were already turning their mounts and trying to flee. But the young Englishman's pride would not permit him to run away. Instead he astonished his friends and amazed the foe by charging straight at the Spaniards, calling on his companions to follow him. They obeyed, probably for no other reason than that there was a ring of authority in his voice and they had been trained to react instantly to commands.

John was well aware of the odds against him, but kept his head. He realized that his rash endeavor could succeed only if he managed to scatter the oncoming horsemen before they overwhelmed him. So, riding at a full gallop, he took aim with his musket and put a bullet into the shoulder of the officer, a lieutenant, who was leading the charge. The man slumped in his saddle, and his horse swerved to one side. But the rest of the platoon continued to move forward.

There was no time to reload, so John snatched a pistol from his belt and fired again. His aim was not as accurate as he might have wished. The effect, however, was the same, for his shot landed between the eyes of a horse in the center of the front rank, and the beast fell, throwing his rider.

By this time the other mercenaries managed to rally and

fired a ragged but effective volley. Two members of the attacking force were wounded, one of them mortally. The advancing horsemen had reason to reconsider, and the line slowed. Then two or three men who had lost their appetite for combat turned back, breaking the solid front of the rank behind them.

John sensed that this was the moment to redouble his efforts. He reloaded his musket frantically, calling on his comrades to do the same, and the mercenaries sent another fusillade in the direction of the cavalrymen. John's aim was poor, and his companions did no better, but the dragoons had lost both their momentum and their appetite for combat. They decided that Amiens was far safer than this open corridor where they were skirmishing with madmen who didn't know when they were beaten. The platoon returned to the city, and the mercenaries resumed their role as sentries.

The Spaniards, John wrote many years later, were among the best soldiers on earth when engaged in an offensive operation. But they were temperamentally unsuited for defensive actions and could always be forced to retreat if their foes took the initiative.

He wasn't alone in knowing the enemy's weakness. The men of Henry's army repeatedly struck first throughout the long siege of Amiens. On most days, of course, John and his companions saw less excitement. Sieges, the young Englishman discovered, were boring work. He stood duty seven days and nights each week, and was so exhausted when given a few hours to eat and sleep that he didn't bother to avail himself of the services of the corps of camp followers who had established their own little tent city near the main army bivouac. He learned the basic military essential, discipline, from the strict Biron; he became increasingly adept in the use of sword and pistol; and he began the study of battlefield tactics that would become a lifelong interest.

He also had a daily opportunity to see the King. Henry of

Navarre, a true warrior, was unique among the monarchs of his time and fully accepted his personal responsibilities as commander-in-chief. He rode out into the field with his men every morning, often shared night patrol duty with them, and made it his business to be on friendly, informal terms with the most humble of his troops.

Henry, a short, slender man who was destined to become one of the greatest rulers in the history of France, had spent his whole adult life fighting for his crown. He had only one weakness, and his fifty-fifth known mistress was sharing his pavilion with him, a fact that in no way made him less of a hero to his men, and certainly did not dim his luster in John's eyes.

The influence of King Henry on John Smith was enormous —and lasting. "Henry," John wrote thirty-three years later, "was the mightiest and wisest of all men. He was calm in adversity, terrible in his anger, which boiled furiously in battle, and was so sweet-natured withal that he treated us whom he hired as his friends and equals. Many are the nobles I have known who have built high walls to shield them from their inferiors, but Henry treated none as his lackey, and we who rode under his banner freely offered up our lives for his cause upon the altar of the god of war.

"He forgave the weak, was just when the service of justice was needful, and dealt with his vassals wisely. In only one thing was he like a mountain that could not be moved. He who showed cowardice was scourged and hanged. Men often err in the heat of battle, and no man who fought under Henry's colors was punished for faults in judgment, but those who turned their backs to the enemy, those who cried aloud and caused others to vomit or empty out their bowels, and those who ran, taking others with them, were treated with the contempt that the strong must reserve for the weak if one's arms are to prevail upon the field of valor.

"Had I not known Henry, I would oft have been tempted to leave off living the life of a man-at-arms, and would have retired to the fair pasture lands that were my heritage. But this grand King among kings taught me the secret essence of manhood, which must be tested, then again tested with steel and ball. Unlike Henry, I had no crown, no great cities to call my own, no lords who bent their knee to me; nought was mine save my own head, yet I gladly followed the precepts he devised and bequeathed me. His cunning and valor were my true heritage, and if I have made my mark on the field of combat, it is because Henry was the tutor and I the pupil."

The siege dragged on interminably through the cold, damp spring and the hot, equally wet summer. Henry's nobles were paying a fortune for the privilege of supporting his campaign, and when they began to murmur in protest, the King knew he had to force the issue. The noose around Amiens was tightened.

The stakes were so high that the Spaniards sent four fresh regiments and a huge supply train to relieve the plight of the garrison. The commander of the column played a trick that should not have fooled as experienced a soldier as Biron, but did. Feinting in strength, the Spaniards drew Biron's troops out of position, then made a wild and successful dash into Amiens.

Duxbury's company of mercenaries recovered sufficiently to lash out at the Spaniards' rear guard and inflict considerable damage on the enemy. No details of this minor operation are known, nor is John Smith's part in the assault. Nevertheless he distinguished himself in action, and later said laconically, "I was promoted, upon this unfortunate occasion, to the rank of sergeant, hence was one of the few who had reason to rejoice." He had climbed his first significant rung on the ladder of military success.

The desperate Henry summoned reserves from Paris, called on units stationed in the south, and demanded fresh levies from his dukes and counts. They responded by the end of August, and he was at last in a position to seal off Amiens from the outside world. Philip of Spain may have been a tyrant, but he was intelligent enough to know when he was beaten. A messenger arrived from his headquarters at Brussels, offering to negotiate for peace, and the besieged garrison simultaneously surrendered, on September 25th.

Only the mercenaries were disappointed. Amiens was a French town, so looting, burning, and the raping of female inhabitants of the town were forbidden on the King's personal orders. Three royal household regiments took up stations inside the walls to make certain the professionals didn't carry their victory celebrations too far. And before October arrived, Biron paid off the company commanders in full, gave them a final bonus, and dismissed them from Henry's service.

The war between France and Spain was at an end, but there was still employment for mercenaries elsewhere. Philip had not yet succeeded in subduing the Dutch, so Duxbury led his men on a march to Amsterdam. Sergeant John Smith rode at the head of his squad, a veteran now with six months of active campaigning under his belt, his purse and belly comfortably filled. Not yet nineteen years old, he was already a leader of men, accepted by professional cutthroats as their superior. And he knew his immediate goal: he wanted to be an officer.

Maurice of Nassau, President of the Dutch Council of State, hereditary Stadholder of Holland and Zeeland, and commander-in-chief of his small nation's army, was a shy, peace-loving young man, a lover of the arts and a promoter of overseas exploration. In 1598 he had no time for literature, painting, or the activities of the Dutch East India Company, however. France was making a separate peace with Spain, and his one nominal ally, England, was not pursuing the war vigorously. Left to his own devices, the diffident Maurice became a raging, cunning lion and overnight demonstrated to an astonished world that he was a military genius.

Eleven regiments of Dutch infantry and two of artillery, augmented by six mercenary companies of cavalry, held the great armies of Spain at bay. Maurice developed an uncanny sixth sense, buttressed by his intelligence agents, and whenever the Spaniards prepared to launch a major surprise attack, he occupied the ground before they could get there. He maneuvered constantly, marching and countermarching, and although not a shot was fired, the Spaniards were unable to take a single square foot of Dutch soil.

Then, suddenly, Philip II died, and in the confusion that followed, the Dutch were better able to prepare their defenses. The powerful princes of the house of Hapsburg, rulers of both Spain and Austria, conferred for months, and finally evolved a cynical scheme. Archduke Albert, Cardinal-Bishop of Vienna, would leave the Church and marry his cousin, the Infanta Isabella, Philip's daughter. They would receive the Low Countries as a wedding gift and would rule the Netherlands and the Belgian provinces together as "independent sovereigns" of a new, "independent" nation.

There were two flies in the Hapsburg ointment. One was Pope Clement VIII, a hard-working, practical statesman who, since his accession to the throne of St. Peter in 1592, had done much to revitalize the Church, and had won a reputation of his own for cynicism. What his critics failed to realize was that Clement was a sincere, pious man. Unable to stomach the Hapsburg scheme, he would neither release Albert from his vows nor, if the Cardinal-Archduke still insisted on leaving the Church, sanction the marriage.

The other deterrent was the army of Maurice, which dared the Spaniards and their Austrian allies to make gifts of territories they did not occupy. The Dutch, with their cherished religious liberty at stake, volunteered in vast numbers for military service. The mercenaries, of course, cared nothing about the issues and were interested only in receiving their wages regularly.

In 1599 the Spaniards launched several abortive assaults, and on each occasion Maurice held them at bay. Captain Duxbury's company took part in each of these operations, and John Smith chalked up still more experience to his credit. Then Albert and Isabella, defying the Pope, were married, and the alarmed Dutch parliament, the States-General, persuaded Maurice to take the offensive.

On July 1, 1600, the Dutch and their mercenaries attacked the Archduke Albert himself at the heavily fortified Flemish town of Nieuport, located about ten miles south of Ostend, on the English Channel. The strong Spanish garrison could have withstood a siege indefinitely, in part because Albert was able to receive reinforcements and supplies by sea. But the wily Maurice lured his foes into the open by sending a pitifully small force toward the walled town.

Albert took the bait and sent several regiments into the open to chastise the impudent Dutch. At that juncture the mercenary companies, Duxbury's included, made a wild charge and placed themselves between the regiments and their sheltering fort. The Dutch corps followed close behind, and Albert had to send the rest of his garrison into the open in order to strengthen the units already dispatched.

Maurice managed to place his entire corps between the enemy and the town of Nieuport and immediately sent his troops into action. The mercenaries led the attack and rode at a gallop, in close formation, against the finest Spanish infantry, veterans who had seen many years of active service. But no men were capable of holding their lines in the face of such a ferocious assault. Duxbury's company was in the center of the cavalry line, and Sergeant Smith, on the offensive for the first time, had to be restrained to prevent him from leading his squad ahead of the others.

At last John Smith was in his element. Indifferent to the fire of musketeers and archers, he stood in his stirrups and wielded his heavy sword as though it were a rapier. Maurice's subsequent report to the States-General tells the story of that first, blazing charge: "The paid horsemen rode in the van, and were inspired by the example of an English sergeant in the Duxbury company, one Jon Smyt [sic], who laid about him with such rapid strokes that he left a path of Spanish dead in his wake. Other horsemen pressed close with matching fervor, and soon the paid listors [companies] reached the enemy rear. Whilst they turned and made ready to ride again, from rear to front, our valiant regiments were upon the foe, who scattered in disarray."

In an action lasting less than an hour, Maurice won a spectacular victory over the Spaniards greater than any ever achieved by Henry of Navarre. And John Smith, now twenty-one years old, had been catapulted into international renown. He was the only individual mentioned in Maurice's report, other than the Dutch regimental commanders.

But there was a sudden, tragic aftermath. The mercenaries rode in pursuit of the Spaniards, cutting them down, and John was seriously wounded when a mounted Castilian officer turned in his saddle long enough to fire a pistol at close range. No details are known other than that John was carried from the field by his comrades.

Duxbury took possession of his horse and equipment on his behalf, and the injured hero was lodged in the home of a Nieuport merchant named De Groet. He was left behind to recuperate when the triumphant Dutch marched back to Amsterdam, their borders secure.

John's wound must have been a nasty one, as he spent six

weeks enjoying the hospitality of the De Groet family. When he mended, however, his recovery was swift. One evening in mid-August, merchant De Groet walked into the "invalid's" room to find John repaying his kindness by entertaining the eldest of the De Groet daughters in bed. The weeping girl, whom John described as "a fair and buxom blonde," and whose name he once spelled Katrina and in his only other reference to her as Karina, was sent to her own quarters.

Her seducer was thrown out of the house in his nightshirt by the De Groet servants, and his clothes followed. The humiliated John was forced to dress in public on the cobbled streets of Nieuport. Then, without a copper in his pocket, he began the long walk through Flanders and Holland to rejoin his company. His journey was unpleasant. Farmers and townsmen had seen more than enough of army deserters who robbed and sometimes murdered the innocent, and few people were willing to open their doors to the traveler or offer him food.

John arrived hungry, footsore, and dusty at Duxbury's bivouac, and was given a riotous welcome by his comrades, who taunted him unmercifully when they learned what had happened to him. The Captain, who cared nothing about his morals and was concerned only with his proficiency as a fighting man, rewarded him for his conduct at the battle of Nieuport by promoting him to ensign, the lowest commissioned rank, and made him third in command of the company. He was at last an officer.

There were rumors that the Spaniards, who had been regaining their strength at their main base, Dunkirk, were taking the field once more before going into winter quarters, and Maurice again marched into Flanders to meet them. Archduke Albert had no intention of repeating his Nieuport mistakes, and now had enough horsemen to prevent himself from being overwhelmed. There were frequent cavalry skirmishes, and in these brief flurries John enjoyed his first taste of independent command, but there was no action that he deemed worthy of detailed mention.

Snow fell in late November; the Spaniards decided they lacked the strength to defeat Maurice and, returning to Dunkirk, sent emissaries to Amsterdam to open tentative peace negotiations. The Dutch were wary but frugal, and the States-General, ignoring Maurice's protests, ordered him to discharge the mercenary companies.

The professionals were dismissed, and the companies, unable to find new employers, disbanded. The grateful Maurice remembered the services John had performed in the battle of Nieuport, and made him the staggering gift of six double *gulden,* a fortune in gold coins with the equivalent of about four thousand dollars, three and a half centuries later.

Most of Duxbury's men decided to go off to Austria with Luis de Toledo. The Hapsburgs, together with the Hungarians and Bohemians, were being menaced by the Turks, and the need for trained fighting men in central Europe was so urgent that, for the first time, Protestant mercenaries were being hired.

John wanted no more of war for the immediate present and planned a visit to his family, whom he hadn't seen in four years. He was in no hurry to leave Holland, however, and lingered for some weeks in Amsterdam with Duxbury.

It was during this brief period that he enjoyed an extraordinary experience, one that would exert an enormous influence on him and, in turn, on Western civilization. In some way that neither he nor anyone else ever bothered to explain, he met or was called to the attention of one of the most remarkable men of the age, geographer Peter Plancius, the Dutch counterpart and associate of England's remarkable Archdeacon Richard Hakluyt.

Plancius was a lugubrious, homely man of middle age who wore a long scholar's robe, lived in a house cluttered with maps and books, and was so fascinated by the discovery and exploration of unknown parts of the earth that he sometimes forgot to eat any meals for days at a time. It is a tantalizing exercise in futility to speculate on the meeting and growing feeling of kinship that sprang up between the great intellectual and the ruthless young professional soldier. Nothing is known of the relationship between the scientist who sparked and directed so many Dutch voyages of discovery, and the young Englishman, except that John spent most of his waking hours at Plancius' house.

During these weeks, presumably, he studied Plancius' maps and charts, and listened to the geographer discourse learnedly on the limits of the known world. By the time the young soldier of fortune left Holland, he, too, was dreaming of finding and conquering new continents. He carried with him a letter of introduction to Hakluyt, written in Plancius' spidery Latin, the universal language of scholars.

John found passage on an English merchant ship en route home from the Mediterranean. Only a few hours after they put out to sea, a frightful gale blew up, and for the better part of a week the vessel was buffeted by the storm. After the first day or two, the sole passenger was pleased to discover that he was no longer seasick, but lived in constant dread that the ship would sink.

Her master, however, was a superb mariner. His name was Henry Hudson, and he had an ability to guess every nuance of change in the violent storm's moods. John had developed a great admiration for him by the time the ship put into the Channel island of Jersey for repairs. While the merchantman was being patched, they spent a great deal of time together and discovered they had much in common. Hudson had sailed as a mate with Captain John Davys on a voyage of discovery that had taken them to Greenland and what was later to become known as Newfoundland, and John was fascinated by

Hudson's stories. The Captain, in turn, absorbed all that John was able to repeat to him of Plancius' theories.

The two were fast friends by the time they sailed up the Thames to London, and John spent a week there at Hudson's home with the mariner, his wife, and four children. There was a hidden romantic streak in the blunt, square-jawed, and seemingly pragmatic Hudson, who secretly shared John's yearning for adventure in far-distant places. They spent hours of speculation on the unknown, and Hudson expounded his idea, later to become an obsession, that there was an unobstructed water passage to the East Indies either by way of the North Pole or across the North American continent. They realized then that they were kindred spirits, and they maintained their close friendship until Hudson's tragic death at the climax of his fourth voyage of discovery.

John also found time during that week to present Plancius' letter to Archdeacon Hakluyt at Westminster, and was deeply impressed by the great geographer's erudition and patience. In his memoirs written three decades later, Smith shows unexpected modesty in discussing his relationship with the gentle, ascetic Hakluyt. He makes no mention of the fact that he must have struck the Archdeacon favorably, too, saying only that he and Hudson were twice privileged to dine at Hakluyt's home.

He infuriates posterity by mentioning nothing of the subjects discussed at the dinner table, and limits himself to the comments that the Archdeacon served inferior joints of beef, but that his taste in wines, which he acquired while living in France, was excellent.

Out of those dinners was destined to grow the single most important friendship in John Smith's life. Hakluyt would remember him when he returned to England several years later, would act as his sponsor and, ultimately, become his associate in the creation and development of an English colony in Virginia. It would be Hakluyt, too, who would spur and guide John's monumental voyage of discovery to New England.

But in December of 1600, the young adventurer wasn't thinking beyond the immediate future. He bought himself a magnificent stallion and a new wardrobe that included a plumed helmet of silver. Then, laden with gifts from Holland and London for his family and the Willoughbys, he rode north to Lincolnshire, confident he would be given a prodigal's welcome. He felt he had good cause to be pleased with his success. No noble owned a finer mount, and few wore more splendid armor. His purse was filled with more money than his father had acquired in a lifetime of hard work, he carried an honorable scar earned in combat, and across his chest he displayed the sash of an officer, which his own efforts had won. Not yet twenty-two years old, he was no longer a frightened, runaway boy, but a man who had carved a niche for himself in the world of men.

V

A Prodigal's Yearnings

"MY MOTHER," A WISTFULLY nostalgic John Smith wrote in 1630, "was unchanged when I returned home to escort her to church for the celebration of Christmas in 1600."

But he found little else in Lincolnshire the same. Francis Smith was married to a girl of whom his brother disapproved, calling her "passing fair, but dull, a dark-haired thing of little wit." Alice was no longer a little girl, and she resented her older brother's attempts to pass judgment on her suitors.

Things were changed at the nearby great house, too. The elder of the Willoughby boys had succeeded to his late father's title and was married to the sweet, placid and, unfortunately, blonde daughter of a baronet. The dowager Lady Willoughby had moved to a smaller house on the extensive property and lived there in quiet retirement, attended by several servants. Henry Willoughby, John's good friend, was in London, having at least temporarily attached himself to the King's household in the hope of winning a diplomatic appointment.

Mrs. Smith prepared all her prodigal son's favorite dishes, among them "a haunch of venison well soaked for four days and nights in Claret Wine and herbs." Young Lord Willoughby cheerfully extended his hospitality to John, too, and entertained him at a banquet held soon after the Christmas season. But the friendship immediately became strained. Young Lady Willoughby, blonde and attractive, soon caught John's eye, or vice versa, according to his version of the story. She flirted with him at the banquet—or vice versa—and he did not dine at the manor house again.

It is unlikely that the relationship with the foolish young Lady Willoughby developed beyond the flirtation stage, as John continued to maintain a friendship, albeit a somewhat cool one, with Lord Willoughby. Had John bedded the bride of his liege, Willoughby would have challenged him to a duel or, at the very least, would have ordered him not to appear at the manor house again. However, the two young men continued to ride together, even though John had no further known contact with his lord's lady.

As a matter of fact, Willoughby granted him an unusual favor. After a short visit with his family, John became bored. He loved his mother, but, in his own words, was "tongue-tied in her presence." He had little in common with his brother and less with his sister. A strange idea occurred to him, and it, in turn, led to the most extraordinary experience of his unique life.

He felt an urge for solitude, and perhaps he yearned, too, for a taste of the wilderness living inspired by his talks on new worlds with Plancius and Hakluyt. At his request Lord Willoughby granted him the privilege of building himself a cabin with his own hands deep in the forests of the Willoughby estate. There he retired for almost six months of a hermit's existence. He took some of his food with him, and augmented it with deer meat and smaller game he shot in the woods.

He came out of the forest once each week to visit his mother for several hours, but saw no one else during his retreat. He built his fires, chopping down trees for the purpose, drew his water from a small stream, and cooked his meals. Aside from these housekeeping chores, he spent his entire time reading, often starting early in the morning and continuing far into the night. By his own account, he used up "more than two one-hundred-lot of tapers."

It may have been that, after brushing shoulders with men of learning, he became conscious of his own lack of education. Whatever his motives, he kept them to himself, and in his book, *The True Travels, Adventures and Observations of Captain John Smith,* completed and published in 1630, he made no mention of his reasons for withdrawing from society. Apparently he took it for granted that his readers would understand and condone his retirement.

John obtained his equivalent of a higher education during his retreat. Many of his books came from the Willoughby library, and others were borrowed from a family friend, Sir Dudley Cahill, whose estate was a few miles away. He specifically mentions only a few works, among them Hakluyt's *Discovery of America, Western Discoveries, The Principal Navigations, Voyages and Discoveries of the English Nation,* and the newly published *The Discoveries of the World,* translated from the Portuguese and edited by Hakluyt, which the Archdeacon well might have mentioned to him at dinner in London.

He also made himself familiar with Plancius' *The World,* a collection of maps published the preceding year, which he must have seen at the Dutch geographer's house in Amsterdam. He spent much time with the "discourses of Plato and treatises of Aristotle." He dabbled in the writings of St. Thomas Aquinas, which were not to his taste, and preferred the philosophy of his great contemporary, Francis Bacon, whose *Essays,*

Colours of Good and Evil, and *Sacred Meditations* had been published a few years earlier.

These works occupied only a fraction of his time, but whatever else he may have read he kept to himself. In any event, he emerged from the forest early in the summer of 1601 a well-read, well-rested young man. Intellectually he was at peace with himself, but he was in a state of emotional ferment and craved adventure after spending so much time in celibate contemplation.

His yearnings were not easy to satisfy, thanks to the cautious foreign policy of King James. Technically, England and Spain were not yet at peace, but the King refused to provoke the enemy openly, preferring the advantages of war to the more obvious hazards. No British troops were stationed overseas, and the Royal Navy took care to avoid Spanish men-of-war. On the other hand, the Crown quietly encouraged privateers to attack Spanish merchantmen, provided the Treasury received eight shillings for every pound of loot captured.

There was little that a young soldier who had just begun to become acquainted with the sea could do for his country and himself. John's thoughts returned to the war still being waged against the Turks in central Europe, and he decided to offer his services as a mercenary officer to the Christian lord who would pay him the highest wages.

His relatives tried to dissuade him, urging him instead to invest his money in farmlands, but the more they argued, the more stubborn he became. In July, 1601, he said goodbye to his mother, and to his everlasting regret never again saw her alive. Before leaving England he showed what was, for him, rare financial acumen, and turned over his fortune to his brother, instructing Francis to hold the money for him until his return.

He traveled to London, where he visited Hakluyt and Henry Hudson, then spent a few days roistering with Henry Willoughby, who vaguely promised to present him at court, but was either unable or unwilling to keep his word. Late in July, John sailed for France, wearing his armor and carrying his sword and pistols, with a double-edged knife in his boot top.

John Smith's account of his experiences on his journey to central Europe, as related in his *True Travels, Adventures and Observations,* was a major cause of the dim view of his veracity taken by his contemporaries and posterity. With no substantiation other than his own word, he told in hair-raising detail of shipwrecks and attempts to fleece him, skullduggery in places high and low, mutinies and piracy on the high seas. It is improbable, if not impossible, that any one man could have undergone so much in the space of approximately six months.

A few facts do stand out, however. John did spend several months as a "guest" on board a privateer manned by Bretons in the Mediterranean. His pinpointed descriptions of the type of ships peculiar to the Mediterranean in the early sixteenth century are accurate, as are his observations of places the vessel visited, among them Sicily and Piraeus, Naples and Alexandria. His circumlocutions, lapses, and evasions lead the reader to believe that the Bretons were pirates, and that he was more than a guest, becoming an active member of their company.

One thing is certain: he learned much about sailing and the sea, and progressed far beyond the level of an apprentice sailor. Finally, in the winter of 1602, he landed at Naples and traveled north to Rome in style, having mysteriously—or not so mysteriously, if he had indeed been active as a pirate—acquired considerable funds to augment the small sum he had taken with him from England.

He spent a few weeks sightseeing in Rome, and says that his curiosity led him to the headquarters of the Society of

Jesus, where he debated theology with the most learned priests in the Roman Catholic Church. John's critics laughed at his claim for almost two hundred years, but the truth of the matter is that he did indeed engage in such debates. In 1792 an English Jesuit working in the Society's archives discovered records kept by Father Johannes Berg, a secretary in the office of the Vicar General of the order at the beginning of the seventeenth century, and found that in February, 1602, "an English gentleman, John Smyth," was a guest of the Jesuits for five days and "did engage in much spirited talk with the Fathers on the nature of the Godhead."

Resuming his journey north, John carefully avoided Venice, which may or may not confirm the impression he gave previously that the Breton privateer attacked one or more richly laden Venetian merchantmen in the Mediterranean. Venice considered herself the undisputed mistress of the Adriatic and Mediterranean, and her rulers kept lists of those who had wronged her. Any such person falling into Venetian hands was usually hanged by the thumbs for days in a public square, tortured for the amusement of the people, and then put to death by slow strangulation. It may or may not be significant that, in all his travels throughout Europe, John Smith never once went to Venice, at that time the most powerful, wealthy, and sophisticated city on the Continent.

He grew tired of travel by public coach by the time he reached Milan, where he bought himself a horse and went on alone to Vienna. He made his way by easy stages, savoring the food, customs, and brothels of strange lands, and at last arrived in Vienna, the capital of Austria, where, to his disgust, he could find no one with the authority to enlist mercenaries. He was told repeatedly to apply to the Archduke Ferdinand, later to become Emperor, who was directing military operations from his provincial capital, Graz, in the southern part of the country.

In Graz, to John's great relief, he found an appropriately martial atmosphere, which was unfortunately complicated by a delicate political situation of which he knew nothing. In brief, the Holy Roman Emperor of the German states, Rudolph, who was also King of Hungary, was a rival of the Hapsburgs who ruled Austria, and the two factions were cooperating with each other only halfheartedly in their prosecution of the war against the Turks.

Rudolph, who enjoyed women, good wine, and strong cheeses, in that order, was bald, bearded, and a bigot among bigots in an age when a man's faith could be a matter of life or death. He had dismissed all Protestant officers from his service, including some Hungarian noblemen who had fought under the imperial banner for more than twenty years. Ferdinand was enlisting these experienced men in his own army, which he intended to send to the scene of the fighting, Transylvania, later to become a part of modern-day Rumania.

John Smith demonstrated that he had visited the Jesuits in Rome for more reasons than a desire to discuss theology. Before learning that Ferdinand was accepting Protestants, he presented the Archduke's adjutant with a letter of recommendation from the Society of Jesus. His foresight called him to the attention of the man who was to become his immediate superior and good friend, the Earl of Volda-Meldritch, to whom John later referred intimately as Meldri.

The Earl, a wealthy Hungarian landowner, was one of the unfortunate Protestants whom Rudolph had dismissed from the imperial service, and may have been the most important of them. He had seen duty for twenty-one consecutive years, and had risen to the rank of major general before being unceremoniously ousted. Now he and his artillery commander, Baron Kizel, were forming a new corps of their own with Hapsburg money and blessings.

Meldritch was a dapper, deceptively mild-mannered man

whose full beard and bristling moustache would inspire John to grow the whiskers he wore for the rest of his days. The Earl's portraits reveal him as round-faced, with gentle, dark-brown eyes and a sensitive, almost feminine, mouth. It must have been difficult for contemporaries who didn't know him to realize that this quiet, unassuming gentleman gave no quarter in his battles with the Turks, expected none in return, and preferred battle with the Moslem hordes who were threatening the Christian nations of Europe to fine food, beautiful women, or any of the other luxuries enjoyed by the aristocracy.

The Earl was amused by John Smith's cunningly won letter from the Jesuits, interviewed him at length, and then hired him as a personal staff member with the rank of lieutenant. An experienced soldier who spoke English, French, and Dutch would be a valuable aide in a corps made up of men from many lands.

Meldritch's unit, the equivalent of an artillery-augmented brigade in later days, marched off to Transylvania in company with an Austrian corps of about the same size raised by the Archduke Ferdinand. On their arrival in the rolling hill country that included some of the most productive farmlands in Europe, they joined the forces under the over-all command of Prince Sigismund Báthory, a member of the royal Hungarian family known to all his subordinates as "the great bear." Sigismund was a courtly, amiable giant with black hair, eyes almost as dark, and a consuming hatred for the enemy, who had killed his first wife and son ten years earlier.

The Turks were unlike any foe John Smith would meet again in his lifetime, a bewildering mixture of the sophisticated and the primitive. Their officers, all high-ranking nobles, were cultured gentlemen—and barbarians. Even in the field, they lived in tents of tapestry-lined silk. They read the Koran and poetry, and sometimes whiled away their leisure time by listening to music played for them by the most accomplished lute players on earth. They also enjoyed subjecting prisoners to unspeakable torture, and calmly followed the example set by their ruler, Sultan Mohammed III, who had nineteen of his seventy-three half-brothers put to death because of his fear that they might connive to steal his throne.

The Turks were superb fighting men, courageous to the point of foolhardiness. Their strategy and tactics were unorthodox by Western standards, and their foes had learned to expect never-ending surprises from them. Their cavalry may have been the best in the world, and John Smith, after seeing them in action, came to the conclusion that their infantry was almost as efficient as the regiments of Henry IV. Their most effective fighting unit was the Janissary Corps, which was made up exclusively of Christian slaves, enemy soldiers who had been captured in combat and then subjected to a complicated training system in which rewards were granted generously and punishment was meted out harshly.

Both armies used one of the most terrible weapons ever devised—"Greek fire,"—which John saw for the first time. Such substances as pitch, sulphur, and burning charcoal were packed in wood-lined copper containers and hurled at the enemy by cannon-like catapults. They produced what was called "wet fire," which gave off an intense heat, was difficult to extinguish, and inflicted severe burns on men who tried in vain to handle it. The cavalry of both sides also used curved Turkish swords, called scimitars. Although the pistols employed were somewhat less efficient than those used in the West, pikes, spears, and javelins had been made by master craftsmen and were remarkably well balanced.

Clashes between the eager, advancing Christians and their equally bloodthirsty enemies were frequent, violent, and fought without the amenities of giving quarter on either side. One day John and several other officers who had not yet been given permanent troop assignments were riding with a small cavalry detachment protecting a sector of the corps's left flank as it moved in the direction of the main enemy body.

These gentlemen, all of them combat veterans, took their ease as they walked their horses through a broad, flat valley virtually devoid of trees. As there was no cover to protect attackers, they assumed the Turks would not molest them. They were wrong.

Preoccupied as they chatted in several languages, they suddenly became aware of a small cavalry force coming toward them at great speed through the knee-high grass. They checked their pistols, drew their sabers and, before they could move into formation, the Turks were upon them.

Veteran officers rarely became flustered, but it was difficult for the Christians to remain calm when a band of scimitar-swinging riders bore down on them. John braced himself, and the others did the same, but their pistol shots did nothing to stop or even slow the advancing Turks. Even those who were wounded continued to press forward relentlessly.

Only one defense was possible against such tactics, and a series of individual hand-to-hand combats developed. John, opposed by a Turkish officer who was relatively short and slender, soon discovered that his own sword was no match for the curved Saracen blade his foe used. Twice he barely escaped decapitation. Only his exceptional agility saved him.

A quick lunge enabled him to wound the man and snatch his scimitar.

Better armed now, he went to the aid of a companion who was in immediate danger of being unseated. To his astonishment, the Turk who had been injured came at him again, brandishing a knife. John had to kill him to put him out of action, something that would have been unnecessary—and certainly would have been considered less than gallant—had the enemy been Christian.

The fight lasted no more than a quarter of an hour, and

John was lucky that he suffered nothing worse than a few minor cuts. Four of his companions were dead, and when the Turks withdrew, riding away at great speed, they left five of their own dead behind. Sigismund's mercenaries realized, as they continued to march toward the main body of the Turkish army, that they were engaging a foe who was ruthless, hard-driving, and totally lacking in the qualities of gentlemanly compassion that men-at-arms normally expected from their enemies in the seventeenth century.

John quickly discovered that virtually every man on both sides was a professional. The tug-of-war between the Emperor Rudolph and his Hapsburg cousins was forgotten at the front, and the men of Prince Sigismund's divisions cared nothing about politics or Catholic-Protestant disputes. Spirits were high, but there were no idealists in the Christian camp. Everyone knew that the war was a nasty business, and the men accepted hardships with good cheer. The Turks were equally resilient, forceful, and brave, and John began to understand why, in spite of constant fighting for many years, neither army had been able to gain a decisive advantage.

The Christians were besieging a town near the Hungarian-Transylvanian border called Stuhlweissenburg by the Germans and Alba Regalis by everyone else. Sigismund and his mercenary French deputy, the Duc de Mercoeur, were besieging the garrison of the Turkish-captured town with a force of approximately thirty thousand men. The defenders were believed to have an army of about equal size.

Meldritch's corps was sent into the front siege lines almost as soon as it arrived, and John Smith participated in several cavalry countercharges against the Janissaries, who liked to ride out at night to break up the Christians' concentrations. He behaved commendably in these skirmishes, but did nothing of note until he conceived an idea that promptly brought him to the attention of Sigismund and Mercoeur.

Greek fire fascinated John, and he showed astonishing ingenuity by proposing a refinement unlike anything utilized since the wet fire had been first used more than a thousand years earlier. Gunpowder, he suggested, should be added to the usual ingredients in the cauldron, then mixed with hundreds of musket bullets, the whole pot to be covered with several layers of heavy searcloth, or canvas.

The advantages were obvious to the delighted commanders of the Christian army: in addition to the usual damage done by Greek fire, exploding bullets would fly in every direction, wreaking havoc. Fifty such cauldrons were prepared in secret, and catapults were placed in position opposite the walls of that part of Alba Regalis where the heaviest Turkish concentrations were believed located. Baron Kizel's artillery was given the honor of firing the catapults at midnight one night, when the Turks were sleeping. The resulting carnage decimated the ranks of the defenders.

The infantry followed the unique artillery barrage with a storming operation, and before dawn the Turkish commander surrendered. Sigismund had won his greatest victory, and Alba Regalis, which had been occupied by the Moslems for years, was restored to the Hungarians. The pasha in charge of the garrison gave his sword to Meldritch. The latter handed it on to Smith, along with a promotion in rank and a new assignment.

Captain John Smith, a title the young adventurer would use for the rest of his life, was given a company of two hundred and fifty men, half of them cavalry, the rest light infantry. He would be responsible only to Meldritch, and his unit would be used for special operational purposes.

Thus, after only sixty days in the field, John had become an authentic hero who had won as much recognition and honor as he could possibly have craved. His name was mentioned in every dispatch sent to Budapest, Vienna, and even Paris, and every soldier in Europe learned the name of the man who had almost miraculously found a way to improve the combat potential of Greek fire.

He also made an attempt to improve the efficacy of catapult fire in other ways, as had scores of artillerymen before him, but his efforts proved fruitless. The catapult, comparable to the heavy artillery of later ages, had been made into a long-range engine of offensive power second to none.

The attack on Alba Regalis illustrated to perfection the many variations that could be applied by imaginative commanders. Huge rocks and boulders were used in some machines, and, when sent over the walls of the town, crashed through roofs, smashed into walls, and endangered the defenders brave enough to venture into the open.

Most of John's time was taken up by specific duties connected with his new command. His company was made up of men from a half-dozen nations, including Hungarians and Austrians, whose languages he didn't know. So he devised a system of signals to communicate his orders in battle. The welfare of his men became his primary consideration, and when the army marched deeper into Transylvania, Meldritch declared in a written report to Sigismund, "The company commanded by Captain Smith has greater spirit than any other in my corps, and will engage in any feat of daring."

John understood his responsibilities, and scores of men from other units wanted to be transferred to his company when an opening occurred. Although a newcomer, he was known by everyone in the army, from the Prince and the Duke to miserable serfs who spent their evenings polishing their masters' armor.

Within the immediate future, the Turks would have good cause to learn John Smith's identity, too.

VI

The Duel

EVENLY MATCHED CHRISTIAN and Turkish armies faced each other across the ramparts of Orastie, a Transylvanian city that changed hands so often in the sixteenth and seventeenth centuries that it lost its influence as a trade center and eventually became a sleepy Rumanian farm town lacking in the glamour and bustle it had enjoyed at its zenith.

The investment of the town was a perplexing and difficult operation. Sigismund had to take Orastie if he hoped to penetrate deeper into Transylvania, but knew the Turks were holding strong reinforcements farther south, and therefore didn't want to risk the lives of too many of his men. An artillery bombardment was out of the question, as some thousands of Transylvanian Christians were inside the walls. Also, the Earl of Meldritch had been born in the city, and he begged his superiors to spare it.

The Turks had their problems, too. The commander of the defense force was one of Sultan Mohammed's younger brothers, Suleiman, who knew the war was placing a great burden on the throne and was afraid, with good reason, that he would be executed if he lost too many men in a protracted siege or had to summon help from still another brother, who was jealous of him and would send scathing reports of his plight to Constantinople.

So the two forces sat and watched each other for several weeks, the Christians digging siege trenches, the defenders firing at them in a desultory manner each day. Neither launched a major offensive, and the men of both armies, with little better to occupy them, shouted insults at each other across the walls. Each day the invectives became sharper, and finally a bored Turkish nobleman named Turbashaw could tolerate no more.

A courier rode out of Orastie under a flag of truce, carrying a challenge to personal combat. Turbashaw, in a long-winded document, offered to meet any gentleman in the Christian army, each of the duelists to be mounted, and each to carry only a lance and sword. The messenger carried a second communication, a letter from Suleiman to Prince Sigismund, suggesting that, if the offer was accepted, a truce be declared so that both armies could watch the sport, together with "the ladies of this city, who are lacking the entertainments due their station."

Many hot-blooded young Christian officers were eager to represent their army, but the first to volunteer, and the most insistent, was Captain John Smith. Sigismund, after some hesitation and with considerable reluctance, agreed to the duel.

The following day a holiday atmosphere prevailed at Orastie. The officers and men of the Christian army marched up to an appointed place less than a quarter of a mile from the city gates, within plain view of the handsomely dressed ladies, who had taken places on the walls and exchanged enthusiastic waves and smiles with their would-be deliverers. Promptly at noon the gates opened, and Suleiman rode into the open, surrounded by members of his staff. He was followed by his entire army, which took up a position opposite the Christians.

The scene was reminiscent of the great days of chivalry, as the commanders of the opposing forces exchanged salutes. Then their principal lieutenants did the same, in a ceremony that lasted the better part of an hour.

Turbashaw was the first of the duelists to appear, and his arrival was arranged with all the pomp that representatives of imperial Turkey could muster. Drums rolled, oboes wailed plaintively, and then a bareheaded Janissary appeared on foot, carrying the lord's lance. As the Janissary was fair-haired—and, of course, a slave—the insult was not lost on the Christians. Next came two turbaned slaves, leading the Turk's horse, a handsome stallion wearing armor and gem-encrusted trappings. Next in the procession marched still more slaves, bearing Turbashaw's personal armor. Bringing up the rear was the duelist, clad in a ground-length cape ornamented with the embroidered wings of an eagle. The cape was so heavily studded with gold, silver, and jewels that the slave boy to whom Turbashaw handed it staggered under the garment's weight.

The Turk took his time preparing for the duel, both armies watching in silence as he donned his armor, except for his helmet, and mounted his horse. His partisans cheered when he took his lance from the Janissary, who dropped to one knee before handing it to him.

At that moment John Smith, who must have been watching from a vantage point behind the lines of the Christian army, came into the open. He was unattended and, following custom, carried his lance under his right arm and his helmet in his left hand. Neither his armor nor that of his horse was ornamented.

The two contestants rode past each other, each bowing courteously. They continued for another seventy-five paces, as had been agreed, each hastily donning his helmet and pulling down his visor. Two judges, one from each of the armies, raised pistols above their heads and fired.

The duelists wheeled instantly and charged at each other, lances ready as they galloped. John struck first, and his aim was true, his lance penetrating deep into his foe's throat in the small space between helmet and body armor. The fight was ended a few seconds after it had begun.

John had been aware of the enemy's insult in sending a Christian captive as a lance-bearer onto the field and returned the compliment by leaping to the ground and drawing a scimitar—rather than a Western-style sword. With a single blow he cut off his adversary's head and, mounting again, carried the grisly trophy as a gift to Prince Sigismund. He left Turbashaw's body on the ground, and neither he nor any other Christian claimed the Turk's armor or horse, which were his by right of combat.

There was a dead silence in the ranks of the enemy, until a handsomely dressed officer named Gualgo rode forward into the open and shouted a challenge to Smith. He dared the victor to meet him in fair duel the following day, with pistols to be used as well as javelins and swords. In a hoarse, shaking voice he called on Allah to hear his vow: he would either regain Turbashaw's head or lose his own.

Several Christian officers, among them the Earl of Meldritch, urged John not to press his luck and advised him to let someone else answer the challenge. But he shook them off, rode again into the clear and, using the limited Turkish he had learned, accepted the offer in a tone of scathing contempt.

The scene was repeated the following day, and the only difference was that Gualgo's cloak was a shade less ornate than the unfortunate Turbashaw's had been. Again the Turks engaged in a pantomime of splendor, while John, appreciating the value of understatement, rode alone and wore plain armor.

The duelists rode hard at each other when the signal was given, and struck with such fury that each shattered his lance on the other's armor. For an instant it appeared as though the Englishman had gained an advantage, and the Christians cheered when Gualgo slipped from his saddle and seemed about to fall to the ground. But the Turk recovered so swiftly that he was the first to draw his pistol.

John, although inclined to behave impetuously at times, was always cool-headed in battle, and conducted himself with great poise. Forcing his horse to sidestep just as Gualgo raised his pistol, he deliberately allowed his opponent to fire the first shot. The bullet glanced harmlessly off the Englishman's body armor, leaving a slight dent in it.

Now it was John's turn, and he put his own bullet between Gualgo's corselet and the crease in his chain-mail shirt, directly above the upper arm. The shot burrowed into the Turk's shoulder with such force that it knocked him to the ground, and although he was not seriously injured, he was at least momentarily incapacitated. John, a ruthless fighting man in a cold-blooded age, quickly drew his scimitar and lopped off his foe's head.

He wanted his slain enemy's horse and armor so he could sell them for a profit, and at a prearranged signal the junior officers of his company raced forward to seize the trophies while he, for the second time in two days, presented Prince Sigismund with a Turk's head as a memento.

The Moslems were angry as they returned to the garrison, and both sides knew the war would begin again in earnest. Less than an hour later, the siege was resumed.

Sigismund's forces threw a strong cordon around the city and resumed the digging of their siege trenches, but, on the Prince's orders, did not return the increased fire of the Turks. The Christian high command still hoped to avoid violence and based its long-range strategy on an attempt to starve the garrison into submission, knowing Suleiman would avoid asking for reinforcements until he became desperate. The siege was effective, and several attempts made by the Turks to send supply trains into Orastie were repulsed. Then a spy who escaped from the city brought word to Prince Sigismund that the garrison's food reserves were dwindling at an alarming rate.

While the Prince and his generals debated what to do next, John Smith came to them with a bold idea. He suggested that he send the proud Turkish officer corps still another challenge to a duel. He would word it in an insulting manner guaranteeing its acceptance, and thereafter his seconds could spend days quibbling with the Turks over the details of the fight. Suleiman would not send for reinforcements until the duel had been fought, in all probability, and in the meantime the stocks of meat and grain would continue to shrink each day.

The Earl of Meldritch was afraid his subordinate's luck would change, so he opposed the scheme, but Sigismund took a less personal view of the situation. The life of only one mercenary officer would be at stake, and Suleiman might be sufficiently intrigued by the prospect of another duel to let his supplies become even more depleted.

John immediately sent a courier to the gates with a contemptuous message, in which he informed any Turkish ladies who might be in the city that "he was not so much enamored of their servants' heads, but if any Turk of rank would come to the place of combat to redeem them, he should have his upon the like conditions, if he could win it."

The challenge was accepted instantly by an officer whom Sigismund calls Buenimolgri, but who is known to posterity as Bonny Mulgro, which is John Smith's phonetic way of spelling his name. The seconds acting on behalf of the Christian challenger at once began to play for time. They claimed that John was ill, and forty-eight hours passed before the alleged invalid recovered his health and negotiations were resumed. Meanwhile the siege continued.

The Turk's seconds proposed that the same weapons be used as those employed in the second duel, but the Christians protested that their duelist wanted a change. He would not specify the weapons he wanted, however, and suggested that Bonny Mulgro name them. For another four days the seconds acted as messengers, going back and forth between their camp and the gates of Orastie under a flag of truce. The siege was not lifted during this time.

At last, when the Turks became impatient, the Christians accepted the weapons Bonny Mulgro wanted: pistols, scimitars, *and* battle-axes. John Smith had never used this most murderous of weapons, and the time of reckoning was at hand.

For the next twenty-four hours, John received instruction in the use of the long-handled, double-bladed battle-ax, and when the time came to fight the duel, was as prepared as was possible under the circumstances. His friends were gloomy, having learned from the gleeful Turks that Bonny Mulgro, a colonel of heavy cavalry, was an expert in the use of all three weapons.

Once again the Turks put on a display of grandeur, but Meldritch noted that virtually all of the defenders who rode out to watch the duel had grown considerably thinner. Bonny Mulgro was a giant, several inches taller than John, with huge hands and a long reach. The Christians gaped at him in awe as he donned his armor.

But John displayed no signs of fear when he rode into the open, and he was politely wooden-faced when he bowed to his opponent. His scimitar was loose in its sheath; he carried his loaded, cocked pistol in his belt; and the handle of his vicious battle-ax protruded from a socket a few inches from his right hand. The combatants rode past each other, each clamping his helmet on his head and pulling down his visor. The signal was given, and they wheeled simultaneously, charging at full tilt.

John had decided to gamble on using his pistol first. It was the weapon with which he was most familiar, and he thought he had a better chance of scoring with it than with either of the others. But early seventeenth-century firearms were notoriously unreliable, and it was exceptionally difficult for a man riding on the back of a lunging stallion to hit a target similarly in motion.

Bonny Mulgro apparently had the same idea, and drew his pistol, too. Both men fired at almost the same instant, as soon as they came within reasonable range, and both missed. John had lost his gamble, and when the Turk drew his battle-ax, had to do the same.

The battle-ax, which had been used since the twelfth century in its advanced form, was the most frightful weapon ever devised for hand-to-hand combat. Its straight-edged and hooked blades were honed to a razor-sharp edge and set in a heavy steel head, from which protruded a sharp point that enabled the user to wield the ax like a lance if he wished. The handle about four and one-half feet long, and the weapon weighed more than one hundred pounds.

The only defense against a battle-ax attack was a counterattack. A man who tried to parry a blow with the shaft of his weapon might find the handle and head separated by a sharp blow, which would leave him at the mercy of an opponent. Therefore a duelist could only hope that his armor would protect him until he could land a lethal blow.

John and Bonny Mulgro hacked at each other, damaging corselets and denting helmets as each tried to unseat the other. A battle of this sort required almost superhuman courage, great physical strength, and expert horsemanship. A duelist needed both hands for his ax, which forced him to guide his angry, plunging stallion with his knees, and the slightest mistake in judgment, combined with a foe's heavy blow, could send him to the ground.

For a time, John Smith gave as good as he received, to the surprised delight of the cheering Christian army, but Bonny Mulgro's greater experience finally won him a sharp advantage. John had just lashed out at his enemy with his ax, and was maneuvering into a new position so he could repeat his tactic, when the Turk's ax crashed against the side of his head.

He lost his balance, and his left foot came out of its stirrup. The Turks gleefully howled for blood, and Bonny Mulgro pressed forward to finish off the Christian. But he was too eager and left himself exposed as he swung around and started to raise his heavy ax high over his head.

In that instant John decided to sacrifice weight for dexterity. Although half in and half out of his saddle, he threw aside his ax, drew his scimitar, and slashed at the straining Turk's exposed neck. The blade found its mark, which was fortunate, for John could not keep his balance any longer and tumbled to the ground. He rolled away from the pawing hoofs of his stallion, and when he regained his feet, his scimitar still in his hand, he saw the crumpled body of his foe a few feet away.

Bonny Mulgro was dead, and John completed his self-assigned task by decapitating the Turk with a second scimitar blow.

Christian officers spurred forward to prevent the enemy from riding down their champion, and for a few moments it looked as though a full-scale battle might erupt before the gates of Orastie. But the personal honor of Prince Sigismund and Suleiman was at stake in the truce, and both commanders, aided by their subordinate generals, finally managed to restore order.

The Turks sullenly marched back into Orastie; regiments

assigned to siege duty quickly surrounded the town; and the dreary business of reducing the garrison was resumed.

Jubilant officers surrounded John, who was still clutching the head of Bonny Mulgro, and hoisting him onto their shoulders, started toward Prince Sigismund's tent. An impromptu procession formed, and more than six thousand cheering officers and men joined in the parade. In that hour John Smith knew one of his greatest personal triumphs. His victory over Bonny Mulgro at a moment when he was himself at the point of death thrilled his colleagues, and even the Earl of Meldritch forgot his noble dignity to caper and shout.

Sigismund showed his appreciation in practical terms. He gave John a magnificent stallion from his personal stable, a scimitar with a gold, gem-encrusted hilt that had been captured from a pasha in battle the previous year, and a purse of three hundred silver ducats. That sum was the equivalent of a six-thousand-dollar prize, three and two-thirds centuries later.

John didn't want to carry so much money with him in a camp filled with professional cutpurses and other rogues, many of whom had served prison terms, so he arranged to leave it in safekeeping with the treasurer of the Prince's household. Although he didn't realize the significance of his decision for a long time, it was one of the wisest and most fortunate he had ever made.

The defeat of Bonny Mulgro by a man who killed three of Suleiman's best officers without losing a drop of his own blood disheartened the Turks. Two attempts were made to send messengers south for the reinforcements Suleiman had been so reluctant to request. Both couriers were captured, and when the second was sent back to the city on foot, the Turks gave up the struggle and surrendered unconditionally.

Orastie was captured, its people were freed from captivity and its buildings were intact. Nearly thirty thousand prisoners had been taken without the need to fight a major battle, and a brother of the Sultan himself was sent to Graz, in Austria.

John Smith's three duels were more responsible than anything else for breaking the Turks' will to resist, and Sigismund, in his order of the day congratulating his troops, promoted the young Englishman to the rank of major and made him the commander of a battalion of seven hundred men.

Why John preferred in later life to call himself Captain, when he had as valid a right to refer to himself as Major, is unknown. It was a mystery he did not elect to explain. At the time of Orastie's fall, however, he was thinking only in terms of his present and immediate future. He had achieved the impossible, and all Europe sang his praises.

VII

The Slave

JOHN SMITH REPEATEDLY DEMonstrated his talent for command in the weeks that followed the Christian victory at Orastie. Prince Sigismund adopted a strategy of seizing and keeping the initiative in the hope that, by the spring of 1603, he could drive the Turks into the recesses of their European stronghold, the area that would in later centuries become Bulgaria. Meldritch was sent ahead with his corps to act as a vanguard, with orders to scout the enemy and, when necessary, clear the region of small bodies of Turks that might harass Sigismund's main army as it advanced into territory long held by the foe.

John's battalion led the corps and fought seven or eight short, sharp skirmishes with the Turks. Most of the units he met were, like his own, mixed cavalry-infantry battalions, and in each engagement he achieved victory by striking very swiftly, with his foot soldiers in the center and his horsemen on the flanks. These brushes had no lasting significance, but did enable the Earl of Meldritch to penetrate deep into enemy territory.

Unfortunately, communications were poor, and Meldritch failed to realize he was far outdistancing Sigismund, who was weighed down by artillery, ponderous siege guns, and heavy baggage trains, and hence had to travel at a much slower pace. The Turks realized that Meldritch was becoming increasingly isolated, however, and their high command, which was still smarting over the loss of Orastie, badly wanted a face-saving victory.

Among the best of the Turks' troops were regiments of Crimean Tatar cavalry and lancers. These men, descendants of Mongolians who had invaded Finland and Hungary hundreds of years earlier, had been living in Lithuania and Poland, where they had retained many of their ancient ways and, in addition, had adopted the Moslem religion. They were magnificent horsemen, recklessly courageous in battle and, under their semi-barbaric code of honor, preferred death to defeat. Six thousand of them were sent north, together with two regiments of Janissaries and three of Turkish dragoons. The corps was under orders to meet and annihilate Meldritch's force, which by now had grown to about four thousand men.

Meldritch was making his way across the rugged Transylvanian Alps, where his progress was slowed until he reached the narrow valleys through which the Oltu River, a branch of the Danube, flowed south. Perhaps success had made him careless; in any event, he was a ten-day march ahead of Sigismund when he reached a wooded valley that was ideal for the Turks' purposes. There were towering hills to the east and west, and a stiff climb directly ahead. On all three of these approaches the Turks stationed archers and musketeers; and then they sent the heavy infantry around to block off the Christian rear.

Too late Meldritch realized he had been hemmed in on all sides. He ordered the vanguard under John Smith to hold the enemy at bay and immediately put his whole force to work chopping down pines to erect a barricade of high stakes that would hamper the foe's cavalry charges. John was able to delay the main body of Turks by striking hard, as though operating from a position of strength, and the Turks were content to fall back and play for time without yet having committed the Tatars to battle.

When the barricade was ready, John's battalion was pulled back behind the makeshift palisade, and the corps braced itself. Meldritch and his officers were well aware of the gravity of their situation. They were badly outnumbered, reinforcements were many days away, and there was virtually no chance they could achieve a victory. Their one hope was that of holding the Turks off until nightfall and then trying to escape to the north through the heavily wooded mountains.

The Turks charged, and the Christians held firm behind their palisade. The stakes slowed the Tatar horsemen long enough to enable Meldritch's musketeers and archers to fire into their solid ranks, and the Christians took a heavy toll of their foes. But the Tatars withdrew just long enough to form their lines again and charge a second time, then a third and a fourth.

In the meantime, pressure was being exerted on the Christian flanks and rear. Meldritch's cavalry was useless, and had to be kept inside the palisades, so horsemen were forced to operate dismounted, on the defensive, which reduced their effectiveness. All accounts of the battle indicate that casualties on both sides were numerous. John's own report, written many years later, declared that "the slaughter was frightful."

The Christians could only stand and fight, beating off the assaults until their infantrymen had no more gunpowder or ammunition, and the archers no arrows. By late afternoon the Turks were able to advance again without serious opposition. Their foot soldiers knocked down the stakes, and the Tatar cavalry rode forward again, galloping wildly as they twirled their scimitars over their heads.

It was to the eternal credit of Meldritch's men that they did not panic. Nowhere did their lines buckle, as they formed a hollow square, and only when the situation became completely hopeless did the Earl allow himself to be led away by several members of his staff, who finally convinced him that the Sultan would like nothing better than to parade him through the streets of Constantinople, naked and in chains. He left his comrades and by hiding in the brush was able to escape to the north that night.

None of his subordinates was as fortunate. John Smith used his pistols until he had no more bullets, and then, still at the head of his troops, wielded his scimitar with such deadly effect that he was soon surrounded by the bodies of Tatar horsemen who had tried in vain to strike him down.

Some of the Christians tried to swim across the river to higher ground, but their armor was too heavy, and they drowned. Most of the corps were killed, and the survivors were taken as prisoners. John would have preferred death to the fate that was ahead. He had been knocked unconscious by a cavalryman's sword and left for dead on the field, where, later that night, the Tatars discovered him and found he was still alive. His silver armor indicated that he was an officer of rank, so he was spared decapitation and was taken into the Turkish camp. In the early hours of the morning he awakened, his head aching, to find he had been stripped naked. He and about fifty other officers in a similar, miserable state were being guarded by Janissaries who regarded them with amusement, as all had suffered the same experience at one time or another before being compelled to join the Turkish army.

John assumed that he, too, would be enlisted in the Janissary Corps, but did not know that orders had been sent from Constantinople to take no more prisoners for this purpose.

Christians captured in the past year or two had been too stubbornly anti-Turkish in their views to make good Janissaries, and this was particularly true of officers. The Turks had other plans for John Smith and his fellow prisoners.

The unfortunate captives were marched south through the Transylvanian Alps in bitter winter weather, all of them stark naked and chained together like animals. Those who stumbled or were slow were beaten with whips by overseers, but none was allowed to die, and to John's surprise, all were given ample food to eat. Most of their meals consisted of fatty lamb stew, heavily flavored with garlic, but the hungry men soon overcame their dislike for the dish. Starving prisoners were in no position to complain.

After a forced march of some days, the captives reached a large town on the Danube River at the southern boundary of Transylvania, which John believed to be Tchernavoda. The headquarters staff of the Turkish army in Europe was spending the winter there, and there were princes of the blood who were related to the Sultan, great lords, and pashas, or generals-administrators, living in the town in large numbers.

The prisoners were taken to a compound where, for the first time, they were given rough clothing to wear. The wounded were treated by physicians, and all were given two meals daily. John tasted flat Turkish bread and a cake made of honey for the first time; he was so ravenous he enjoyed both. The greatest hardship, he later wrote, was that he and the other prisoners were denied spirits, even weak beer. The Turks were supposedly devout Moslems and therefore neither drank nor served alcoholic beverages, but in practice the lords, pashas, and other high-ranking officers did what they pleased.

After being held for more than a month at Tchernavoda, the prisoners finally discovered what was in store for them. One day they bathed for the first time, and were given an oil of pine tar to remove body vermin. Then, completely unclad, they were marched to the slave market, where scores of officers had gathered. The proceeds of all sales would be split between the Sultan, the general who had commanded the victorious corps, and the men who had actually captured the prisoners.

The slaves-to-be were separated, and each was chained to a stake set deep in the ground. The Turkish officers examined them with interest, looking inside their mouths to see if they had teeth, insuring that they weren't diseased, and making certain they were sound of limb. One young English lieutenant, Thomas Milimer, who had served in John's battalion, became so indignant over his treatment that he struck an elderly Turkish officer, who drew a scimitar and decapitated him.

John, who saw what had happened to the unfortunate Milimer, suffered his own indignities in silence. The high-ranking Turks paid particular attention to him, knowing he had been a major. Several wondered whether his strength was as great as it appeared, so he and several other prisoners were unchained and required to wrestle, lift weights, and otherwise demonstrate their prowess.

A pasha named Timor purchased John Smith for three gold coins, the highest price paid for any of the prisoners. John, in his later observations, did not feel honored. Timor, a heavy-set man with broad shoulders, a pointed beard, and dark, brooding eyes, was the governor of a Turkish province in Bulgaria, and John assumed he would be taken off to his master's own headquarters. But the mocking laughter of the soldiers who stood guard over him made him feel that Timor had other plans for him. He was right.

He was given a loincloth and a rough peasant's cloak of wool, and was then taken south, his guards on horseback, while he rode a donkey. He was grateful that he wasn't forced to walk, but at best his journey was unpleasant. He wore chains on his wrists and ankles, and when his captors halted for a meal or a night's rest, he was compelled to prepare their food and serve it to them. He was allowed to eat scraps, when any were available. On those occasions when the guards finished the food, he went hungry.

They took the prisoner through Macedon, the rugged hill country of Alexander the Great, and south through Thrace to the great city of Adrianople, which stood about one hundred and thirty miles from Constantinople. In spite of his misery, John was fascinated by the blending of the cultures of East and West. He saw minarets and temples, severely handsome Grecian buildings, and the more ornate structures built by the Romans.

He was led down crooked, narrow, and evil-smelling streets, littered with refuse, past the great mosque, recently completed, built in honor of Sultan Selim II. At the Ali Pasha bazaar, which had been famous for centuries and would know still more renown in the years ahead, he was dazed by the beauty of the merchandise offered by jewelers and leatherworkers. Among the many items displayed in booths were the helmets and corselets of Christian warriors, and he wanted to weep.

Adrianople was a city of Turkish men—and of male slaves. Very few women appeared on the twisting, cobbled streets, and without exception they were heavily veiled. John was curious about them, but did not dare raise his head to look at them. He had already been cuffed a number of times for demonstrating too lively an interest in his surroundings.

At last his guards brought him to a great palace, known as Eski Serai, which was maintained as a royal residence, although no sultan had visited it in many years. Doorframes were arched, floors were tiled, and although the high walls were bare in the austere Moslem traditions of the Turks, the covers of embroidered divans were encrusted with gems, and jewels glittered on the rugs casually thrown over benches. The gardens were breathtakingly lovely, but utilitarian. Fruit and almond trees, date palms and other food-bearing plants abounded, but beauty was not cultivated for its own sake. At one time during John's sojourn at the palace, he was told that more than a hundred and fifty slaves, most of them Christians and all of them emasculated, worked there.

He was afraid his captors intended to castrate him, too, and for several weeks lived in dread. Certainly the treatment he received was unusual. Timor, along with other high-ranking Turkish officials, had an apartment of his own at Eski Serai, and John was taken immediately to his master's suite, where he was handed over to the eunuchs who maintained the quarters. These beardless, giggling, grossly overweight creatures lived in a world of their own, and John soon discovered that they were "as meanly tyrannical in their demands and as variable in their moods, one moment gay and the next dour, as the most common shrews in England."

The eunuchs saw to it that John bathed in steaming hot water, a humiliation he deeply resented, as he—like most Western men of his age—usually washed in cold water. Then the eunuchs shaved off his beard, which was the pride and symbol of his manhood, and subjected him to the further humiliation of scraping his body "with a fine pumice," which "removed all hair from my chest, arms, legs, and other parts." He was then forced to submit to yet another degradation, that of painting the soles of his feet and the palms of his hands with henna, a Turkish practice ordinarily reserved for women —and eunuchs. It was no wonder that John thought his days as a man were numbered.

He had good cause for his apprehension. His thick eyebrows were removed with an instrument he later called "a small pliers invented by Satan," and smaller brows were painted on his face. His already shaggy hair was oiled, curled, and perfumed, and the eunuchs then attired him in what he referred to, very briefly, as "a gown of silk," apparently a woman's dress.

There was a faint glimmer of hope, however, that his masculinity might be saved. His identity had become known prior to his purchase, he learned from one of the eunuchs who spoke French, and Timor had realized that he had bought the renowned winner of three celebrated duels against Turkish champions. The pasha had, therefore, made up a story of his own, claiming he had himself defeated John in hand-to-hand combat on the field of battle. By means of this totally false assertion, the Turk was trying to present himself—to those who didn't know better—as a greater warrior than the men John had defeated.

After a stay of several weeks at Adrianople, remaining the entire time in Timor's apartment at the palace, John was moved to his ultimate destination. Dressed in the "gown" and an outer garment that covered him from the top of his head to his feet, completely veiling his face and body, he was taken to a palanquin, a litter consisting of a coach-like box, with a seat, that was carried on poles by four brawny slaves. John rode alone, behind closed curtains, and several eunuchs as well as guards accompanied the party. He was given no information, and the eunuchs kept him apart from others on the journey. It is possible that the guards and slaves didn't know the identity of their veiled passenger.

After spending more than a week on the road, the party came at last to the greatest Islamic city, Constantinople, once the most glittering metropolis in Christendom and, since the final fall of the Roman Empire in 1453, the capital of the powerful Ottoman Empire.

Founded by Constantine the Great in A.D. 328 on an older town, Byzantium, seventeenth-century Constantinople may have been the most spectacularly beautiful city in the civilized world. Like Rome, it was built on seven hills, and its superb harbor bay, known as the Golden Horn, was filled with triremes, merchant ships from Lebanon, humble fishing boats with multicolored sails, and sinister fighting vessels manned by chained slaves. The domes and minarets of the mosques towered high above the walls and palaces built by generations of rulers and their generals. Ancient aqueducts erected by the Romans still brought water to the city from the hills, and there were gardens everywhere, even in the yards of Christian churches now being used for purposes other than worship.

Constantinople, the last outpost of Europe, may have been the world's largest city in John Smith's day, and certainly was the busiest. Games were held every week in the hippodrome and smaller arenas for the entertainment of the people, a practice begun under the Romans and continued by the sultans, who found races and circuses an inexpensive substitute for bread.

Soldiers in the many uniforms of troops from all parts of the far-flung empire wandered through the narrow streets and in the great bazaars, the marketplaces. Black Africans and Orientals came to Constantinople to trade, and the most outrageously brazen strumpets on earth searched everywhere for clients. The city was a bewildering jumble of sights and sounds and odors. In the poorer quarters, which had often been burned to the ground, people lived in ramshackle wooden huts under conditions of unspeakable poverty.

The little that John Smith saw of Constantinople he viewed from his curtain-shrouded palanquin, which was not the most satisfactory way to see the sights. But he had other matters on his mind besides the wonders of Constantinople, and his worst fears seemed about to be confirmed when he was delivered to a substantial house of red stone from the Turkish highlands and there given into the care of a group of slave women.

To his great embarrassment, the women bathed and perfumed him, tinted his eyelids with dye, and rimmed them with black antimony. One of these women was young, blonde, and attractive, and John was horrified to discover that she was an English girl named Elizabeth Rondee, who had also been captured by the Turks and sold into slavery. He had an opportunity to exchange only a few words with Elizabeth, who showed pity for him.

Then, naked again and with slender ceremonial chains of gold at his ankles and wrists, John was taken to the great court of the house and made to prostrate himself on the tiled floor. Only at that moment did he learn he was being presented as a "gift" by Timor to his mistress, Lady Charatza Tragabigzanda, a Turkish noblewoman.

According to John's subsequent account, Tragabigzanda was fair-skinned, with delicate features and fair, reddish hair. Inasmuch as members of the Turkish nobility were dark, it may have been that she colored her hair with henna. Her only portrait, a sketch drawn by John himself, shows her to have been heavier than the attractive women of England and western Europe, but sweet-faced, with grave eyes and a faint smile on her small mouth.

Tragabigzanda was delighted with her new possession, and after inspecting John, decided not to have him emasculated, but instead to have a servant who was completely male perform the services of a servingmaid.

Other captives of the period reported that they had been treated in a similar fashion, which appears to have been much in vogue. Certainly it was difficult for Turkish ladies of the seventeenth century to amuse themselves. They were not permitted to attend the games at the hippodrome or other arenas, could not dine in public places and, even when veiled, risked maltreatment and possible open assault if they went to the bazaars.

Consequently they spent most of their time at home with their relatives and found relief from the monotony of daily existence by calling on their friends, who were in similar situations. Tragabigzanda was more fortunate than most. She was an only child, her father was dead, and she was therefore free to live a relatively unrestricted existence. As a pasha's mistress, she was a woman of some influence and could reasonably expect to marry Timor either when he requested her to join him at his headquarters in Cambia, later known as Bulgaria, or when he was recalled to the capital.

In all probability, Timor expected Tragabigzanda to have her new slave castrated, but her failure to do so need not have alarmed or upset him, inasmuch as other women of her class were entertaining themselves in a similar fashion. After all, Timor had been boasting by sending her the Christian champion he claimed to have defeated in single combat.

As for John, he was fortunate—and knew it. He willingly endured the humiliation of attending Tragabigzanda in her chamber and bath, in company with slave girls wearing flimsy attire identical with his. It was somewhat more disconcerting, however, to be summoned by Tragabigzanda when she had guests, to appear before them similarly dressed, and then be made to strip naked in their presence and serve them honey cakes. He suffered intensely in this perverted atmosphere, and his pride was shattered.

The tortures he endured, he later wrote, were even worse than the agonies he would have felt had he been emasculated. A healthy, virile male had been thrust into a world of women whose manners and attitudes he was expected to imitate. His inevitable failure, and the mockery to which he was subjected as a consequence, kept him in misery.

His one friend during this trying time was Elizabeth Rondee. The daughter of an official in the British diplomatic service, she and her parents had been passengers on a London-bound ship after spending several years in Portugal. The vessel had been attacked by Moslem pirates from North Africa, and she had seen both her mother and father killed. To the best of her knowledge, she had been the sole survivor of all who had been on board the merchantman. Her Moslem captors had taken her to a city on the south shore of the Mediterranean, where she had been given into the custody of a slave dealer, and after suffering a variety of frightening experiences, she had been transported to Constantinople, where Timor had purchased her for his mistress.

John and Elizabeth exchanged confidences in snatches. At no time were they able to spend more than a few moments alone, since the slaves' activities were strictly supervised by three eunuchs in Tragabigzanda's employ. Slaves were whipped for offenses real and imagined, and it is unlikely that the English couple made love. Their situation was so precarious that neither would have been willing to take the chance. Their mistress had the power to do what she pleased with them, and was accountable to no one but herself; had she chosen to have them executed, the law would have required her to file a registration of the facts with a minor government official who kept records of such trivia, and that would have been the end of the matter.

Tragabigzanda must have realized that John and Elizabeth were growing more friendly, and she undoubtedly knew, too, that the English girl was exceptionally attractive. A portrait painted twelve years later, after Elizabeth had become a person of consequence, depicted her as a slender, high-bosomed woman with blonde hair, intense blue eyes, and unusually pale skin.

Whatever Tragabigzanda's reasons, she took surprising action and got rid of the slave girl by giving her to a cousin who was marrying a pasha stationed in the far western reaches of the Ottoman Empire, in the land later to become known as Morocco. Female Caucasians in their late teens and early twenties brought higher prices in the market than any other slaves, and Tragabigzanda must have enjoyed a unique distinction in her circle of friends because she owned one. So it is safe to assume that something in their relationship disturbed her to the extent that she rid herself of a slave who gave her considerable prestige.

Elizabeth's departure was so abrupt that John knew nothing of it until she had gone. Now he was completely alone in an alien, morally corrupt land. He thought of escape, but soon realized that such dreams were not practical. Man's clothing, which would be essential for the purpose, was unavailable. He had no way of getting his hands on either weapons or money, and soldiers stationed at the gates of the city were always on the lookout for runaway slaves.

No matter how difficult and disgraceful his lot, he was forced to remain in the house of an imaginative, high-strung Turkish lady who treated him as a toy, pampering him one moment and ridiculing him the next. Many guests came to the house to see the humiliation of the Christian hero, and apparently Timor heartily approved of his mistress's conduct, which increased his own stature and renown in Constantinople.

John was afraid, too, that Tragabigzanda would grow tired of him and sell him to someone who would treat him with even greater cruelty. According, he began to search for some way to preserve his sanity, masculinity, and life, and eventually found the most simple and obvious of solutions.

VIII

"Freedom Is Priceless"

FREEDOM IS PRICELESS, THE most precious of possessions," John Smith wrote in his *Generall Historie of Virginia,* twenty years after his enslavement, and he meant every word. Only one who had known the degradations he had suffered could appreciate and savor liberty as he did.

Desperation and his instinct for self-preservation impelled him to seek a new route that would lead toward an improvement in his status. He discovered that Lady Tragabigzanda knew a little Italian, a language he had picked up during his brief sojourn in the Italian states and his subsequent service with officers from Milan, Florence, and Rome in the Christian army of Prince Sigismund. Using his own limited knowledge of the tongue as a base, he began to teach the Turkish lady French.

She, like Smith, apparently had an aptitude for languages, and before long they were able to communicate. Eventually they understood each other sufficiently well for John to tell

Tragabigzanda the true story of his capture in the Transylvanian Alps. It is difficult to determine whether disgust for Timor or a new appreciation of her slave caused a change in attitude, but whatever the cause, John's situation improved dramatically.

He was no longer compelled to wear feminine attire and paint his hands and feet with henna. Instead, Tragabigzanda dressed him in a loincloth of silk and stopped exposing him to her friends. Their daily conversations in French grew longer, and sometimes they were closeted together for hours at a time. It is safe to assume that Tragabigzanda had reason to be grateful that she hadn't ordered her slave emasculated.

In any event, she treated John so well now that he never forgot her, and twice in later life he went out of his way to honor her. After making his second voyage to the New World, he named a portion of New England Cape Tragabigzanda, but less romantic men called it Cape Ann instead, in honor of an English queen. And in 1624 the Turkish lady was one of two persons to whom he dedicated his *Generall Historie,* writing, "The beauteous Lady Tragabigzanda, when I was a slave to the Turks, did all she could to succour me."

No secrets are safe in a house filled with servants, and soon Tragabigzanda's eunuchs and slaves began to whisper about her relations with the strapping young Englishman. These rumors came to the attention of the lady's mother, who was alarmed. A noblewoman's reputation would be ruined if she had an affair with one of her slaves, and in Tragabigzanda's case there might have been even more serious consequences. Timor would have broken his bethrothal vows had he heard the stories, and Tragabigzanda would have been disgraced for life.

The old woman made strong, determined efforts to break off the affair, but the harder she pressed, the more tightly Tragabigzanda clung to John Smith. The risks had become enormous, however. The mother was incapable of keeping her mouth shut, and if she had said something to the wrong person, the slave would have been put to death under a strictly enforced imperial law.

Tragabigzanda decided that the best way to protect John from harm would be to send him away from Constantinople for a time, and she cunningly thought he would be safest if he joined Timor in Cambia.

She took John into her confidence, and he agreed with her scheme. It did not occur to either of them that he might be mistreated, and he stressed this point at some length in his *True Travels,* written a generation later.

The beginning of his journey was actually pleasant. He wore neither chains nor a slave collar, and was dressed soberly in boots, breeches, and a heavy shirt, so that anyone seeing him might have mistaken him for a free Greek or Serb, two of the Western people under the rule of the Turks. Nothing, in fact, prevented him from trying to escape other than the letter Tragabigzanda had sent to Timor, telling her official lover she was sending the slave to him. John had no wish to cause any embarrassment to his benefactress.

He traveled by ship up the western shore of the Black Sea, and, his passage having been arranged by Tragabigzanda, he slept alone in a private cabin and ate his meals with members of the Turkish gentry, none of whom suspected his true status. When he went ashore and rode inland to the great stone castle where Timor made his headquarters, however, his standing changed abruptly and harshly.

Timor had nothing more to gain by giving the Christian hero special treatment, and John, like hundreds of other captives, was made a field slave. His hair and beard, which Tragabigzanda had allowed him to grow again, were shaved off, he was stripped and lashed on principle, and then a heavy iron ring was riveted around his neck. He was given a coarse "hair coat" to wear, and was sent to the pens where the miserable prisoners lived under conditions that, according to John's account, "not even a dog could have lived to endure." He, as the newcomer, was mistreated by his peers and "was slave of slaves to them all."

Timor believed in working his captives, and the slaves were driven into the fields before dawn every morning by whip-wielding overseers and made to labor without rest until long after sundown. The food served the captives was vile, and the men survived only because they stole vegetables and roots, which they hid and consumed late at night. They worked seven days each week, were beaten for the slightest offense, and slept in squalid wooden huts, on the bare ground.

John's fellow prisoners were men from many lands, among them Hungarians, Austrians, Bohemians, and a few Russians —the first of that nationality he had met. When out of their guards' hearing the men spoke constantly of escape. Few, however had ever tried to break away, and none had succeeded. Runaways were tortured and then beaten to death in the presence of all, and this treatment discouraged even the most courageous.

One day in February, 1604, after having spent considerably more than a year as a slave, John unexpectedly found himself in a new situation. He was working as a thresher in a field located about three miles from Pasha Timor's castle, and since he was alone at the time, had thrown himself onto a pile of hay just inside a barn door. It was his luck that Timor was making a tour of inspection and came upon him while he was dozing.

The pasha slashed at him with a riding crop and cursed him so intemperately that John could stand no more abuse. Losing his own temper, he picked up the crude threshing-bat of heavy wood he had been using, and literally beat out Timor's brains with it. Only when he saw his master's body at his feet and realized what would happen when the deed was discovered did he recover his wits.

Then, because he had no choice, he stripped Timor's body, which he hid beneath the hay, and dressed in the pasha's clothes. He also took the Turk's pistol, scimitar, and short knife, and hastily stuffed his pockets with rye he had been threshing. Timor's gelding was haltered outside the barn, and in a moment John was in the saddle.

His mind working rapidly, he considered his situation from every angle. He was still wearing his heavy, conspicuous slave collar, and had neither the tools nor the time to get rid of it. Therefore he did not dare ride toward the west, for that entire region was occupied by his captors. There were Turks to the south, too, and his only hope of escape lay to the northeast, across the border of a vast nation virtually unknown to the outside world it shunned—Russia.

Unhesitatingly he started in that direction, avoiding Turkish army patrols and not daring to halt near any man, free or slave. He continued far past nightfall, and stole some feed for the horse from a farmer's barn. A side of beef was hanging in the barn, curing, so he cut off a slice with his knife and ate it raw before pressing on.

The next sixteen days and nights constituted the worst nightmare John had ever known. He made his way north through the eastern portions of Transylvania and pushed up through Moldavia, which was under Turkish domination. He crossed the Russian border without realizing it, and later estimated that he had spent forty-eight hours on Russian soil before it finally crossed his mind that he was no longer in Turkish territory.

Everywhere, he had to steal food for himself and his horse, and his situation did not improve in Russia, where foreigners were regarded with intense suspicion. Peasants fled when the dirty, tattered man on horseback approached them, and the few travelers he saw would have nothing to do with him. The gates of walled towns remained closed to him, and only after he had spent two and a half weeks in flight did he obtain relief —of a sort—when he reached the city of Rostov.

He had found it by traveling almost due east along the northern shore of the Black Sea and its extension, the Sea of Azov. Rostov, which was located a few miles from the Sea of Azov on the estuary of the Don River, had been occupied several times by Turks and Mongols in its long history, but had retained its completely Russian character.

It was a seaport, the capital of a grain-producing district. The country's ruler, Tsar Boris Godunov, who had seized the throne by questionable methods, had established a strong garrison there. Rostov was a city of contrasts. There were many churches there, but none resembled Christian houses of worship that John had seen elsewhere in his travels. These edifices somewhat resembled Turkish mosques, and they had some of the characteristics of pagan Greek temples, too. Not until he had spent some time there did he learn that the Russian bishops refused to accept the authority of the Roman Church.

The wealthy lived in some of the most magnificent homes he had seen anywhere, and he noted that "the most insignificant lord dwelled amidst splendors unknown to the greatest of English dukes." The higher nobles owned castles that studded the Don on both sides, and John, observing them with a professional soldier's eye, saw that each was capable of independent self-defense.

The poor of Rostov, however, lived in squalor worse than that suffered by the most miserable of Turkish slaves. Thousands of mud huts were crowded close together on the estuary lowlands, and a heavy rain, in John's opinion, would have washed them away. Half-naked children played in the dirt, and their elders resembled grimy savages. All had long, matted hair and were dressed in shapeless rags.

John was taken into custody at Rostov's walls by fierce, evil-smelling soldiers. He was unable to communicate with them in any of the languages he knew, and they handled him so roughly that he was afraid they intended to kill him on the spot. Instead they took him to the Governor of Rostov, Baron Reshdinski, one of the most cultivated barbarians John Smith ever knew.

The Governor was a remarkable, contradictory man. He spoke Greek, Turkish, and Latin as well as his own tongue. His collection of portraits painted on porcelain was sent, after his death, to the Kremlin in Moscow, where archivists preserved it for posterity. He loved good music and fine food, and was also a student of French poetry. At the same time, he was a bloodthirsty monster who often entertained his dinner guests by having a serf tortured for their amusement during the meal. He was said to be the father of forty or more illegitimate children, and attractive peasant girls of the neighborhood smeared mud on their faces and clothes in order to escape his notice.

John Smith's obvious erudition struck an immediate responsive chord in Reshdinski, and the Baron listened sympathetically as the young Englishman told his story in several languages. An armorer was called in to strike the slave collar from John's neck, a barber trimmed his growing beard and hair, and he enjoyed his first bath in months, although he noted that Russian soap was so caustic that it had a tendency to peel the skin from his body.

Few outsiders had ever come to Rostov, and John was one of a very small number of foreigners the Governor had ever met. Their fascination was mutual, and the fugitive stayed on at the castle as an honored guest. John wore suits trimmed with fur, ate huge meals at a table laden with more food than he had ever seen, and drank wines so potent that he often felt dizzy and a little ill.

Reshdinski sometimes took the visitor hunting, and John was horrified by the Russian nobles' custom of using serfs instead of dogs to flush their game. One day two unfortunate peasants who had cornered a wild boar in a fir forest were killed by the beast, but the tragedy left the Governor and the officials of his court unmoved. Life in Russia was cheap. Yet these same blue-bloods wept when a minstrel who entertained them at dinner sang them a sad ballad about a bird crippled by a broken wing.

John's friendship with the Governor took second place to a far more significant relationship he formed in Rostov with Reshdinski's niece, the Lady Camallata, who may have been the one real love of his life. Several portraits of her, painted on porcelain, are still extant in the Kremlin collection and reveal her to be blonde, of course, and unusually slim and willowy for a Russian. There is humor as well as character in her eyes; although not a beauty, she is certain to have commanded attention.

Camallata was almost as learned as her uncle, and John communicated with her in both Latin and French. They became constant companions, and by the time John ended his three-month sojourn in Rostov, Camallata had taught him a passable Russian, which he spoke to the end of his days.

"The Lady Camallata," he wrote in his *True Travels,* "was the loveliest and most constant of women, and to her Captain Smith gave his heart." Thus he summed up his romance with her, and at no time indicates whether they had an affair or whether he was able to refrain from bedding her.

Late in the spring of 1604, Camallata made a trip to Moscow, and John accompanied her there. They traveled with a trade caravan, and the Englishman was astonished to find that camels as well as donkeys and horses were used as pack animals. Because of the Governor's high rank, his niece was provided with an escort of Cossack cavalrymen. These hard-riding soldiers, descendants of noblemen who traditionally had guarded the tsars, attracted John's attention to the extent that he commemorated their horsemanship with a brief mention in his *True Travels*. Otherwise, although usually sensitive to his surroundings, he was conscious only of Camallata on the journey.

Moscow proved to be a drab city of wooden houses that spread out on both banks of the Moskva River in the middle of a seemingly endless pine forest. The most imposing buildings in the metropolis were the many structures that made up the Great Kremlin Palace, a huge fortress surrounded by high walls. Here the Tsar, Boris Godunov, lived and worked. Virtually all members of the nobility residing in the capital had apartments there, too. At least three divisions of infantry and several independent regiments of cavalry were stationed inside the Kremlin, which was the political, military, and social nerve center of Russia.

The only other buildings of consequence were two ornate cathedrals located just outside the Kremlin walls, both of which reminded John of Constantinople. Beyond the Kremlin stood another walled compound, the Kitai Gorod, where the city's merchants lived and worked. Adjacent to it was the Vasili Cathedral, begun during the reign of Ivan the Terrible, which was not yet completed.

John Smith saw literally nothing of Moscow beyond the Kremlin walls. He was given a small suite of his own in the apartment set aside for Camallata's use, and a day or two after his arrival his curiosity impelled him to go out into the city on a tour of inspection. To his amazement he was halted at the gates set in the high walls by heavily armed Cossacks, who turned him back with the curt explanation that foreigners were not permitted to roam at will through the capital.

The attitude of Russians toward outsiders bewildered and irked John, who found the atmosphere far different from the conviviality he had enjoyed at the Governor's palace in Rostov. His hosts regarded him with bristling suspicion, and he made no friends among the nobles he met. Most, he noted, went out of their way to avoid him. He concluded that Muscovites were cold people, and shrewdly realized, too, that an unstable political situation was at least partly responsible for the chill of his reception.

Boris was a competent monarch, but had almost no personal following, and many of the aristocrats regarded him as an upstart. There were rumors that dissidents were forming armies in Poland and elsewhere in the hope of overthrowing him, and a mood of tension pervaded the Kremlin. At no time during the four weeks of John Smith's stay there did he see, much less meet, either the Tsar or any other high official of the government.

He spent a portion of each day and most of his evenings with Camallata, who seemed to have few official duties to occupy her. But he was relieved when a chamberlain named Tsilovitch came to him with a firm "invitation" to leave the country. Foreigners were no more welcome in Russia in the early seventeenth century than in later times.

John intimates in his *True Travels* that he asked Camallata to accompany him to England as his wife. She refused on the somewhat vague grounds that it would be inappropriate for her to leave her homeland. John never forgot her, and he dedicated the first edition of his *True Relation,* the story of the Jamestown colony, to her. He also included her in the dedication of his *Generall Historie,* and in later years confided to the Duchess of Richmond, who may have been one of his mistresses, that Camallata was the only woman he had ever wanted to marry.

Even with all of his charm and powers of persuasion, John failed to sway Lady Camallata, and was forced to leave Moscow alone. Baron Reshdinski had provided him with clothes, a horse, and a little money, but since he had no other funds at hand, he immediately set out to recover his fortune from Prince Sigismund's treasure.

The Cossacks escorted him on a long, uneventful ride to the ill-defined border on the Dniester River, and he rode alone across the passes in the Carpathian Mountains into Hungary. There he discovered that an undeclared truce had at least temporarily halted the fighting between Turks and Christians. Accordingly, he went on to Graz, in Austria, where Sigismund was visiting the Archduke Ferdinand.

He was on familiar soil as he rode west across Hungary. Everywhere he met brother officers who opened the doors of their manor houses to him. His reunion with these men was pleasant, but lacked verve. His writing in the *True Travels* indicates that he was still grieving for Camallata, and he knew no joy. He seemed to realize, too, that a chapter in his life had ended. He had escaped from slavery only to lose his heart to a woman who would not have him. With the Christian army disbanded, he had no employment and literally did not know what to do next.

IX

Damsel in Distress

PRINCE SIGISMUND HAD LEFT Graz for Prague by the time John Smith reached Austria, so he continued his journey without delay. When he arrived in the Bohemian capital, he was dismayed to learn that the Prince had gone on to Leipzig, in the kingdom of Saxony. Now without funds and once again reduced to begging for his meals, John did not tarry in Prague long enough to form any impressions of the place.

Finally, in Leipzig, he was reunited with both Sigismund and the Earl of Meldritch, who was traveling with him. The reunion of old comrades was one of the memorable occasions of John's life. He was the guest of honor at a banquet and sat between the Prince and the Earl. At the conclusion of a meal that lasted for hours, Sigismund presented John with a coat of arms, which, after his return to England the following year, was duly recorded in the official Register of Heraldry by Sir William Segar, England's Garter King of Arms.

The award of this seal was a gesture that John appreciated

to the last of his days. It made him a gentleman entitled to write *Esquire* after his name, and raised him, in a class-conscious era, above the common herd.

He received other rewards equally dazzling. Sigismund gave him a purse of one thousand ducats, and Meldritch added another five hundred to it. Although these sums, added to his previously acquired nest egg, did not make John truly wealthy, he could live in comfort for the rest of his days. Sigismund also presented him with a personally signed and sealed safe-conduct pass, the seventeenth-century equivalent of a passport, which other ruling princes and kings were required by courtesy to honor.

His pockets filled with money, and with a passport entitling him to consideration everywhere in Christendom in his wallet, John set out on a leisurely Grand Tour of western Europe. He traveled by easy stages, lodging at comfortable inns and dining at the best taverns. He journeyed south into Italy, where he chanced to meet Lord and Lady Willoughby and his old friend, Henry Willoughby, at Siena. Henry accompanied him into France, but was less curious about the world than his boyhood companion from Lincolnshire, and John went on alone to Spain.

He visited many of the great cities in the nation that, until recently, had been England's great enemy, and in his *True Travels* duly reported his tourist's impression of Bilbao and Valladolid, Madrid and Toledo, Cordova and Seville and Cadiz. Everywhere he viewed the sights with enthusiasm, and by the winter of 1605 he had become one of the most widely traveled men of his age. Not even he realized that his most important journeys were still to be made.

Perhaps the proximity of southern Spain to Morocco across the narrow western end of the Mediterranean reminded John of Elizabeth Rondee, his fellow slave in Constantinople, or it may be that he had enjoyed too little excitement for too long.

Whatever the reason, he was reminded of her, and he made up his mind to rescue her from captivity.

The adventure into which he plunged following this decision was one of his most fantastic experiences and would be unbelievable if it were not for the indisputable fact that the verification of the lady herself renders it authentic.

Morocco was populated by Spain's ancient foes, the Moors, a ferocious and piratical people who ruled the western portion of Islam, the Barbary, under the overlordship of the Ottomans. Unlike the sophisticated Turks, who had continued to develop a complex civilization in spite of their many cruelties, the Moroccans had allowed their culture to decline. The beys, or rulers, were petty tyrants, and the nobles were so corrupt that pashas had been sent from Constantinople to rule each of the nation's sparsely settled districts in the name of the local lords.

John knew only that Elizabeth Rondee was a slave in the household of the wife of the pasha who governed El Araish, a town whose named was later given the western name of Larache. It was a port on the Atlantic, located about fifty miles from Tangier. Portuguese merchant ships occasionally put in to the harbor there to buy the wine that was the principal product of El Araish. Apparently the grape growers of the area paid little attention to the Moslem injunction against the drinking of spirits.

Portuguese captains frequented the taverns of Cadiz, Malaga, and other Spanish ports, and John questioned them, but they knew nothing of an English girl living as a captive in El Araish. All they could tell him was that the town, a community of perhaps fifteen thousand people, was protected by two forts set high on the terraced cliffs directly above the port. One, the Kibibat, was an extension of an ancient Roman fort and had so many domes it resembled a mosque. A battalion of infantry was stationed there, but since it had no cannon, it was useful only as a garrison for troops. La Cigogne, the new fortress, was twenty-five years old and had been built by the Portuguese themselves when they had occupied the town for a time. It was virtually impregnable, and was protected by both cannon and slings. The pasha, Mahomet ben Arif, lived there with his family, and so did the local lord. The masters of the Portuguese merchantmen had dealt with both men, and thought them stupid and greedy.

For more than six months John tried to find a ship that would take him to El Araish. During this period, according to his own unverified account, he put to sea several times and continued his education as a sailor. He claims to have enjoyed many spectacular adventures, some on an English man-of-war commanded by a Captain Merham, of whom no other record exists, and some on a Spanish privateer commanded by a Captain Cordoba, whose name also appears only in the *True Travels*. If John is to be believed, he survived several tempestuous storms and took part in several spirited naval engagements against the Turks and their subjects, the Tripolitanians and the Moroccans.

Elizabeth Rondee later confirmed as a fact that John arrived at El Araish on board a Spanish vessel in September, 1605. Presumably this ship was commanded by Captain Cordoba. The harbor master was astonished to be greeted in Turkish by John, who was attired in the robes of a great lord and attended by eight retainers. These men, two of them English, two French, and the rest Spanish, were former mercenary soldiers who had accepted employment for a specific purpose. Like John, they wore armor beneath their flowing gowns and carried concealed weapons.

John informed the harbor master that he wanted to pay his respects to Mahomet ben Arif, for whom he had brought a gift. The word was carried to La Cigogne, and the unexpected visitor was invited to climb the cliff to the fortress. John had arranged the details of his visit with care. Although the day was warm, his cloak was fur-trimmed, rings sparkled on his fingers, and he wore the scimitar with the gold, gem-encrusted hilt that Prince Sigismund had given him. His men were also handsomely dressed, in order to impress the luxury-loving Turks.

Mahomet ben Arif, an overweight, middle-aged man who was slow of speech, was delighted that a visitor had come to relieve the monotony of his existence in this far outpost of the Ottoman Empire. He replied at length to a speech in Turkish that John had prepared, and graciously accepted a "costly" ring, actually a worthless glass bauble that John had brought with him for the purpose.

The pasha and the local lord entertained their guest at dinner, with members of their own staffs and John's retainers sitting cross-legged around a steaming cauldron. John dipped his left hand into the pot repeatedly, and found the lamb exceptionally good, but his men ate little of the highly seasoned dish.

After the meal, Mahomet ben Arif and his guest retired to the pasha's private rooms to continue their talk. John, in a gesture of seemingly spontaneous generosity, presented his host with still another glass ring. Mahomet ben Arif believed him to be a ruling prince of one of the far-distant German states, an illusion which John carefully nurtured.

At an opportune moment, John casually asked the question that had brought him to El Araish: was it true, as he had heard, that there was an English slave girl in Mahomet's household? When the pasha carefully sidestepped the query, John immediately took another tack. He had been certain from the moment he had heard the rumor that it was false, he declared scornfully.

Mahomet ben Arif was stung, and protested that there was

indeed such a girl in his possession. She belonged to his number one wife, and was both comely and useful as a servingmaid.

John now knew that Elizabeth Rondee was at La Cigogne. But he realized, too, that even though he had confirmed her presence, he and eight men could not overcome a strong garrison of Turks and Moors, augmented by still another, smaller garrison at the other fort. If he tried to invade the women's quarters, or harem, an alarm would be given, and he and his men would be killed. Therefore he had to proceed with care.

Still following the same approach, but speaking lightly so he didn't offend his host, he continued to profess his disbelief.

Mahomet ben Arif reacted precisely as John had hoped. Would His Excellency like to see the wench with his own eyes?

John agreed that if he saw her and heard her speak English, a language of which he claimed an imperfect understanding, he would be satisfied.

The pasha immediately sent a servant for the girl, and John hoped that his men, who were being entertained in a nearby room, were alert and sober enough for the attempt to escape with her.

Elizabeth appeared, wearing the same sort of flimsy clothing she had used in Constantinople, and dutifully prostrated herself before the pasha, who smiled at his guest in triumph.

John pretended to be dissatisfied, and asked for the privilege of questioning her.

Elizabeth had not recognized him, and tears came to her eyes when he informed her in English, speaking very quickly, that he had come to rescue her.

The girl's sudden tears made the pasha suspicious. He rose to his feet, intending to pull the bell rope that would summon members of his staff.

John threw aside all pretense. Reaching beneath his robe,

he drew a knife and plunged it into Mahomet ben Arif's body, killing the pasha instantly.

As the man slumped to the tiled floor, Elizabeth was unable to control a scream of terror and revulsion.

Turks, Moors, and John's mercenaries ran into the room from the nearby chamber where they had been talking and drinking wine. John's men enjoyed an advantage, having known there would be trouble, and at his direction they attacked their hosts with cold fury. It was essential that no alarm be given, and the men, fighting for their own lives as well as for Elizabeth, used their swords and knives to good advantage.

John led the attack, first seriously wounding a giant Moor who leaped at him, then engaging in a brief, vicious duel with the captain of Mahomet ben Arif's guard. Both men used scimitars, and although the Turk was an excellent swordsman, he was no match for the veteran soldier. Twice John beat aside his opponent's blade, then swung his own sword sharply, inflicting a shoulder wound that rendered the captain helpless. Displaying the ruthlessness that he showed in battle throughout his life, John calmly decapitated the man, an act that Elizabeth later described as the most horrifying exhibition of violence she had ever witnessed.

In a few minutes the fight was ended. All of the Turks and Moors were either dead or so badly injured they could neither move nor cry out. One of John's Spaniards was dead, and one of his Englishmen had suffered a superficial but painful cut on his hand and arm. There was subsequently some confusion regarding the number of Moslems who took part in the brief battle. John, in his *True Travels,* refers to a score. Elizabeth, probably more accurate, says there were nine or ten.

The immediate objective had now been accomplished, but Elizabeth's rescuers were still high on the cliff above their waiting ship. Leaving the dead Spaniard behind, after first thoughtfully taking his weapons and fur-trimmed hat, they descended to the inner courtyard of the fortress, where their borrowed horses were waiting. John wrapped his own cloak around Elizabeth, jammed the Spaniard's hat onto her head in order to hide her blonde hair, and thrust the Spaniard's sword into her hand.

There were nine horses—and nine riders. But Elizabeth's clumsiness aroused the suspicion of a groom, and the man shouted a warning to one of the sentries stationed at the gates of La Cigogne. All pretense had to be abandoned, and John spurred forward, wielding his scimitar. The startled Moors on guard duty leaped backward, leaving the gate untended, and the entire party rode through, unharmed.

Someone fired a pistol shot after them, and John knew that a chase would soon be organized. The road leading from the fort to the streets of El Araish below was so narrow that it was impossible to ride two abreast, so John placed Elizabeth in the center of the column. He himself brought up the rear and encouraged the others to ride faster.

Several times the terrified Elizabeth was in danger of being thrown, but she clung to her saddle with all her strength and managed to keep her seat. By the time the group reached the bottom of the hill, they could see a party setting out from the fort in pursuit.

The nine horses thundered through the twisting streets of the ancient Moorish city, scattering its astonished inhabitants, and soon reached the waterfront. At this point, a gig from the ship was waiting for them. John lifted Elizabeth into the boat, and the men began to row as a crowd gathered on the shore to watch them.

The captain of the ship had failed to obey John's specific instructions. The vessel was still riding at anchor, and her sails were neatly furled. A half-hour of frantic labor awaited her crew before she could put to sea. John shouted orders as the boat approached the ship, and the captain awoke from his lethargy. Elizabeth was handed aboard, and John sent her to a cabin below while his own men and the crew members not otherwise engaged made ready to repel boarders who might follow.

But the Turks had other ideas. A cannon high in the ramparts of La Cigogne boomed. The crowd on the shore promptly lost interest in the affair and departed in haste. The crew worked frantically, as the gunners opened fire with a second cannon, then a third. Only their poor marksmanship prevented them from shattering the frail privateer and transforming it into kindling.

"The Almighty," Smith declares in his *True Travels,* "kept watch over the wayfarers and preserved them from the infidel's harm whilst they made ready for sea."

The breeze was light, but strong enough to enable the ship to crawl slowly out of the El Araish harbor. Not until the privateer began to move did the Turks and Moors realize their quarry might escape. The cannonading was abandoned, and men raced down from the two forts on the cliffs to a small fleet at anchor in the harbor.

The captain of the privateer made up for his carelessness by handling his ship ably, and he was well out in the Atlantic by the time several of the Moslem ships, far clumsier than his own, slid from the harbor into open water. For all practical purposes the chase was ended. The privateer easily outdistanced her pursuers and lost sight of them several hours before nightfall. The Moors were not seen again.

John Smith refers briefly to Elizabeth's gratitude, but his comment is confined to a casual phrase; on the surface, at least, he seems far more interested in the tides and winds off the coasts of North Africa and Europe. The voyage was uneventful, and the privateer reached Cadiz without further incident. John paid off his mercenaries and took lodgings for Elizabeth and himself at an inn—separate quarters, as he was careful to emphasize in his *True Travels*. Presumably Elizabeth acquired a respectable wardrobe there.

A new problem developed in the sleepy Spanish town that was also a major operational and training base for the Spanish navy. John wanted passage to England, but no Spanish ships would sail into the den of the lion with whom no formal peace treaty had yet been made. Though John was acceptable to the Spanish government, thanks to Prince Sigismund's letter, the masters of British merchantmen were reluctant to put into Spanish ports for fear of possible complications, including the confiscation of their cargo.

The dilemma was solved when a Portuguese bark of two hundred tons, the *Leonora,* put into Cadiz for water and repairs after being blown off her course at sea by a storm. Passenger quarters were limited, and only one cabin was available. John engaged it, and he and Elizabeth shared it. Presumably she demonstrated her gratitude to him in practical terms on the voyage to England, if she had not already done so.

The *Leonora* sailed up the Thames, arriving at London on October 4, 1605. John Smith came ashore with a bulging purse, world renown, and an attractive blonde on his arm. His arrival created something of a sensation. Many of his countrymen had learned of his daring exploits, and he was applauded at the various taverns he visited.

Soon after his return he called on Richard Hakluyt, to whom he reported in detail on the geographical features of the many lands he had visited. His information concerning Russia was of value to the Archdeacon, little being known of Russian topography in England, but he contributed nothing of consequence concerning other lands. His visit strengthened his relationship with Hakluyt, however, and it may have been that he renewed his acquaintance with Henry, Prince of Wales, through the great geographer.

The Prince, who was strongly interested in exploration and

the expansion of British colonial possessions overseas, was an extraordinary young man. Had he lived to mount the throne, he would have been a far more able monarch than his younger brother, who became Charles I. Henry was the most handsome of the Stuarts, and had a warm smile, eyes that could be either relaxed and inquiring or regally glacial, and a healthy appetite for everything English.

He loved food, and often ate in the taverns frequented by merchants, much to the dismay of King James, who instinctively distrusted people and kept himself at a distance from his subjects. Henry was capable of consuming enormous meals, washed down with large quantities of spirits, but not until his later years did he grow obese. He enjoyed violent physical exercise, and rode, wrestled, and engaged in other competitive sports with his associates, whom he chastised if they deferred to him.

He was by far the most popular member of his family, in part because his tastes were similar to those of his father's subjects, and in part because of his insatiable curiosity. Certainly he must have been interested in John Smith, about whom everyone in London was talking or writing. It may also be that Hakluyt, with whom the Prince was friendly, arranged an audience for the young adventurer.

In any event, John was summoned to the quarters Henry maintained at Number 17 Fleet Street, where he conducted the business of the Duchy of Lancaster, one of the hereditary holdings of a Prince of Wales. The heir to the throne also had a large suite of his own at Whitehall, his father's palace, but received no visitors there and, in fact, rarely went there himself. He happened to be on bad terms with the moody James at the moment, and was not welcome at court.

It was unfortunate for John Smith that he and Henry should begin to see a great deal of each other at this period. James was a man who harbored grudges, both real and imaginary.

Although he forgot, in later years, why he did not care for the adventurer, he never trusted John.

The contrary was true of Henry. At their first meeting, he was so entranced by John's forceful personality and the stories he told of exciting events in far places, that the Prince kept other visitors waiting for hours as he listened to the tales.

John was in his true element at last. He was receiving a hero's welcome, and although he had become friendly with many nobles in his travels, his new one-man audience was his own Crown Prince. No record was kept of his conversations with Henry, but it would have been surprisingly out of character had he failed to embellish and garnish his accounts of all that had happened to him.

Certainly his reputation was made when, less than a week after his return to England, he was seen in Prince Henry's company at various London taverns, among them the Eel, the White Stallion, and the sanctuary of the great lords of the land, the Whitefriars, which burned to the ground in the Great Fire.

In a breathtakingly short time, John was consorting with the Dukes of Buckingham and Norfolk, and was universally regarded as a man with a bright future. It was also taken for granted by many in society that he would marry Elizabeth Rondee, their romantic association and its dramatic climax having become public knowledge.

Numerous letters written by members of the small literate class in the late autumn of 1605 speculate on the possibility of such a marriage. There were some who took it for granted that they would soon be married. Elizabeth herself may have imagined that she would soon be Mistress Smith. In any event, she made no attempt to conceal her regard for John or her attachment to him.

If she was thinking in such terms, John quickly disabused her of the idea. There is no indication in his own writing, the letters of others, or any other historical accounts that he saw Elizabeth, called on her at the home of cousins with whom she was living, or acted as her escort after they reached England.

Perhaps he ignored her until she realized he had no honorable intentions toward her. On the other hand, he may have been gentleman enough to maneuver and scheme until she jilted him. The latter is more likely, for Elizabeth subsequently bore him no grudge.

In the following year she became betrothed to Sir Philip Graham, a prominent landowner and country squire, whom she married a few months later. Sir Philip invested a large sum of money in the company John helped to form that was planning to establish a colony in the New World, and thereafter the two men were friendly business associates for many years. And on at least two unknown occasions, the latter in 1613, John was a guest of the Grahams at their Dorsetshire estate.

It is improbable that Elizabeth would have been pleased by the friendship of her husband with a man who had rejected her, and it is even more unlikely that she herself would have entertained such a man in her home. The only conclusion to be drawn is that John found some way, without hurting her pride or feelings, to avoid marrying her.

He had found her sufficiently attractive to enjoy an affair with her, but her rescue had been far more exciting and had given him a greater sense of satisfaction. To be sure, a sense of propriety could have been responsible for his discretion when, many years later, he wrote his *True Travels,* although he made no attempt to hide the relationship from his readers.

In the absence of other testimony, his own protestations on the subject of matrimony must be accepted at face value. Lady Camalatta of Rostov-on-Don and Moscow was the only woman he had ever wanted to marry. All the others, Elizabeth included, were just mistresses, never potential wives.

A man as self-centered as John could not have thought in terms of taking a wife in the first triumphant months that followed his return to England. He had achieved a position of financial stability, and by his family's standards was wealthy. He consorted with the Prince of Wales, had won the respect of Richard Hakluyt, and was the friend of some of the most powerful and prominent nobles in the land. He was hailed everywhere as a hero. On at least one occasion, when he attended a performance of the significantly named comedy, *Eastward Ho!,* to which Ben Jonson contributed some passages, the entire audience greeted him with such a wild ovation that officers of the nightwatch had to be called to the theater to restore order.

Even Sir Walter Raleigh, the great Admiral and explorer who was being held in the Tower of London by the suspicious King James on the grounds of treason, expressed a desire to meet the gallant soldier who had fought with such valor in far places and had seen so much of the world.

Shortly before Christmas, 1605, John scaled even greater heights. Queen Anne, the plump and frowsy, sometimes kindly, and occasionally imperious consort of King James, summoned the social lion to Whitehall for an audience.

John was at his best, and he captivated the Queen and her ladies. Anne, who could be moved to tears by anyone except her husband, wept copiously as she listened to the wanderer's tales of his suffering. John had made still another important friend, and it was small wonder that Elizabeth Rondee was forgotten.

During this hectic time John made only one enemy, but fortunately wasn't aware of it. King James must have heard his courtiers talking about Captain John Smith, but stubbornly became deaf when the man's name was mentioned. John was inadvertently rubbing salt in the King's emotional open sores, and James had many of them.

Noblemen who tried to win the King's favor were taking care to avoid Prince Henry, who was in such deep disgrace that he used a side entrance to the palace when he paid an occasional visit to his mother. But the bold adventurer who had established his credentials as a gentleman only a few weeks earlier was seen everywhere in the Prince's company, thereby proving to the paranoid James that he placed no value on the King's good opinion.

Even more damning was his attitude toward Raleigh. Sir Walter had been found guilty of treason in a trial that had been an almost ludicrous mockery of justice, and the entire nation sympathized with the dashing Admiral. Yet few men, including those who had been his close associates, dared to call on him. John, however, was recklessly indifferent to such subtleties.

He found a kindred spirit in the satanically handsome fellow adventurer who had once captivated Queen Elizabeth I. Raleigh recognized the bond, too, and after listening to John's stories, reciprocated with tales of his own about his life on the high seas and his New World explorations. John discovered in Sir Walter an even more persuasive talker than himself. His imagination was fired by the Admiral's descriptions of the expeditions he had dispatched to Virginia, the vast territory between French and Spanish possessions in the New World, and his own voyage to South America.

John and the graying Admiral were remarkably alike in many ways. Both were poseurs, yet they achieved far more than ordinary mortals. Both were natural leaders of men and had such dynamic personalities that they made as many enemies as friends. Both were supreme egoists, indifferent to others when their own interests were at stake, and women found them both fascinating.

Sir Walter cast a spell over John, who visited the Admiral in his gloomy Tower of London suite regularly, paying no attention to those who warned him that he would incur the King's displeasure. Like Raleigh himself, John found a perverse pleasure in exerting his own will, even when it might prove costly to him. In the month of December, 1605, he paid six known visits to the Admiral, and continued to see him often the following year.

Each of these visits was duly reported by Raleigh's keepers to the brooding monarch at Whitehall. Henry Hudson urged his friend to be more careful, but John elected to disregard the warning. In time to come, he would pay for his impetuosity, yet he never regretted it. Although he may have been a cad in his relations with women, he was always loyal to the men he regarded as his friends, no matter what the cost.

Sometime in the busy autumn of 1605, John paid a brief visit to Lincolnshire. Apparently he had already been informed of his mother's death during his absence abroad and was not surprised to find her gone. "The tears froze on my cheeks," he wrote, "when I stood beside my mother's grave. I have felt her loss sorely each day of my life."

He felt no such love for his surviving relatives, who bored him. Francis and his wife were interested only in their own narrow world, and their interminable gossip about neighbors put John to sleep. His only consolation was that they had named their eldest son after him. He gave the child a scimitar, which was passed down from father to son for generations and became an heirloom about which many legends were told, all of them fictitious.

Alice had married, too. She had found happiness with a yeoman farmer who had never traveled farther from home than the city of York. The young couple regarded the famous Captain with gratifying awe and were so tongue-tied in his presence that John became irritated. He noted that Alice had become an excellent cook, however, and he approved of her kidneys with blood dumplings, which she made from a recipe of her mother's.

The Willoughbys were still enjoying a sojourn abroad, and John discovered that he had outgrown all of his other boyhood companions. He cut short his stay after paying several more visits to his mother's grave and returned to London, taking with him the money that Francis had so carefully hoarded for him. More than twenty years would pass before he traveled again to the place of his birth.

London had become his home, and on his return to the city he was caught up in a swift tide of adventure far exceeding the bounds of his own lively and colorful imagination. Within a short time he would embark on a career for which his previous experiences had been only a prelude.

X

The Pot Boils

AN EXTRAORDINARY SENSE OF anticipatory excitement was in the air of England at the time John Smith came home from his travels in Europe and Africa. In London, as in other great capitals, nobles and merchants were awakening to the realization that there were tremendous profits in store for those willing to risk their lives and fortunes in overseas exploration and trade.

Since the reign of Henry VII, sea captains sailing under the British flag had gone to distant, hitherto unknown lands in search of gold, yet Spain, France, Portugal, and the Netherlands were taking the lead in colonization. The national pride that had been so strong under Elizabeth I was still rampant, and England was moving rapidly to make up for lost time.

The groundwork had already been done. Raleigh's expeditions, together with those of Davys, Bartholomew Gosnold, and others, had established a British claim to the lands lying between the Spanish colonies in Central and South America and the French settlements in Canada. The East India Company had been chartered by Queen Elizabeth in 1600, and the few ships that had gone to the Far East under the Company's banner had earned handsome profits.

Now, thanks to the untiring efforts of Hakluyt and his disciples, the enthusiasm of Prince Henry, and the clamor of London merchants, efforts were being made to expand British dominion on a massive scale. What the French, Spanish, Dutch, and even Portuguese could do, Englishmen could do better and more thoroughly. The impractical and uninitiated dreamed of gold, silver, and precious gems to be found in profusion. The realists thought in terms of furs and timber, spices and silks, for which they knew there was a market. And a very few, among them John Smith, took the word of Sir Walter Raleigh that tobacco, cultivated in the right climate by colonists willing to establish large plantations, could earn greater profits than any other products to be found in exotic places.

One group of influential investors in London formed the Muscovy Company in 1606, with Hakluyt its guiding spirit. These wealthy nobles and men of business believed that a sea route to the East Indies could be opened somewhere on earth, and in Henry Hudson they found a sea captain whose views were identical to their own. In 1607, after more than a year of preparatory work, Hudson would sail for the Muscovy Company on the first of his four great voyages of exploration.

Other men, also led by Hakluyt, preferred to concentrate on North America. Undeterred by Raleigh's failure, two decades earlier, to establish permanent settlements on the shores of the virtually unknown continent, they believed in setting up self-sustaining colonies that would enhance the power, prestige, and wealth of England. The Prince of Wales was one who held this view, and for once his father agreed with him. King James was jealous of the French and Spanish monarchs whose subjects were creating vast overseas empires.

A company was formed for the purpose of exploring and

settling continental North America, and so many men wanted to invest in shares of its stock that it soon had more money than it needed. Sir John Popham, the Lord Chief Justice, was the President of the Royal Virginia Company, and the first to purchase stock was Prince Henry. A day or two after he sent a bag of gold to Sir John, Captain John Smith invested five hundred pounds in the organization, a large sum by any standard.

The directors quarreled amiably at their initial meetings, some wanting to concentrate on the north—the region that would subsequently bear John Smith's name, New England—while others thought the chances of success would be greater if a colony were established farther south, in what later became Virginia itself. A compromise was reached by dividing into two interlocking groups. The second, that which wanted to set up a southern colony, called itself the London Company.

An application was made to the King for a patent, but James was annoyed because he had not been consulted by the directors when they had made their plans, and for months he refused to sign the charter. It was not until several alarmed subjects warned him, saying that if he failed to act soon, the British claim of suzerainty would be lost to energetic men from other nations, that he finally did sign and seal the patent.

The northern branch was plagued by misfortune from the outset. Its directors hoped to send out an expedition in 1607, but it bought ships that were unseaworthy, hired too many troublemakers, and lost some of its essential supplies in a storm. The leader of the expedition, which finally sailed in 1608, was Sir John Popham's brother, who died at sea. His subordinates found the weather so cold they turned back after spending a few weeks on "a bleak desert"—a beach somewhere in New England.

The members of the London Company were more cautious and thorough than their colleagues. And their ambitions were boundless. They set multiple goals for the expedition they were planning: they intended to set up a permanent colony in Virginia, send out groups to occupy as much territory as possible in the name of the Crown and, simultaneously, find a navigable river that would lead to the Pacific Ocean and thus establish a sea route to the East Indies. These gentlemen, like most of their contemporaries, Hakluyt and Plancius included, believed North America to be a very narrow continent, no more than one hundred to three hundred miles wide.

The directors hired one of the nation's most competent seamen, Captain Christopher Newport, to act as commodore of the fleet they would send to Virginia. This blunt, ruddy-faced man had spent all of his life at sea, and the judgment of the stockholders was not misplaced. He knew his business. As his deputy they engaged the lean, dyspeptic Bartholomew Gosnold, somewhat younger and more impetuous, who enjoyed the distinction of having made a successful voyage of discovery to the New World in 1602. On the recommendation of these two officers, they also hired Newport's onetime mate, Captain John Ratcliffe.

Ratcliffe, who resembled a Viking, with blonde hair and light-blue eyes, was handsome and eager to please and made a good impression on the directors. They had no way of knowing that he was a moody man whose competence was hampered by violent fits of anger and a cruel streak he was unable and unwilling to control.

Three ships were purchased, the largest of them a relatively new vessel, the hundred-ton, square-rigged *Susan Constant,* which Newport intended to use as his flagship. It was sufficiently large, by seventeenth-century standards, to carry huge quantities of supplies in her hold, two cannon on her deck, and seventy passengers. Gosnold's ship was the older, more cumbersome *God Speed,* of forty tons, and Ratcliffe was given a tiny, twenty-ton pinnace, the *Discovery.*

John Smith made up his mind from the start that he would be a member of the expedition. There was never any question in his mind on the subject, and the directors were delighted. He was a soldier who had proved his worth, he had learned enough about the sea to assume command of a ship in an emergency, and he was a recognized leader of men. He and the three sea captains jointly supervised the purchase of supplies, and John insisted on inspecting all merchandise, as merchants were inclined to sell rotting canvas, spoiled food, and rusting iron utensils and tools to the unwary.

The four were joined by several others in what became the high command of the expedition. Edward Maria Wingfield was an austere, high-minded gentleman who was hampered by narrow views on virtually every subject on earth. He was earnest and dedicated, but was a bumbler in all his endeavors. He was mentally slow and physically awkward, and although the directors liked him because of his patrician airs and patriotic attitudes, he proved to be more of a liability than an asset to the expedition.

Master George Percy, another of the command echelon, was the bearer of one of England's oldest and proudest names. A black-haired, brown-eyed playboy, Percy had dissipated most of his considerable inheritance on gaming and women. He became a member of the expedition at the instigation of his brother, the Earl of Northumberland, who was one of the Company's directors, and who was embarrassed by his presence in England. Percy was amiable, wanted to become useful, and was too easily influenced.

Captain John Martin, about whom little is known, had served as an artillery officer in the army, and was an honest, conscientious man. Unfortunately he was in frail health, which limited the contributions he was able to make to the colony's welfare.

Captain George Kendal, who applied through his friend

Ratcliffe for a place in the expedition, was a former infantry officer. Narrow-faced, silent, and vindictive, he made no friends, spent much of his time alone, and enjoyed setting the others at odds. He was such a mischief-maker that he almost caused the downfall of the colony and eventually was executed on somewhat ill-defined charges of treason.

The Reverend Robert Hunt was a member of the party of gentlemen, but had no voice in the secular affairs of the colony, in large part because he wanted none. A large-boned man with a long face, he was pious and self-effacing and repeatedly demonstrated such great physical and moral courage that he won the undying admiration of John Smith.

The last to join the ruling gentry was Captain Gabriel Archer, the youngest son of a baronet. Archer's father had purchased a commission for him in a Household regiment in which he served briefly. Later he had fought as a mercenary in the Netherlands at the same time John was there, although the two never met. Archer was ruggedly attractive, with a commanding personality and a flamboyant air. He considered himself a leader and might have become a proficient one had his judgment been sound. He was inclined to be rash in making decisions, rarely weighed the consequences, and preferred action, for its own sake, to contemplation. He was proud and ambitious, and it was almost inevitable that he and John Smith should clash.

Others in the total party of one hundred and fifty who volunteered as members of the expedition included a number of artisans, among them bricklayers, carpenters, dock hands, and stonemasons. There were two surgeon-barbers, a few former sailors, a onetime drummer in a military band, and a number of boys still in their teens who were seeking adventure.

Newport insisted on carrying large quantities of ship's stores, and was supported by Gosnold and John, who made fervent pleas to the directors at a special meeting called for the purpose of curbing the steadily mounting expenses. The three were successful, and the holds were filled almost to overflowing with provisions.

Wheat and rye flour spoiled on long voyages, so rice and oatmeal were carried instead, and the only wheat on board was in the form of hard sea biscuits, which were made with water instead of shortening. There were tubs of butter, to be sure, but these were used at once. Newport ordered kegs of sugar, prunes, raisins, and a variety of spices to make food palatable. At his request the directors reluctantly supplied him with jellies, marmalades, candy, and roasted, salted nuts.

Meat was the heart of shipboard diet, principally pickled beef, and it was customary to use the vinegar in the barrels of beef after other vinegar supplies were exhausted. Heavily salted pork and fish were common fare, too, and the three ships also carried smoked bacon. A fairly unusual item was mutton, which had been chopped, stewed, and then packed in large earthenware pots. Unfortunately these pots were lined with butter, and the mutton that wasn't eaten in the first weeks of the voyage spoiled.

Beer and cider were provided for liquid refreshment, and the gentlemen, like the ships' officers, also enjoyed wine with their meals, principally claret, Canary, and Madeira. Newport and Gosnold also carried casks of water, but these were reserved for emergency use. No one in the seventeenth century drank water when anything else was available. There were no hard spirits on board the vessels, experience having proved that men often became troublesome if they drank brandywine or gin while living at close quarters for many weeks.

The directors of the London Company prepared infinitely detailed instructions covering every conceivable subject, from their own expectations to the type of government the colonists were to establish. Even such matters as the treatment to be accorded any natives who might be encountered were carefully outlined.

These orders were drawn up at a secret meeting of the council, as the directors now called themselves, transcribed, and locked in a strongbox, which was given to Captain Newport with directions not to open it until he reached his destination. The secrecy was intended to prevent rivalry between gentlemen-adventurers who might compete for the leadership of the colony. The lack of specific instructions on the long voyage, however, had the opposite effect.

The year 1606 was one of the most pleasant and productive John had ever known. He was still popular with both peers and commoners. It was known that he would participate in an enterprise that stirred men of imagination, and he was in demand as a dinner companion. He spent much of his free time at the taverns of the aristocrats, although he drank sparingly, and the correspondence of others indicates that he tried his luck at the gaming tables in a gingerly way on a few occasions. But one who was willing to risk his life on a battlefield, on the deck of a privateer, or on bizarre missions, found dice and cards dull.

He was also busy with a new mistress, the glamorous Frances, Duchess of Lennox, whose husband, Ludovic Stuart, was one of Scotland's leading noblemen and was related to the King. Frances, two years John's junior, was a ravishing blonde who, with good reason and justifiable pride, wore some of the lowest-cut gowns in the British Isles.

How she and John first met is not known, but he could have been presented to her at any one of a number of the great houses where both were frequent guests. Either they made no secret of their liaison or, if they tried, they failed. The affair was common knowledge in court circles and elsewhere, and they were sometimes seen together at the theater, strolling on fashionable promenades, or shopping.

The Duke, whom James later made Earl and then Duke of Richmond in the English peerage, was one of the financial sponsors of the London Company, and John saw him frequently. He was a man with such delicate features that it was sometimes said he was almost as pretty as his wife. Ludovic could not have been ignorant of Frances's romance, but apparently he didn't care. In any event he was occupied elsewhere, sometimes with beauties less celebrated than his wife, sometimes with young men of effeminate refinement.

It is unlikely that John and Frances imagined themselves in love with each other. Both were cynics in a hard world, and each was attracted by the other's physical charms and renown. The Duchess, like her lover, enjoyed the limelight. On several occasions she had offended the pious Queen Anne and upset the easily shocked King James by appearing at Whitehall in gowns with bust lines that left little to the imagination. She was an impudent young blue-blood, and in her portraits the mischievous expression in her green eyes and her provocative smile are always in evidence.

John's relationship with her was unique, and he neither abandoned nor forgot her. Frances had no children and, in later years, after settling down, she devoted a great deal of her time to charity. The poor developed a great affection for her. It was said, perhaps in an exaggeration of the truth, that she was the only beauty in England who could walk unmolested through the streets of Southwark, the rough district across the Thames from London, which was a sanctuary frequently used by criminals. She and John were friends long after they had been lovers, and remained close to each other, often exchanging confidences, until the end of their days. In fact, only Frances's illness prevented her from attending John's funeral.

He enjoyed her company for other than the obvious reasons. She could read and write—accomplishments that few young ladies of her era could boast. In addition, she was a student of philosophy and the natural sciences. Her wit, often mentioned by her contemporaries, was so caustic that other women were afraid of her and men sometimes became uncomfortable in her presence. But John had endured too much real suffering and hardship to be thin-skinned, and he enjoyed her conversation.

By the latter part of the year he was too busy to see much of the Duchess. Preparations for the great voyage were in their final, hectic stages, and when he wasn't busy interviewing applicants for the expedition he was conferring with the sea captains, the other gentlemen-adventurers, and the members of the council.

His relations with the directors were beginning to cool, principally because he was a pragmatist who had little patience with daydreamers. He was contemptuous of the hopes expressed by the council members that the explorers would find vast quantities of gold, diamonds, and emeralds. In an impassioned speech to them—of which no record was kept—he pointed out that not since the days when the Spaniards had struck it rich in South America almost one hundred years earlier had anyone returned to the Old World with precious metals and gems. As for the insistence of the council that there must be as yet undiscovered lands of plenty in the South Seas, he reminded them that the colonists would be fully occupied establishing a settlement in Virginia. Only when they had made their base secure, he declared, would they be in a position to push deeper into the unknown.

On the last day of December, 1606, John dined with Prince Henry, Richard Hakluyt, and "several other gentlemen of rare quality" in the private room of an inn. Soon thereafter he and the other leaders of the expedition were received in a formal audience at Whitehall. The dyspeptic King James, who was suffering from a head cold, cut the interview short after making a few banal remarks. Apparently neither he nor anyone else quite realized that these courageous, somewhat foolhardy, men would lay the cornerstone of what was to become the most powerful, far-flung empire in all human history.

At dawn on January 1, 1607, the entire company attended communion services at Westminster Abbey and listened to three sermons, one delivered by their own clergyman, Robert Hunt. Various members of the council were present with their families, as were the wives and children of the married men in the expedition. Ludovic Stuart sat with his colleagues, bundled in a fur-lined cloak that protected him from the damp chill of the great cathedral, but Frances was conspicuous by her absence.

The entire party then repaired to the wharves on the Thames, where the sailors immediately went on board the three ships. The weather was foul, as it had been for two weeks. Winds were adverse, and a snowstorm threatened, but the investors in the enterprise didn't want to be deprived of their own moment of glory, and a number of speeches were delivered by Sir John Popham and others.

A final inspection of the ships by the directors and their families had been scheduled as part of the farewell ceremonies, but the wind shifted unexpectedly, and Captain Newport cut short the celebration by piping all hands aboard. Favorable weather was far more important to the commodore than the momentary satisfaction of the directors.

Most of the gentlemen, John Smith included, were lodged on the *Susan Constant,* and it was John's misfortune that his cabin mate in a tiny, cramped cell should be Gabriel Archer. It would not be long before these two ambitious, hard-driving men would become rivals and bitter enemies, as they jockeyed for the exclusive leadership of the expedition.

The weather remained relatively good as the little flotilla sailed down the Thames, and only one incident of note occurred, seemingly insignificant at the time. Captain Newport dined with his own officers and the gentlemen-adventurers on the first evening of the voyage, and someone, whose identity has never been passed down to posterity, mentioned an interesting tidbit in the past of Captain Ratcliffe of the *Discovery*. Ratcliffe, the company was informed, had once served a brief prison term under the name of Sicklemore. The nature of his offense was not mentioned.

It is unlikely that anyone was unduly disturbed by the news. The age was a rough and bawdy one, and seamen, like soldiers of fortune and other excitement-seekers, were no saints. Certainly John, who by his own admission had been a pirate, would not have been upset. But someone subsequently told Ratcliffe about the exposure of his past and hinted that one of the gentlemen-adventurers had urged Newport to send the ex-convict ashore, replacing him with the *Susan Constant*'s mate, who also acted as flotilla lieutenant. The mysterious busybody told Ratcliffe it was John who had exposed him.

John, who was completely innocent, suspected that either Archer or Kendal was the troublemaker, but was unable to learn which of them went to Ratcliffe with the lie. Wingfield, Martin, and Percy were also present; at a much later time, they insisted they had heard no such comments, but the damage had already been done by that time. Captain Ratcliffe, instead of directing his animosity at the man who had revealed his past, instead joined the rapidly growing band of John Smith's foes.

The weather grew worse before the ships could move out into the English Channel. The winds soon reached gale proportions, forcing Newport to lie at anchor in the Downs. Ships' officers were sent ashore in boats to obtain meat, bread, and beer in order to conserve the precious supplies on board, and the eager adventurers were compelled to curb their impatience as they waited for better seas and lighter winds.

The expedition was off to an inauspicious start, but conditions would become far worse before they began to improve.

XI

The Long Voyage

FOR SIX INTERMINABLY LONG weeks the little ships remained in the Downs, straining fitfully at their anchors as the weather remained "unprosperous," as John later called it. Day after day, there was nothing to do but stand on deck for a few minutes, stare at the choppy seas and feel the blustery winds, then go below again. Occasionally a few of the gentlemen and ships' officers went ashore to stretch their legs and buy provisions, but they didn't dare venture far, because Captain Newport swore he would sail the instant he sensed a change in the weather.

Archer, Kendal, and Ratcliffe spent a good deal of time together and founded an insecure friendship based on a mutual loathing for John Smith, who seemed to be taking it for granted that he would act as military leader of the colony when the expedition finally reached Virginia. All three were connivers who probably would have caused trouble under any circumstances, but John had no one but himself to blame for his growing unpopularity. He had become so renowned and had enjoyed so much flattery since his return to England from his European adventures that he was insensitive to the feelings of others, and his unnecessarily arrogant attitude irritated even Wingfield, ordinarily the most mild-mannered of men. Only Percy and Martin remained friendly with the ambitious hero from Lincolnshire.

Meanwhile, the Reverend Mr. Hunt fell ill. When his condition worsened, Captain Newport considered sending him to his home, which was only a few miles from the Downs. Hunt, however, refused to abandon his new comrades, and displayed such stubborn courage in his determination to sail with the expedition that John supported him. Hunt eventually recovered his health and was grateful to John, now shunned by most of his colleagues.

In mid-February the weather improved suddenly and dramatically. The skies turned blue, an unusual phenomenon at that season of the year. Although the winds were strong, experienced seamen could maneuver their ships without too much difficulty. Accordingly, Newport ordered the flotilla to weigh anchor and sailed to the Canary Islands, reaching them without incident.

There he took on fresh supplies of water and additional meat, because most of the minced, stewed mutton packed in butter had spoiled. Many members of the company, particularly those who had never before gone to sea, were unhappy, and there was some talk of turning back. But the Reverend Mr. Hunt spoke at some length with the restless passengers on all three ships, and the grumbling subsided.

The flotilla set out on a run across the Atlantic. Although the weather remained surprisingly good, the passengers had now grown tired of seeing each other, and John, who had already aroused the ire of his comrades, provided fresh excitement. He, too, was bored. Instead of ignoring the unpleasantness of Archer and Kendal, he reacted vigorously to their nasty comments.

His relations with them became increasingly strained, and one day, inevitably, tempers flared. According to John's version of what happened, one of the others cursed him, calling him "names so foul that no man could tolerate such abuse." Archer and Kendal, on the other hand, insisted that he drew his sword without cause and threatened to cut them down.

Captain Newport was forced to intervene in order to restore order. The following day Wingfield was persuaded by several of the other gentlemen-adventurers, the vacillating Percy among them, to preside over a "court of inquiry" that would determine what punishment, if any, John should be given for breaking the peace.

Newport and his officers refused to participate, and the disgusted John absented himself from the "trial," which was held in the main saloon of the *Susan Constant*. His colleagues, egged on by Archer and Kendal, solemnly voted to hang him after they reached land. John then made another error. Instead of pretending to accept the verdict and going through the motions of "apologizing," he laughed at the farce. His actions naturally hardened the opinions of the others.

On March 24th, land was sighted, and that afternoon the flotilla cast anchor off the island of Hispaniola in the Caribbean. The island was claimed by Spain, Columbus having discovered it in 1493, but only a few Spanish missionaries were on the island, and all of them lived inland.

Like so many of the West Indian lands, Hispaniola was a lush, deep-green paradise. Its lowlands were almost insufferably hot and teeming with insects of every description; its cool mountains, their peaks hidden behind pure-white clouds, were almost unattainable mirages in the distance.

The entire company went ashore, and scores of small, wiry men with dark skins, members of the Carib Indian tribe, appeared from the bamboo jungles to greet them shyly. Soon a brisk barter had begun, the ships' officers and colonists trading colored beads, hatchets, and knives for freshly killed wild boar, huge fish with very white meat, and a variety of succulent but strange-looking fruits. On Captain Newport's strict instructions, no firearms or alcoholic spirits were allowed to pass into the hands of the "naturals," a policy thereafter employed by the British for more than a century and a half.

John Smith's enemies had not forgotten their "verdict," and after trading to their satisfaction, they started to build a gallows. He contemptuously paid no attention to them and went off down the beach with several of the Caribs, with whom he sat down, making an earnest effort to begin learning their language.

When the erection of the gallows was completed, the gentlemen-adventurers had only two tasks still ahead—they had to take John into custody, and then hang him. The former promised to be a formidable undertaking. He was wearing both his scimitar and a razor-sharp smallsword. In addition, he carried a brace of French dueling pistols in his belts, and the hilt of a knife protruded from a boot top. He was wearing light armor and a helmet, too, in spite of the heat, and it occurred to them that he had come ashore prepared for any emergency.

They knew that if they tried to rush him he would dispatch several of them, and they began to suffer second thoughts about carrying out the death sentence. Captain Newport also realized that any man who attacked John would be committing suicide, and with the assistance of Martin and the Reverend Mr. Hunt he dissuaded the others from attempting to carry out their foolish plan.

At no time was John fearful. "I had oft faced far greater odds," he wrote in his *True Relation,* an account of the colony's first days, "and knew that there was no swordsman in that miserable lot who could stand up to me with impunity."

The crisis eased, the entire company turned its attention to a more exciting spectacle—a fight between a swordfish and a small thresher whale in the outer reaches of the harbor. The battle lasted for two hours. When the fight reached its climax, the Indians went out in small boats and killed both fish with their spears. John was impressed by the courage of the natives, who showed no fear as they attacked the whale.

Then a feast was prepared, the naturals cooking over hot coals. John tasted whale meat for the first time, and liked it. He enjoyed the swordfish even more, and predicted that, if the fish were plentiful in cooler waters, they could become a major source of food for the colonists.

The flotilla put to sea again and on March 27th anchored off Guadeloupe, later to become a French colony. There they found a spring, heated by an active volcano, that sent up small geysers of boiling water. John, who was being snubbed by most of the gentlemen-adventurers, went hunting with Martin and shot two wild boar. The company enjoyed the pork cooked over the water of the springs, and John enjoyed increased popularity with the commoners. His peers ate the meat, but thought no more highly of him.

Two days later the ships arrived at Nevis Island, where Captain Newport saw natives in the jungle behind the beach. Everyone carried arms ashore, and they marched in military formation. John brushed aside Gabriel Archer's claim that he had the right to act as commander of the force and arbitrarily took charge. The company marched through jungle to higher ground and found some mineral springs. There everyone bathed and washed his clothes, half of the men standing guard while the others removed the sweat and grime accumulated during their long voyage.

Newport was afraid the savages might attack, but the Indians respected the foreigners' fire-sticks and kept their distance. Nevis was the most pleasant of the tropical islands the party had yet seen. Wild fruit grew in abundance, there were strange, sweet berries on bushes in the highlands, and the roots of several plants proved edible and delicious when cooked. In tiny, placid bays the men saw hundreds of fish beneath the surface of the clear water. There was game on the island, too—rabbit and wild boar and small, swift tropical deer.

Nevis was a paradise, and Newport allowed the men several days' holiday, with everyone doing as he pleased. The fruit the company enjoyed helped to prevent an outbreak of scurvy, although no one knew it. Many decades would pass before ships' captains discovered that the cause of scurvy was a lack of ascorbic acid.

For six days the company enjoyed a tropical holiday, and none of the ships' stores were touched. Some went hunting, and others fished. Everyone picked berries and fruit, and it was a joy to stretch legs that had become cramped on the voyage. No one went swimming, however, because people in the seventeenth century believed salt water was poisonous.

The natives remained at a distance, and Smith ordered that no one fire on the savages unless attacked. The Indians started no trouble, and the holiday was undisturbed. Spirits rose somewhat, and Percy, mellowed by the sun and fresh meat, juicy tropical fruits, and mealy roots, went to John with an apology. Kendal and Archer still refused to speak to John, however. Wingfield, somewhat influenced by Ratcliffe, kept apart, too.

On April 3rd, Newport set sail again. The next day the three ships reached the Virgin Islands, where the gentlemen-adventurers went ashore on Eustatius. They snared dozens of "succulent fowl," captured a two-hundred-and-eighty-pound turtle, and caught large quantities of fish. They also encountered an iguana, which John called "a loathsome beast, like a crocodile." He killed the big lizard, and when no one else would touch it, he threw it into a sand pit.

A brief search was made for springs or a river, but neither could be found. Nevertheless, they remained at anchor for two days in a large and pleasant bay. Putting to sea again, they found it necessary to call at the small islands of Mona and Moneta, between Puerto Rico and Haiti, because the drinking water they had taken on board at Nevis had developed odors so foul that every drop had to be spilled overboard.

The first real tragedy occurred on one of these small volcanic islands. A gentleman named Edward Brookes, who was very much overweight, died of his exertions while hacking his way through the jungle under a blazing sun. He was buried with full military honors.

His death caused only a momentary lowering of the company's spirits, however. Birds "flew over our heads as thick as drops of hail," and scores were killed. The nests of these birds were discovered, too, and for the first time since leaving England there were fresh eggs to eat. That night everyone feasted.

Even more important, two of Newport's sailors found a stream of cool, clear water. The water kegs were thoroughly rinsed, then filled, and the flotilla was ready for the last stage of the long voyage. On the morning of April 10th, the ships sailed due north, the *Susan Constant* in the lead, and four days later reached a point east of the southern tip of Florida, where the Spaniards had established several small but active missions.

As the squadron sailed north in the Gulf Stream, a fierce gale blew up. For a full week the officers and men of the three vessels fought the storm, losing much of their gear overboard. Most of the passengers were seasick, but John Smith remained on deck and acted as one of Newport's lieutenants.

On April 22nd, the weather cleared, but Newport could not pinpoint his position. He took soundings, but found none at one hundred fathoms, and therefore believed he had been blown far out into the Atlantic. Neither he nor other navigators of the time realized that the waters were very deep along portions of the North American continental shelf. The few charts on board the vessels were virtually useless, too, as they had been made by imaginative cartographers with no knowledge of the American coastline.

For three days Newport continued to sail toward the northwest, but was still unable to sight the mainland. He called a meeting of his fellow captains on board the *Susan Constant,* and Ratcliffe proposed that the squadron return to England, obtain fresh supplies, and start out again.

Newport called in the gentlemen-adventurers and asked their advice. All but John Smith hesitated. He made up for the silence of the others and expressed his opinions with his usual vigor. If the company returned to England, he said, many months would pass before a new expedition sailed. At least half of the men who had been recruited as settlers would lose heart and would have to be replaced. Even more important, the investors would be disgusted, and some would undoubtedly withdraw their financial support.

It was absurd, he argued, to admit failure when success was so close at hand. No matter how far the ships had been blown out to sea, he declared, they were certain to reach land if they continued to sail toward the west. He cajoled and begged his comrades to listen to reason, but his principal weapon was scorn. Those who wanted to turn back, he said, were cowards, and even the eunuchs he had encountered in the Ottoman Empire were more manly.

His stinging words shamed Ratcliffe and his supporters into silence, and when Newport finally proposed that they continue their search for the North American mainland, no one opposed him. John was responsible for the decision, but few of his colleagues appreciated his efforts. His rebuke had been so harsh that Ratcliffe, Archer, and Kendal hated him even more venomously.

On the night of April 25th, another gale blew up, driving the ships before it, and the sea captains, completely at the mercy of the storm, let the wind drive them where it would. They devoted all their efforts to remaining afloat and staying within hailing distance of each other.

The gale died away as abruptly as it had arisen, and a sailor who went aloft soon after dawn stunned the company when he called down from the crow's nest in the *Susan Constant's* mainmast, "Land ho!"

Newport climbed the rigging himself and discovered that he was indeed off a peninsula. Beyond it, as far as he could see, was a deep green forest, and he realized he had found the mainland. Devout members of the company felt certain the Almighty had created the storm in order to guide the ships to their destination.

A few hours later, Newport led his squadron into the entrance to what would become known as Chesapeake Bay when John Smith gave it that name. A small party went ashore, and the men were overwhelmed by the sight of pleasant meadows, tall, stately trees, and numerous brooks. The group decided to spend the night on shore and continue their explorations in the morning.

Soon after sundown they were subjected to their first Indian attack. A large party of savages crept through the forest toward them as the men warmed themselves around a campfire they had built. The warriors approached silently, then launched a sudden assault, firing scores of arrows. Gabriel Archer received minor flesh cuts in both hands, and a sailor, Matthew Morton, was seriously wounded.

John's quick thinking may have prevented a catastrophe. He realized that the members of the landing party made perfect targets in the firelight, and repeatedly ordered them to scatter. Some were so terror-stricken they were unable to move, and he shoved them into the shadows beyond the clearing. Captain Newport had the presence of mind to fire his musket and both of his pistols at the savages. The Indians, who had never before heard the sound of firearms, retreated in panic.

The injured were sent out to the anchored ships, and the rest elected to spend the night on shore. On the morning of April 27th, the instructions prepared by the directors in London were read for the first time. The colony was to be governed by a council of seven, which included the three ships' captains—Newport, Gosnold, and Ratcliffe—and four of the gentlemen-adventurers—John Smith, Edward Wingfield, John Martin, and George Kendal. They were directed to hold office for one year, electing their own president. All questions of importance were to be decided by a majority vote, with the president casting two votes and each of the others one.

Ratcliffe and Kendal insisted that John be denied his seat on the council and persuaded Wingfield and Gosnold to support them. Newport and Martin pleaded with the others to behave sensibly, but were ignored. John was too ambitious and, perhaps, too dictatorial in his attitudes to suit the majority. He accepted the decision quietly, but made it plain that he was accommodating his colleagues only temporarily. At the appropriate time, he declared, he would claim his seat.

That day, work was begun on a small vessel that could navigate inland waters. Sometimes called a *sloop* and sometimes a *shallop,* it had a mainmast and foremast and could carry approximately twenty-five men. When completed, it would prove to be a useful little vessel that belied its clumsy appearance. It resembled a barge, John said, but was seaworthy and could be maneuvered easily.

While the sea captains supervised the construction of the shallop, John paid no attention to the snubs of his fellow council members and led the better part of the company on an eight-mile march inland through the forest. He proved adept at following the trail of the savages, and they came at last to a campsite where the natives had been roasting oysters. The Indians fled as the Englishmen approached, and the delighted explorers found several large vine baskets heaped high with oysters. They ate some raw and roasted others, and John found them large and "delicate in taste."

They discovered other pleasures in the forest, too. There were spring flowers everywhere, "of so many colors and hues that I cannot find words to describe them," as John later wrote. They also found wild strawberries four times larger than any grown in England, and it was John's opinion that their taste was four times better.

Work on the shallop progressed so rapidly that it was completed on April 28th, and Newport went for a brief sail on the lower part of Chesapeake Bay. Most of the gentlemen-adventurers accompanied him, and everyone ate his fill of oysters and mussels, which they found in vast numbers.

Then they began a search for a permanent anchorage. Luck was with them, for they discovered a channel with six to twelve fathoms of water—the mouth of what was to be called the James River. They named the point of land adjoining it Cape Comfort, and John drew the first of the sketches that would be included in his remarkably accurate maps of the area. To the east of Cape Comfort was the open Atlantic, and to the north lay Chesapeake Bay.

The peninsula that jutted out at the southern end of the bay was called Cape Henry, at John's suggestion, after the Prince of Wales; on April 29th, a cross was erected there. A peninsula to the north was called Cape Charles, after Henry's younger brother, the Duke of York.

The land that the company had discovered was pleasant in every way. The climate was warm, but at night the air became bracing. As far as the eye could see, there were sandy beaches from which oysters, mussels, and a small creature unknown in Europe—the North American clam—were found by the thousands.

The endless forests of pine and fir gave off a sweet-smelling scent, and the explorers were impressed by the giant oaks and elms they saw further inland. Those who knew something of farming, and John was one of them, declared that the soil was as rich as that found in the most productive regions of England.

Here, John wrote, "is a country that may have the prerogative over the most pleasant places of Europe, Asia, Africa, or America, for large and pleasant navigable rivers: heaven and earth never agreed better to frame a place for man's habitation being of our constitutions, were it fully manured and inhabited by industrious people. Here are mountains, hills, plains, valleys, rivers and brooks all running most pleasantly into a fair bay compassed, but for the mouth, with fruitful and delightsome land."

On April 30th, a large party of natives was seen at Point Comfort, so Newport ordered his ships to shift their anchorage there from the mouth of the James, and John led a group of gentlemen-adventurers, settlers, and sailors ashore in the shallop. Although prepared for trouble, he ordered the men not to show their weapons. Standing in the prow of the ship, he indicated in pantomime to the Indians that he sought friendly intercourse with them.

The warriors outnumbered the band of strangers bearing down on them, which gave them a feeling of security, and the broad gestures of the smiling man in armor further convinced them that they had nothing to fear. They held their ground, half timidly, half defiantly.

As John leaped ashore, he reached into a sack he was carrying and flung a handful of colored beads in the direction of the braves. The warriors eagerly snatched the gifts, and he took still others from the bag—small knives sharper than any that the Indians carried, a variety of worthless trinkets, and a dozen little mirrors—the first the natives had ever seen—that soon had them shrieking and laughing in childish glee.

The meeting was a great success. The Indians invited the strangers to share their meal, which consisted of roasted venison, which had not been marinated in the European manner and therefore was very difficult to cut and chew, bread made of a paste (of American corn) that was cooked on heated rocks, and several small animals that the Englishmen at first believed to be pigs. When they discovered they were eating roasted dog, some gagged, but at John's insistence they manfully ate everything placed before them so they wouldn't offend their hosts.

Then the warriors lighted pipes, which they passed to the strangers, and John was secretly elated that tobacco was grown in the area. "There was joy in my heart to find here green gold, so much in demand by the merchants of London that its value is as great as the most precious metals," he wrote.

The Indians then danced for their visitors, and John persuaded Martin to help him repay the compliment by staging a mock duel. Several of the settlers wanted to return to the shallop for their muskets, but John knew the noise the firearms made would frighten away the Indians and undo all that had been achieved. He threatened to cut off the head of any man who dared discharge a weapon, and spoke in such deadly tones that he was obeyed. No one doubted that, if provoked, he would keep his word.

The educated members of the expedition—sea captains, their mates, and the gentlemen-adventurers alike—all believed that the Pacific Ocean lay only a short distance inland up the rivers that flowed into the Atlantic. The directors in London had ordered that a water passage to the Pacific be found as quickly as possible, and everyone was eager to carry out this mission. Therefore, the friendship of the savages having been won, John formed a party of exploration to make its way up the James and find the world's largest ocean.

On May 4th, the group ventured a short distance up the James in the shallop and came to the home of the Indians who had entertained them, a large village called Paspahegh. John was fascinated by the savages' mode of living. The majority slept in longhouses of wood, mud, and animal skins, unmarried braves in two of the houses, unmarried women in others. Married braves and their wives also lived in longhouses, but their children were taken off at the age of seven to live with the unmarried.

Elderly men and old women were allowed the luxury of dwelling in tents of their own, but were treated as outcasts. They were allowed to approach the communal cooking pots only when everyone else had eaten. The chief of the village was a ruggedly handsome man of early middle age, with high cheekbones, dark, intense eyes, and a regal manner. He lived apart from his people in a small version of a longhouse, and with him were three wives and their children, among them two sons who appeared to be in their late teens.

John utilized his flair for languages and spent most of his time with the chief. With him was Percy, also a student of foreign tongues, who had learned Latin, Greek, and French at Oxford. Between them they made rapid progress in communicating with the Indian. He told them his name was Powhatan, and he was proud of the fact that the river, which the explorers were calling the James, had been named after him. Further inquiry revealed that he was not only headman of the one village, but was chief of chiefs of a confederation of savage nations that included his own, the Chickahominy, as well as three to the north—the Pamaunke, the Rappahannock, and the Potomac.

The visitors were disturbed by his revelation that he also exercised suzerainty over nations that lived far to the west, the Chawon, the Monacan, and the Mannahoack. If the claim was true—and Powhatan did not strike John as an idle boaster—the continent stretched farther to the west than anyone had suspected, and the chances of finding a sea passage to the Pacific were reduced.

That night John and Percy courageously remained at the village as Powhatan's guests while the rest of the party cautiously returned to the ships. The two Englishmen pretended to enjoy the food, but actually found only the unleavened corn bread palatable. John recognized the grain, found only in the New World, from descriptions written by Spanish explorers, who had called it maize, a corruption of a Caribbean Indian word, *mahis*.

He was so curious and so extravagant in his praise of the corn that Powhatan graciously presented him with several full gourds of kernels. The sachem, as he was called by his own people, managed to communicate the idea that this was the best season of the year to plant maize.

John kept his advice in mind, and the corn planted at his insistence soon thereafter was a major contribution to the prevention of famine during the colonists' first winter in the New World.

The two visitors noted that the Chickahominy wore clothing made of animal skins, much of it as soft as cloth. The women, whose modest appearance impressed John, a man never unaware of the opposite sex, also wore garments made of woven rushes or vines. Villagers who died were placed on platforms made of wooden planks and supported by high poles, which were set deep in the forest. There the earthly remains of the departed decomposed, safe from wild animals that roamed through the wilderness.

As a badge of office Powhatan wore a magnificent cape of feathers that stretched from his neck to the ground. Assuming that John was the chief of the strangers, the sachem presented him with a similar cape, a gesture that would arouse violent jealousy in the breasts of other gentlemen-adventurers when they learned of it. Not to be outdone by his host's generosity, John gave Powhatan a smallsword with a sharp steel blade.

If John met or saw Powhatan's little daughter, Pocahontas, during this visit, he does not mention that fact in any of the three books he subsequently wrote about his experiences: *A True Relation; A Map of Virginia, With a Description of the Country;* and *The Generall Historie of Virginia.* Nor does Percy refer to her in his *Journal,* a letter-diary he kept for the edification of his family and friends. Ordinarily the omission of the name of an eleven- or twelve-year-old Indian maiden from such recitals would not be surprising, but in view of the romantic furor made in later years it may be significant.

On May 5th the shallop returned. John and Percy rejoined their comrades, and the boat moved farther up the river. They were cordially received by the chief of another village, Powhatan having sent word ahead that the strangers meant no harm. Percy was impressed by the clear water in the brooks that ran down from the mountains and by "the goodliest corn fields that ever was seen in any country." He, like the others, was also amused by John's persistent efforts to learn the language of the Chickahominy.

The river proved to be navigable far upstream, and the men paddled deeper into the interior each day, accompanied by guides provided by Powhatan. At the village of Appamatuck, John concluded that the waters were becoming much shallower. Beyond the Indian town the river narrowed to a width not much greater than that of a brook. He doubted that the James would lead to the Pacific, and reluctantly turned back downstream.

On May 13th the shallop reached the anchored ships, and John, still excluded from the council, made a point of submitting his report only to Captain Newport. The snub did nothing to improve his relations with the other members of the council.

The following day, the squadron sailed up the James to a point not far from Powhatan's village, anchoring close to the shore in six fathoms of water. Virtually everyone went ashore. While a few men acted as sentries, the rest went to work to build wooden houses, storage sheds, a meeting hall and, far more important than all the rest, a fort.

A few days later, while work was still going on, Powhatan paid a visit of state to the camp of the strangers. He was surrounded by his warriors, his approach was heralded by savage drummers, and all of the Chickahominy had faces daubed with ceremonial paint for the occasion. John hastily donned his own feather cape and gravely presented the ships' officers and the other gentlemen-adventurers to the sachem. Newport was impressed by John's growing ability to speak the tongue of the Chickahominy, and Percy no longer laughed at his friend.

The natives carried with them the carcasses of several freshly killed deer, and both Englishmen and Chickahominy went fishing for several hours. When there was enough food at hand for a feast, meat and fish were cooked on fires that others had lighted. Powhatan seemed to enjoy himself, but John irritated Archer and Kendal by reminding them in rather stringent terms not to serve alcoholic spirits to the savages. Wingfield, commenting on the incident in his own book, *Discourse of America,* says the advice was unnecessary.

Perhaps his observation is accurate, but it may be that he was justifying his own antipathy to John. Wingfield had been elected president of the council earlier that same day, and felt sufficiently guilty about John's exclusion from the body that he deemed it necessary to include a long report in his *Discourse* on the hostility of the members toward John.

Wingfield insisted on making a speech to the guests, and John tried to translate it to Powhatan in a form so abbreviated that the new president became annoyed. John blandly informed him that he hadn't mastered the Chickahominy tongue well enough to make a verbatim translation.

A short time before dusk, the Indians prepared to take their leave. At that moment one of the settlers discovered that an Indian warrior had stolen his ax. He snatched the tool from the thief, striking the brave on the arm. This act so incensed another warrior that he threatened to beat out the brains of the Englishman with a crude hammer of stone that he was carrying. The combatants were separated with great difficulty, and everyone began shouting.

John urged his comrades to remain calm, but they paid no attention to his pleas and ran for their muskets. Powhatan was apprehensive of the power of these strange weapons, even though he had never seen one used. He called his warriors to him, and they responded with remarkable discipline as they formed in ranks behind him.

The sachem, very angry at what he considered a breach of hospitality, withdrew with his men after making a short address, punctuated with broad, self-explanatory gestures. What he said in effect was that he considered John Smith his friend, but all other Englishmen were his enemies. On that ominous note he departed.

The colony, which the council had that very day given the name of Jamestown, in honor of the King, was threatened with extinction on the day it was founded.

XII

Jamestown

THE MIRACLE OF JAMESTOWN, the first English settlement in North America, was that it survived. Not only did the powerful sachem of the Chickahominy confederation, Powhatan, become its enemy, but it was torn by internal dissension. The exclusion of Captain John Smith from the colony's council, in defiance of the directors' orders, was the result of a long-standing feud, and other quarrels soon erupted, and further disturbed the peace.

Wingfield, who was neither a leader of men nor an experienced administrator, did not like the site that had been selected for the settlement, claiming it was inaccessible and difficult to defend. Gosnold, one of the most seasoned mariners of the age, laughed at Wingfield's fears. Jamestown, he said, had a splendid deepwater channel that made it as easy to reach as London via the Thames. High palisades were being built around the entire town, cannon would be emplaced in the fort, and Jamestown would soon be impregnable.

The president took umbrage at Captain Gosnold and sullenly declared in his *Discourse* that he did not believe the site appropriate for the founding of a great city.

He changed his mind, however, in an even angrier dispute he had with Gabriel Archer. Excluded from the council by London's orders and refused a place of honor in the ranks of the gentlemen-adventurers, Archer was spoiling for a fight. He went to Wingfield in great anger, saying he had been refused a voice in the selection of the town's site because Wingfield had disapproved of the plans he had drawn up for the defenses of the community while on board the *Discovery*. Archer's naiveté in assuming he could lay out a town's defenses before he even knew its location indicates his incompetence. Wingfield reveals his own lack of stature by countering Archer's arguments with the very comments Gosnold had previously made to him.

The worst of the Wingfield-Archer conflict was sparked by Wingfield's refusal to give the Captain a place on the council. In his *Discourse,* the first president of Jamestown rightly declared that it was not in his power to grant Archer a seat. He added that, in his opinion, the soldier of fortune did not deserve it.

A far more serious difference of opinion split Wingfield and the other members of the council. The president was so afraid of offending Powhatan again that, acting on his own authority, he ordered construction of the fort and palisades halted. He would allow no defenses other than a prettily ingenious intertwining of tree branches devised by Kendal. Having been thrust into the limelight with his foolish defense scheme, Kendal naturally cast his vote with Wingfield, who had two ballots of his own. They persuaded Ratcliffe to join them, which the junior sea captain did, chiefly because he believed that Newport and Gosnold disliked him.

There were four votes against the building of the fortifications and four in favor. Had the council been fully manned, as the directors in London had anticipated, no tie would have been possible, but John Smith's exclusion led to the deadlock. Therefore Wingfield claimed that, since his wishes had not been vetoed, they would be observed. Sensible men wondered whether to impeach and depose him, but John and Newport calmed the rebels by promising them that construction would be resumed in the near future. They had already learned that Wingfield was not one to maintain a stand, and they thought it wiser to let him save face by changing his mind quietly after the hubbub subsided.

This he did, precisely as they had anticipated, and on May 19th construction work on the fort was resumed. John, although officially holding no office, had already become the co-leader of the colony with Newport. Perhaps his greatest source of strength was the popularity he had achieved with the commoners in the colony. These men recognized his qualities of decisiveness and common sense, and came to him with their personal problems. They sought his advice when they discovered that the houses they were building had roofs and windows that leaked. Despite the fact that he was neither an architect nor a carpenter, John soon corrected the defects.

There were many in the company who were totally unfamiliar with the use of firearms, so John set himself the task of teaching them how to load, fire, and clean the muskets they had been issued. Lacking such instructions, the weapons would have been useless for purposes of either hunting or self-defense.

Wingfield claimed that John was trying to "curry favor" with the commoners, and ordered that no "exercises at arms" be held. John replied that he was not conducting such exercises and, quietly supported by the dependable Newport, he continued to teach the neophytes how to use their weapons.

Late in May a party of twenty-three men started up the James River again on a journey of exploration in depth. Newport placed himself in charge of the company and gave John Smith command of the land party that would range through the forest whenever the shallop was anchored.

Several accounts of this journey were later written. The best known was John's, which appeared in his *True Relation*. Another, by Percy, was printed sixteen years later in a book compiled and edited by the Reverend Samuel Purchas, an English divine who loved exploration and liked to imagine himself Hakluyt's successor, although he lacked the Archdeacon's ability to separate accurate fact from delusive fancy. A third point of view was presented by Archer. Jealous of everything John did, he kept a journal of his own for more than a month.

The Newport-Smith party traveled approximately seventy miles up the James River, moving through the same territory John had covered previously. But this group made its journey at a much slower pace, pausing frequently so that John, accompanied by everyone except Newport and his sailors, was able to venture far inland on both sides of the river.

The James flowed through a deep forest wilderness, so the explorers discovered virtually nothing of consequence. But the trip was of tremendous importance to the future of Jamestown because of their frequent meetings with the savages of various sub-branches of Powhatan's Chickahominy. It is curious that John, who was so often brusque and sometimes even brutal in his impatient treatment of his fellow Englishmen, should have shown genius in his dealings with the Indians. He was gentle, calm, and generous, knew how to appeal to the natives' child-like but often subtle sense of humor, and had a remarkable talent for winning their friendship.

The first stop was made at Paspahegh, and there John, with Newport's assistance and encouragement, made strenuous efforts to end the rift with Powhatan. He presented the sachem with still more gifts, among them several pairs of shears, brass bells that made "a pleasingly musical sound"—and his own razor, which Powhatan admired. John didn't mind parting with it, since he used it only to trim his luxurious beard. Powhatan had even less need for a razor. Like most North American Indians, he had only a few whiskers, and it was the custom of the savages to pluck stray hairs from their faces. Nevertheless, the razor accomplished its purpose, and Powhatan was mollified.

Another gift was equally successful and had far-reaching effects. John produced paper, a jar of ink, and a quill pen, and drew a rough sketch of the river and the territory adjacent to it. Powhatan and his sons were fascinated and suggested changes in the crude map that were of inestimable benefit to the explorers. Because of the sachem's great interest, John gave him the writing implements. Incidentally, Archer claimed in his journal that it was *he* who drew an outline of the river and presented the tools to Powhatan. Inasmuch as he had never before shown a talent for cartography and never demonstrated such skills later in life, the allegation may be taken with a pinch of salt.

Powhatan provided the travelers with five guides, one of them his own younger son, and the Englishmen visited eleven other Indian communities as they sailed up the James. Some of them were tiny hamlets set deep in the forest; two or three of them were villages of considerable size. Everywhere the visitors were well received and were feasted at banquets, where the main dishes were roasted venison, fish, and oysters. They also ate quantities of unleavened corn bread and a dish John describes as a porridge of coarsely pounded corn meal and water, sweetened with a thick, scarcely edible syrup made of sap from maple trees.

The Indians also grew wheat, which was less delicate than that of England and Europe, and used it to thicken their stews. Their strawberries and mulberries were infinitely superior to those of the Old World. The visitors were also introduced to a berry that was new to them and which they found particularly delicious. It was about the size of a large pea, had a smooth skin, and was blue in color, leaving a temporary blue stain on the insides of their mouths. They enjoyed another New World agricultural product, too, a nut that was sweet to the taste and somewhat resembled an acorn.

The party penetrated as far inland as a village that would become, in the eighteenth century, the site of Richmond. Newport optimistically held a ceremony in which he claimed the entire area, as far west as the Pacific Ocean, in the name of King James, and a cross was erected on a hill just beyond the village. An inscription burned into the wood informed other Old World travelers who might come this way that the territory was English.

The forest enthralled even the unimaginative members of the party. John says that nowhere in his many travels had he seen trees so enormous. Percy identified beech, oak, cedar, cypress, and walnut trees as particularly impressive, and made an attempt to give names to other varieties unknown to the party. It was still spring, and the wildflowers everywhere were in full bloom, making some of the younger men homesick.

The return to Jamestown was leisurely. There was ample game in the forests, John was learning more about edible plants and roots each day, and the explorers, under the spell of the wilderness, saw no reason to hurry. When they finally reached Jamestown, however, they discovered that tragedy had struck the infant colony only twenty-four hours earlier.

Several hundred Indians of the Chesapeake tribe, a nation not affiliated with Powhatan's confederation, had launched a vicious surprise attack on the settlers. The partly completed defenses had been inadequate to protect the town. Wingfield, who was responsible for the failure to prepare for such an emergency, had made still another error that had seriously compromised the settlers' ability to defend themselves. Most of the company had been scattered over a fairly wide area outside the partly erected palisades, sowing corn, when the Indian assault was launched. Though John Smith had urged that everyone who wandered away from the compound for any purpose should carry a musket with him at all times, Wingfield had issued a contrary order forbidding anyone to carry arms.

Consequently, when the Indians struck Jamestown, the colonists were helpless. Most of them managed to dash to the safety of the completed buildings, but twelve had been wounded, and two—a man and a teen-age boy—had been killed. By the time the defenders had organized themselves into a semblance of a military company, the Chesapeake warriors had gained sufficient momentum to carry the day.

Fortunately, however, Captain Gosnold had remained calm. He had ordered the crews of all three ships to board at once and unlimber their cannon. The roar of the big guns had frightened the savages. They fled in terror just as they had been at the point of annihilating the entire company. All the council members in Jamestown at the time, except Wingfield, had been wounded. An arrow had whistled through his beard, but had left him unscathed.

John felt certain the Chesapeake would return, and a number of others agreed with him. Wingfield stubbornly insisted that his policy of placating the Indians by not building strong fortifications was correct. John, however, supported by virtually all the commoners, ignored his orders and went to work at once on the task of completing the fort.

In the next three weeks the Chesapeake returned to make four separate raids. All of these attacks were made at night, two shortly after sundown and the other two an hour or so before dawn. In each attack, the savages employed the same tactics, sending flaming arrows into the town in the hope of starting a fire that would force the defenders to flee into the woods, where waiting braves could slaughter them.

But John was prepared now, and acted accordingly. He set up sentry schedules around the clock, with two gentlemen-adventurers in command of each detail. He paid no attention to Wingfield's foolish order to the effect that no muskets were to be discharged unless the savages tried to climb over the palisades, which had just been finished. If any warrior was seen loitering in the vicinity of Jamestown at any time, under any circumstances, John directed, he was to be killed instantly.

The two policies were so radically different that they created a new furor of controversy. Most of the members of the company stood with John. Only Kendal, Ratcliffe, and the meek, shortsighted Wingfield continued to favor pacification at any price. On the third of the Chesapeake raids, another settler was killed. When one more settler was wounded during the fourth attack, the entire colony rebelled. Percy and Martin finally drew up a formal petition demanding the immediate reformation of the council. Even Gabriel Archer signed it, and those commoners who could neither read nor write put their marks in the appropriate place.

President Wingfield, pressed by Newport and Gosnold, and faced with an insurrection that threatened to sweep him out of office, surrendered. On June 14th John Smith was finally admitted to the place on the council that should have been his from the start.

Once granted his seat, he lost no time in taking charge. Men worked day and night to strengthen the palisades and put two new towers on the fort. Land was cleared for several hundred feet from every approach to the town in order to make new sneak attacks impossible.

Furthermore, John did not allow himself to forget that the directors in London expected the colony to show a profit. The tallest and sturdiest of the oak, beech, and white pine cut down were sawed into lumber and stored in the holds of the ships.

Wingfield still held the title of president, but John had assumed active charge of Jamestown's affairs, and for the first time the settlement enjoyed relative security. He well realized that further dissension would weaken the little community, so he turned to diplomacy and made an effort to win Wingfield's confidence and good will. When he elected to use his charm, John was able to dazzle anyone, and the confused president was no exception. Newport later asked Wingfield in so many words whether he felt secure in his office, and the president replied that only two men wanted to take his seat from him. One was Gosnold, he said, and the other was Archer. He felt no threat from John Smith.

In any event, the settlers' chances of survival had brightened immeasurably, and in late June Newport made ready to take advantage of calm seas and warm weather for his return voyage to England. Artillery pieces had been mounted at each of the corners of the triangle-shaped fort. The men were drilling daily under the watchful eye of John, who strained his newly utilized statesmanship almost to the breaking point by appointing Archer as his deputy field commander. He calmed the ambitious Gosnold, too, by nominating the sea captain for the post of artillery commander. Ratcliffe was unwilling to oppose a fellow sailor, and only Wingfield and Kendal dissented.

At the end of June, the *Susan Constant* was ready for her voyage, and Captain Newport entertained the colony's gentlemen at a farewell dinner of boiled salt pork and peas, augmented with venison, fish, and berries. Wine flowed freely, and most of the guests were in a merry mood. John had good reason to feel pleased with himself, since he had just concluded a barter deal with Powhatan for beaver and fox pelts that greatly enhanced the value of the cargo that Newport was carrying to England. The furs alone would show the directors a substantial profit on their investment to date.

Despite these accomplishments, John was silent and worried. Before the party ended, he demanded that the council hold a final session with Newport. The members reluctantly adjourned to the master's cabin. There John presented them with some sobering facts. A total of 105 men were remaining in Jamestown, he said, and even though all corn, beans, and peas had been planted, there was a chance the colony might starve that winter. The Indians had told him that game would disappear from the forest when the cold weather came, and there would be neither berries nor edible roots in the forests until the following spring.

Supplies that Newport was leaving behind were limited; there was no guarantee that the corn crop would be good; and fishing might prove hazardous in cold, stormy weather. Therefore he proposed that the council send a petition to the directors in London, asking for provisions. He drafted the petition then and there. It made so much sense that the council passed a resolution in favor of sending it by a unanimous vote, the first time all members had been in agreement.

Newport sailed off to England, carrying the petition with him. He reached London in mid-August, and the directors accepted his report with mixed feelings. They happily accepted their profit on the furs, but apparently failed to recognize the value of the lumber. At least, they made no mention of it.

They were deeply disappointed because the explorers had found no gold, silver, and precious gems, and prepared fresh instructions ordering that the search for metals and stones be increased. John's request for food, coupled with Newport's personal description of conditions in the colony, made the directors aware of the gravity of the situation. As a result, arrangements were made to send out two ships laden with provisions as rapidly as they could be purchased.

Affairs in Jamestown deteriorated rapidly after Newport's departure. Wingfield had been somewhat in awe of the fleet's commodore, but was now determined to make himself master in his own house. He issued a long list of rules, most of them injurious to the welfare of the colony. Any man in the settlement who wanted to go hunting or fishing was required to apply for a written permit from the president, who intended to let no more than three go out into the wilderness for either purpose on any given day.

Houses were to be made "snug," and new homes were to be built for additional colonists who might arrive at some as yet unknown future date. Meanwhile, all work was to stop on the new outer line of palisades on which John had started construction. No more than twenty men were permitted to engage in military drills during the course of a single week. The firing of muskets and pistols for training purposes was to be halted at once, because it "wasted" ammunition and powder.

John Smith lost his temper when the president's rules were posted on the door of Wingfield's house. Apparently Wingfield had consulted no one other than Kendal before issuing his instructions, and the other members of the council were angry, too. John demanded that a full-dress council meeting be held at once, but Wingfield procrastinated until the others, in exasperation, sat down without him in the little house that John and Gosnold shared.

Wingfield learned that the meeting was being held without him and stormed into the house, declaring that the session was illegal. The others countered by saying that his arrival made the session legal. They asked him to act as chairman, which he did with bad grace.

Gosnold called the construction schedule absurd, pointing out that it was imperative to protect the current members of the community rather than prepare for those who might some day arrive. Ratcliffe was unable to follow Wingfield, and only Kendal voted with the president in an attempt to emphasize the building of new houses. First priority was given to the new outer palisades.

John confined himself to the subject of food and cited some basic figures that were frightening. There was only enough wheat and barley for another fourteen weeks, he said, if every member of the settlement was rationed, and received a half-pint of wheat each day and an equal amount of barley to boil with water.

He had established a new sentry system, assigning men to duty in each of the fort's three turrets. He pointed out that colonists who worked in the fields or built palisades all day were inclined to fall asleep at their sentry posts at night when they had too little to eat. It was an urgent and obvious need, he said, that the rations be supplemented by meat and fish. For that reason, he suggested that everyone not otherwise occupied take part in the search for food.

The council accepted his ideas, Wingfield and Kendal again dissenting. But the members balked at his plan to send trading missions to barter for food with the Indians. His scheme was too bold, they felt, and they wanted no more to do with any of the savage tribes than was necessary.

By the latter part of July, the council regretted its refusal to obtain provisions from the Indians. The weather became unbearably hot, and the dampness was all-pervading. Men worked for a few hours, then fainted. Game disappeared from the forests overnight, and schools of fish that had been so plentiful in both the Atlantic and Chesapeake Bay vanished. John and a few others put clams, mussels, and oysters in their barley, thus making the first American clam chowder and oyster stew, but most of the colonists could no longer abide the taste of shellfish.

Then, one by one, members of the company fell ill. "The sickness" was unlike anything that anyone in the colony had ever experienced. One moment a man felt well enough to do his chores; suddenly, without warning, he broke out in a rash, ran a high fever, and was so weak he could not stand. A variety of remedies were tried, but none were effective, and the number of those suffering from the ailment grew larger each day. By the end of August, more than half of the men lay sweltering and moaning in their huts.

Those who remained healthy had to do all the work, including the standing of sentry duty, but they were so weak on the thin diet of wheat and barley that they frequently fell asleep. John Smith had rarely proved his worth more than he did during this trying period. His energy was inexhaustible. Although he had no more to eat than anyone else, he snatched a few hours of sleep when he could, and he worked tirelessly, day and night, to prevent the colony from disintegrating.

On August 22nd, Captain Bartholomew Gosnold died of "the sickness." Within the next twenty days, forty-five others also expired. John fell ill, and Martin, Percy, and several others were afraid they would lose him, too. However, he rallied swiftly and insisted on returning to the fort after spending only two days on his pallet of pine boughs. Ratcliffe was also ill, but recovered, thanks to the ministrations of John, the man he had so consistently opposed.

As Ratcliffe convalesced, he had time to mull over all that had happened since leaving England, and for the first time he wondered if John had really attacked him so bitterly at the beginning of the voyage. He brought the matter into the open when John visited his house, and accepted the reply that "Captain Smith cared nought what any man had done to save his own life, since all men will fight like wild beasts when they are endangered by death."

Ratcliffe's change of heart had rapid and far-reaching consequences. The colony's survivors were inclined to blame Wingfield for the tragedy, which was unfair, of course, but contained enough elements of truth to be realistic. Kendal, Ratcliffe saw at last, was a schemer who sowed dissension and mistrust everywhere. The sea captain finally had a long talk with Wingfield, who was so shocked by the perfidy of his friend Kendal that he called a meeting of the council.

Formal charges of treason were lodged against Kendal, his fellow council members acting as prosecutors, judges, and jury. By unanimous vote Kendal was discharged from office, placed under arrest, and given into the hands of John Smith for safekeeping. John had to hold the prisoner in his own house for two days while some of the men built a cell in the fort.

The death of so many settlers made it possible to increase the rations of the survivors, and some of the men were strong enough now for serious work. John, acting on his own authority, asked for volunteers to accompany him on a tour of the Indian villages in the vicinity. Both Ratcliffe and Percy responded, as did eleven of the commoners. The party of fourteen took large sacks of glass beads and other baubles with them. After a journey of seventy-two hours, they returned to Jamestown, the deck of the shallop piled high with baskets of corn and quarters of venison. The expedition had been successful.

During John's absence, however, Wingfield and Martin had been wrangling. The president had made another of his blunders, declaring that victims of "the sickness" should receive no food until they were strong enough to apply for their rations at the warehouse in person. The order was so ridiculous and unfair that some of the commoners were openly threatening to lynch Wingfield.

John and Ratcliffe consulted with Martin, and the three council members realized that drastic steps had to be taken immediately. They voted to depose Wingfield and place him under arrest. At John's suggestion, Ratcliffe was chosen as president to replace him. Then the trio called on Wingfield to break the unpleasant news to him.

He accepted his fate silently, but wept when he was banished to the *Discovery,* a precautionary move taken to prevent disgruntled settlers from murdering him. He was given the freedom of the ship, a small concession, and was directed to remain on board until a squadron arrived from England, at which time he would be deported.

The sentence was harsh, but the age was a cruel one, and members of the tiny colony were fighting for their lives. Wingfield had done nothing evil, and certainly intended harm to no man. His worst offense was that he was a bungler, but he had made more mistakes than Jamestown could afford, so he was deposed by his colleagues, who didn't bother to put him on trial or allow him to speak a word in his own defense.

During his captivity on board the *Discovery,* Wingfield began to write his book, *A Discourse of Virginia.* This account was honest and candid, and matches much of what John wrote in his *True Relation.* It was natural that Wingfield should feel bitter toward his colleagues, both living and dead, but it was surprising that he wrote with relatively little hostility about John, reserving most of his scorn for Gosnold, Ratcliffe, Kendal, and Gabriel Archer, who was not yet a member of the council.

The three men in charge of Jamestown knew they had their work cut out for them. One of their first acts was the election of new council members. At John's suggestion, all gentlemen-adventurers would serve for terms of a few months until the directors in London appointed a new, permanent board of governors.

John, Ratcliffe, and Martin were aware of the impropriety of sentencing a man to prison without a trial, so they hailed Wingfield before a jury of his peers one Sunday late in September. He was charged with having kept large quantities of sack and other alcoholic spirits for his own use and that of his friends. He pleaded guilty. He was also charged with having made slanderous remarks about one of the commoners, having falsely accused the man of planning to abscond to Newfoundland with the shallop. He pleaded guilty again, but declared himself innocent of the charge of having administered the affairs of the colony badly.

The jury of gentlemen-adventurers found him guilty on all charges and fined him several thousand pounds. Since he had no money to pay, they seized all his personal property, which was then awarded to those whom he had maligned or harmed at one time or another. John was given goods worth two hundred pounds, as recompense for having been denied his seat on the council for so many weeks.

This property consisted of weapons and clothing. John, embarrassed by the award, immediately gave it to the community at large, directing that all the items be stored in the common warehouse to be used when needed.

Ratcliffe, meanwhile, was conscious of his own limitations and realized that he had few supporters in the colony. Therefore, in order to strengthen his own hand, he made John his deputy and put him in complete charge of all work done outdoors.

John had legitimate authority at last, and he drew up schedules for all the men. He gave the lightest task, that of preparing new thatched roofs for the houses, to those still convalescing from "the sickness." Men who were healthy again were directed to strengthen the fort, expand the clearing, and tend the growing crops. (There were, of course, no women among the original Jamestown settlers.)

John, accompanied by a small band of personally selected assistants, made another food-hunting expedition up the James. The Indians had admired the settlers' axes, so he took a number of tools with him, along with iron cooking pots. The shallop had lost its sails in a gale, and there was no cloth for replacement purposes, so the men had to row upstream, a grueling task.

John visited five Indian villages and used his most persuasive powers of salesmanship on the natives. It was fortunate, Percy later wrote, that by now he was sufficiently familiar with the language of the Chickahominy to speak it fluently. His charm, shrewd bargaining talent, and persistence paid dividends in the first four villages he visited. At the fifth, however, the Indians said they had no desire to trade. John immediately ordered a demonstration of force, and his companions, at his command, fired their muskets into the air.

Squaws and children fled in terror, and some warriors vanished into the forest, too. But the chief of the village was quick to understand John's point and changed his mind, agreeing to barter with the foreigners. Neither then nor later was John concerned over the ethics of the tactics he had used. He cared only about results.

His achievements on the journey were spectacularly successful. He and his companions returned to Jamestown with thirty bushels of corn, twenty of wheat, and seventeen of "coarse Indian rye, too strong in taste for bread, but nourishing when made into a paste with water and sweetened with the gum of the maple tree." They brought sides of venison and pungent bear bacon, wild turkeys, fish, and oysters. Equally important, they carried sacks of salt found at a deer lick, which they would use to preserve the meat and fish not eaten immediately. Then the threat of starvation was eased.

A few weeks later the corn, peas, and beans the colonists were growing ripened, and everyone in the colony was put to work reaping the harvest. No one was excepted. John set the example, starting to work at dawn and continuing with only short pauses until sundown every day. The precious provisions were stored in the common warehouse, which was equipped with a lock. Only Ratcliffe and John had keys. Two sentries were stationed outside the building, with orders to shoot anyone who approached.

In the autumn John made several additional trips to Indian villages, all of them successful, before he began to grapple with a new problem. The men were still wearing the clothes they had brought with them from England, and shirts, breeches, and coats were growing threadbare. The ships the optimists expected daily from England failed to arrive, so John emulated the savages. He learned to cure deerskin and the heavier, less malleable skin of the buffalo that roamed the valleys of the interior.

The other gentlemen-adventurers refused to wear shirts and trousers of skins. John, however, refused to be so particular and set the example for the whole community by appearing daily in such attire. As the weather became colder and the dampness more penetrating, others were glad to do the same.

It was inconvenient and difficult to take care of a prisoner at the fort, so President Ratcliffe transferred Kendal to the *Discovery*. This proved to be a mistake, because Kendal and Wingfield were given the opportunity to conspire, which they did. They held surreptitious conversations with members of the ship's crew, who took turns guarding them, and it was easy to persuade these seamen that life in the New World was hazardous and unpleasant beyond endurance. Scheming in secret, the two deposed members of the council planned to steal the ship and sail with her crew to England during one of John's absences from Jamestown.

Supplies were smuggled on board, the sailors having dug a tunnel into the rear of the warehouse, and one day in October the plan was put into operation. Ratcliffe was shocked when he saw the *Discovery* ready to leave Jamestown. Going down to the water's edge, he pleaded in vain with his sailors and with the two prisoners. The sails were hoisted, and everyone in the colony hurried down to the bank of the James to watch the vessel's departure.

Before the anchor could be weighed, however, John and nine companions unexpectedly returned to Jamestown in the shallop. They had obtained all the supplies they needed from Powhatan and had cut short their journey into the interior. Informed of the situation, John took charge and summarily ordered all hands on the *Discovery* ashore.

The men refused to obey him, so he fired two pistol shots, one of them grazing Kendal's ear. Then he directed every man on shore to fire at will at the outlaws on the deck of the pinnace. This was too much for the sailors and Wingfield, who surrendered. Kendal tried to hold firm, but buckled when John drew a scimitar, leaped on board, and personally took him into custody.

The mutiny, combined with the theft of provisions, could not be tolerated, and John, having saved the colony, was determined that the offense would not be repeated. He insisted that a trial be held at once, with a jury to be made of six gentlemen-adventurers and six commoners. Ratcliffe presided as judge, while John acted as prosecutor.

Kendal was found to be the principal conspirator and was sentenced to death by hanging. James Read, a member of the *Discovery's* crew, cursed at Ratcliffe when called to the witness stand, and then tried to attack the president with a knife. John wrenched the weapon from him, thus saving Ratcliffe's life. A short time later, Read was also sentenced to be hanged.

Both men were executed one raw, gray morning in November, and there were no more mutinies.

But life was hard, men grumbled, and even Ratcliffe yearned for the chance to go back to England. He and Archer toyed with the idea of making an "official" voyage to London in the *Discovery,* but abandoned the scheme when John heard of their intentions and told them bluntly that he would not hesitate to put them on trial, too, if they persisted.

Whenever possible that autumn, John went out in the shallop on trips of exploration and food bartering. He sailed up the Chickahominy River, a major tributary of the James, and traveled overland through the forests as far north as the Potomac River. He kept extensive notes and sketches, and never returned empty-handed. The corn he obtained, Percy later wrote, kept the men of Jamestown alive that autumn and winter.

The vast wilderness became John's real love and delight. "There is a peace in that cathedral," he wrote in the first edition of his *True Relation,* "as sublime as the tranquility obtained in the sacrament of communion. Standing alone beneath towering trees, one feels the presence of the Almighty Lord, and stands close to Him."

The winter of 1607–8 came early to Virginia, and the cold brought ducks and geese, swans and cranes from the high waters of the hill country to the somewhat milder climate near the mouth of the Chickahominy. There, in a single expedition, John and seven companions brought down so many birds they finally exhausted their ammunition. They were cheered on their return to Jamestown, and the colony enjoyed a welcome change in diet.

John's trips of exploration were remarkably thorough. He made notes on the kinds of trees he found, drew accurate maps of the territory through which he traveled, and even studied the soil in order to determine the kind of crops that would grow best in different localities. His journeys were hazardous, and on more than one occasion his life was threatened. He was taken prisoner by a sachem of the Potomac named Opechancanough, but saved his life by showing his compass to the sachem. The Indian was fascinated by the instrument, and was so grateful when John presented it to him that he set his prisoner free.

Twice John escaped ambushes. On one of his trips a gentleman-adventurer, Jehu Robinson, was killed, as was a carpenter, Thomas Emry. Late in December, George Cassen, one of his companions, was captured and put to death by slow torture. John was taken prisoner, this time by the Chesapeake, who recognized him as the "chief" of the strangers and therefore spared his life.

John learned they intended to launch a new surprise attack on Jamestown and begged his captors to let him send a message to his friends telling them he was alive and being treated with consideration. The savages naively allowed him to prepare such a note, and sent off three braves to Jamestown, carrying with them John's curt warning that a major attack might be made at any time.

It was during this captivity that Pocahontas, Powhatan's daughter, allegedly saved John Smith's life. The record, however, is smudged, and for more than three and a half centuries no one has known precisely what happened. An examination of contradictory claims appears essential at this point.

XIII

Princess Pocahontas

A True Relation of such occurrences and accidents of note as hath hapned in Virginia since the first planting of that Collony was John Smith's first published book, and it won an immediate success, enhancing his reputation from the time of its publication. It concerned events in the history of Jamestown from its inception to early June, 1608, and John sent it home for publication in that same month. It was officially registered at Stationers' Hall, in London, on August 13, 1608, and appeared in print about eight weeks later.

Nowhere in its pages does the name of Pocahontas appear. Instead, John calmly explains that his three weeks of captivity came to an end early in 1608 when, after the colonists received his message warning them of an impending attack, they put on an exhibition of artillery fire that dumfounded the Chesapeake couriers who waited at the settlement to bring a reply to him. The description of the big guns' power so awed the sachem and his elders that they set their prisoner free without further ado.

Edward M. Wingfield's *A Discourse of Virginia,* published soon after the unfortunate first president's return to England in 1608, is also silent on the subject of Pocahontas. Percy makes no reference to her, nor does *The Proceedings of the English Colony in Virginia,* by William Simmonds, published in Oxford in 1612. Her name is also absent from the writings of Gabriel Archer and the seven other colonists who kept journals or diaries.

She first steps onto the stage in 1617, a few months after she and her husband, John Rolfe, arrived in England. A charming, attractive, and exceptionally intelligent young woman, she created a sensation everywhere she went. Not only was she the daughter of a king and the first Indian woman ever to visit the British Isles, but as a convert to Christianity she aroused interest in circles that otherwise would have ignored her.

She discussed theology with bishops and with those learned scholars who were engaged in the monumental task of translating the Bible from Hebrew and Greek for King James, who had ordered a new edition published. She proved to the doubting dons of Oxford and Cambridge that she was an independent, stimulating thinker. Her beauty and sweetness endeared her to the court, where Queen Anne became her patroness, and even the sour James unbent and chatted with her by the hour.

While Pocahontas was enjoying her triumph, a new edition of John's *True Relation* was published. It was substantially the same book that had been printed eight years earlier, and the text was not altered. But there was something new in the form of a series of running footnotes in the section that dealt with his capture by the Chesapeake late in 1607. These notes tell the story, subsequently learned by generation after generation of children, of Pocahontas' courage and heroism.

According to this account, John's captors took him to the

sachem of sachems, Powhatan, who demanded to know why he was intruding on Chickahominy soil. The prisoner was unable to give an answer that satisfied the chief, who ordered his head smashed against a rock. Before this terrible command could be carried out, however, Powhatan's courageous daughter raced forward out of the crowd watching the scene, and risking her own life, threw herself across the defenseless John's body as she begged her father to show mercy. Powhatan, who was so fond of the child that he could deny her nothing, granted the request. John was set free, and thereafter Pocahontas, his little friend, often visited him at Jamestown.

Without making the claim in so many words, he hints that he taught her to speak English and that she acquired her love of the Bible from him. He also takes credit, indirectly, for the taming and domestication of a young savage.

A longer, more smoothly written version of the story appears in *The Generall Historie of Virginia,* which John completed in 1624 and published in that same year. In it he expands on the theme that she rescued him at the risk of her own life. "Princess Pocahontas hazarded the beating out of her own brains to save mine," he declares. "Not only that, but she so prevailed with her father that I was safely conducted to Jamestown."

In another portion of Book IV of that same work, he says, "Jamestown with her wild train Pocahontas as freely frequented as her father's habitation; and during the time of two or three years, she next under God, was still the instrument to preserve this Colony from death, famine and utter confusion." He does not elaborate, and makes no attempt to explain the ways in which she was helpful to the colonists.

The romantic Pocahontas legend did more than all of John Smith's proven exploits to win him immortality. But the timing of his publication of the story lays him open to the suspicion that he opportunistically tried to win greater renown for himself at a time when she was the toast of England.

Perhaps the most damning evidence against John is the fact that the most complete of contemporary histories of Jamestown, *A True Discourse of the Present Estate of Virginia,* written by Ralph Hamor and published in 1615, makes no mention of the story.

Also, John damns himself by presenting contradictory evidence. According to his own accounts in both his *True Relation* and *Generall Historie,* as well as the chronicles of other writers, the Chesapeake Indians were the sworn enemies of the Chickahominy. He does not explain why the Chesapeake would have handed a valuable prisoner to their deadly foes.

Even more important, he makes it appear in the legend that he and Powhatan met face to face for the first time when he was hauled before the sachem as a captive. Yet he writes previously, at length and in detail, of his friendship with the Chickahominy chief. In his own words he says that he has paid many visits to Paspahegh, Powhatan's town, and he offers full accounts of the barter deals he has made with the sachem.

Why should Powhatan, who had engaged in mutually profitable trading operations with the intrepid Captain, have become offended because John was traveling in the interior of Virginia? After all, the sachem had himself provided the Englishman with guides to assist him in his explorations. The alleged ire of Powhatan and his order condemning John to death do not jibe with the consistently friendly attitude he had displayed previously.

It must be remembered, too, that the Jamestown colony was established only a short distance from Paspahegh. The Chickahominy were sufficiently friendly with the colonists for various residents of the Indian village to pay frequent visits to the foreigners' town, which they did. Certainly Pocahontas was such a visitor, although it is not known whether she started going there as a child or as a young woman in her teens.

The known historical facts speak for themselves. John Rolfe was a widower with two small children who arrived in Jamestown after the colony had become solidly established. He was the first to plant tobacco on a large scale and experiment with various types of leaf in order to increase his yield. It would not be amiss to call him the father of the American tobacco-growing industry. With a farm to tend and two children to rear, Rolfe had no time to travel extensively in the interior. Yet he and Pocahontas met, fell in love, and married. She was familiar enough with Jamestown and its ways to have gained at least a basic understanding of English by the time she met Rolfe, and she was attending worship services regularly.

Whether she started visiting Jamestown while John was still there, and whether she became acquainted with him during that period, are facts hidden in mist and probably will never be known. Some of the embroidery that has been added to the Pocahontas–John Smith legend can be dismissed, however.

Seventeenth-century writers who enlarged on the tale spiced the story by claiming that John was responsible for Pocahontas' attendance at worship services in Jamestown, that her father and brothers objected, but that she became a convert to Christianity in spite of their opposition. No established facts indicate any basis for such statements. Precisely how Pocahontas became a convert, much less how her family reacted, has never been revealed.

Some of John's contemporaries may have laughed behind their ruffled cuffs at his tale of the Indian princess who had saved his life, but no one questioned his story in print for more than a half-century after it first appeared. The first to suggest that his enthusiasm for good fiction was stronger than his love of fact was the Reverend Thomas Fuller, whose posthumously published book, *The Worthies of England,* which was edited by his son, appeared a few years after the Restoration, in the 1660s. Fuller rather indignantly called John a liar.

His charge fell on deaf ears, however, and the legend of the gallant twenty-eight-year-old Captain whose life was saved by a demure and courageous Indian maiden of twelve became part of the folklore of the English-speaking people. If John did make up the story out of whole cloth, he dreamed up fiction that endured.

His one documented meeting with Pocahontas, which took place during her visit to England with Rolfe, will be discussed in detail in its appropriate chronological place. All that need be said here is that nothing happened at that meeting to prove or disprove the truth of John's claim.

The end of the story is also somewhat suspicious. John does not mention this aspect in his *True Relation* footnotes of 1616, but dwells at some length on the matter in his *Generall Historie* of 1624. Powhatan, he says, finally agreed to set him free on the condition that he promised to send the Chickahominy two cannon and a millstone. Several warriors were sent to Jamestown with him, and were instructed to kill him if he changed his mind about the gifts.

The settlers had given him up for dead, and rejoiced when he appeared one morning in the custody of several braves. He explained what had happened, he writes, and then filled two mammoth demiculverins—the largest cannon in the colony—with stones. He fired the guns with devastating effect, the stones crashing deep in the forest and knocking down several trees. The terrified warriors tried to lift the cannon, but found them "somewhat too heavy," and were happy to return home without the awful weapons.

Inasmuch as the safety of Jamestown depended more on its artillery than on any other single factor, it is inconceivable that the colonists would have permitted any cannon to be carted off by the Chickahominy. It is also doubtful that John, who was always mindful of the settlement's defenses, would have made any such promise except under duress, and it is inconceivable that he would have tried to keep his word.

A demiculverin was a piece usually mounted on a large warship, and was as cumbersome as it was large. Made of iron and brass, it weighed between four thousand and five thousand pounds and was capable of firing a nine-pound shot approximately one thousand yards. The two demiculverins in Jamestown's fort had been carried ashore from the *Susan Constant* under the most difficult of conditions. Twice the special hoists made for them broke, and one was feared lost when it fell into the James River. It was retrieved only after several days of back-breaking work.

Had John made Powhatan such a promise, even if he privately intended to break his word, the exhibition he describes for the benefit of the Chickahominy warriors would have been an event of prime importance in the early history of the colony. No mention is made of the incident in the chronicles of Wingfield, Percy, Hamor, or anyone else writing on the subject of the settlement of Jamestown.

John's picture of the startled braves watching the firing of the cannon is colorful, but cannot be seriously regarded as an accurate statement of fact. It must be considered only as the fitting anticlimax of a romantic story. John had attended the theater often enough in London to know that the last act of a good play should end on a dramatic note, and he was too proficient an author to disappoint his audience.

In any event, regardless of the veracity of the whole story, Pocahontas remained in the wilderness when John returned to Jamestown on January 7, 1608. Even if she had saved his life, as he claimed, he had good cause to wish she had been less valiant. And he was far too busy to think of her again for a long time. The year 1608 was the most crowded he had ever known, and the experiences he suffered during the first forty-eight hours after his return—a period far too frantic for artillery demonstrations held for the benefit of savages—were more exciting and dangerous than anything that had happened earlier in his busy life. Not even he could have invented a series of events so bizarre.

XIV

The Year of Great Decisions

When John Smith returned to Jamestown on January 7, 1608, he found the little colony in a ferment. Gabriel Archer had persuaded President Ratcliffe to give him a seat on the council, in spite of John Martin's objections. And Archer had talked Ratcliffe into making an "official" voyage to England two days later.

John immediately spiked the plan by declaring he would use every cannon, musket, and pistol in the settlement to prevent the sailing. Archer, who had thought him dead somewhere in the interior, promptly retaliated by charging him with responsibility for the killing of Robinson and Emry by the Indians. John was placed on "trial" the following morning, and although no details are known, what followed must have been a mockery of justice.

In less than an hour he was found guilty and sentenced to be hanged at dawn the next day. Archer also saw to it that Wingfield would be executed by hanging at the same time. Then he and Ratcliffe would be free to leave for England later in the day, precisely as they had planned.

The neat scheme exploded that same afternoon, however. A ship was sighted, and a short time later Captain Newport sailed up the James in the *Susan Constant*. He had left England six weeks earlier with another ship, the *Phoenix*, commanded by Captain Francis Nelson, but they had become separated during a storm.

Newport's first act was to set John and Wingfield free. Then, after forbidding Ratcliffe and Archer to leave, he took stock of Jamestown's sad plight. Of the original 105 members of the colony, only 38 had survived. Until now, no reinforcements had come to the New World colony. There was a shortage of ammunition and gunpowder. All were in need of clothing, and supplies of such minor but useful items as lamp oil had long been exhausted.

The *Susan Constant's* hold was filled with provisions of every kind—from munitions and tools to clothing, blankets, and hogsheads of food. Equally important, Newport had brought 80 eager, healthy recruits to the settlement; 40 more were expected on the *Phoenix*, which also carried large quantities of badly needed supplies.

John, who was restored to his place on the council by Newport's timely intervention, put the newcomers to work at once. Some began the construction of new houses and erected the skeleton of a new, permanent church where services could be conducted in dignity. John had long been ashamed of the "miserable hovel" that the Reverend Mr. Hunt had been required to use as a church.

Less than a week later, however, a new catastrophe set back the building program. A fire broke out in one of the thatch-roofed houses, spread to several others, and destroyed one section of the fort. A dozen of the men lost most of their clothes and personal possessions.

The worst sufferer was the Reverend Mr. Hunt, whose precious library was entirely consumed by the flames. He made no complaint, however, and held a service of thanksgiving in the open, inviting everyone in the community to join in offering prayers of gratitude to the Lord because no lives had been lost.

John stopped all other building and put the construction gangs to work repairing the damage to the fort. While he was preoccupied, Archer became busy behind his back. Anxious to win the approval of Newport, which in turn could lead to an appointment to a post of trust by the directors in London, Archer set out to prove that John wasn't the only one capable of dealing with the Indians. He made a quick journey into the interior and returned with considerable quantities of food. On the surface his performance appeared impressive—until it was learned he had paid four times as much as John had taught the savages to expect in barter deals.

The members of Newport's crew also helped to ruin the native market. Eager to take home bows, arrows, Chickahominy spears, and other souvenirs, they sneaked off to Paspahegh in defiance of John's local standing orders and the general instructions of the directors in England. They spoiled the warriors so badly that, as John told Newport, he now had to pay the Chickahominy one pound's worth of trinkets for supplies that had formerly cost him a penny's worth.

Among the newcomers to the colony were three gentlemen of stature and ability—Matthew Scrivener and the Phettiplace brothers, William and Michael. Scrivener, a tall, almost painfully thin young man with lugubrious eyes and a wispy beard, was given a council seat on the instructions of the London directors. He was so reserved that Archer and Ratcliffe were contemptuous of him. John, a far better judge of character, believed him dependable and scrupulously honest. He was also impressed by Scrivener's superior marksmanship and ability to handle a sword. In the months ahead, Scrivener would become the most loyal and useful of John's lieutenants.

John took Newport and Scrivener with him on several trips into Indian country, and Newport later reported to the directors that "the Naturals do trust Captain Smith as they do none other. When we did approach a village, all the inhabitants thereof did run away and hide. But Captain Smith did walk alone and unarmed toward them, and they went to him with joyous cries, like ducks begging for crusts from a friend."

Winter was not the best season of the year to obtain furs and lumber for the profit of the investors in England. Fox and other game were hard to find, and the beavers had vanished, as they were hibernating. Men could work only for limited periods in the deep forests, as the damp cold numbed and exhausted them. Therefore the hold of the *Susan Constant* was not filled until April, and Newport delayed his sailing until the 10th of the month.

By that time most of the provisions he had brought with him from England had been consumed, and the colony again faced the problem of obtaining enough food for survival. The *Phoenix,* which had been carrying a cargo consisting of only foodstuffs, had not yet arrived and was presumed lost.

At the insistence of the council, Newport gave passage to former President Wingfield, and at John's quiet suggestion he also took the trouble-making Gabriel Archer back to England. Never vindictive against defeated enemies, John pushed a motion through the council dropping all charges against both men, in order that "they might find gainful and useful employment elsewhere."

It would have been helpful had Ratcliffe returned to London, too, but he was determined to keep his place as president. Unfortunately, twenty-four hours after the *Susan Constant* sailed, he blew off his left hand while cleaning his fowling piece, a musket with a muzzle shaped like a horn. The surgeon was able to save his life, but thereafter he was a weak, sick man, unable to govern, and the full burden fell on John's shoulders. In Scrivener he had a competent assistant; Martin was useful when his frail health permitted; and the mercurial Percy was also valuable—when it suited his mood to work.

The new colonists dreamed of finding gold, thanks to the false information disseminated by the enthusiastic but ignorant directors in London, and were not eager to engage in such mundane work as sowing Indian corn and English wheat, or planting vegetables.

On the morning of April 12th, John suddenly faced a rebellion. The newly arrived men refused to accept the day's schedule he had drawn up for them, and their spokesmen told him that, instead, they planned to spend the day searching for gold.

The veteran colonists gathered in front of the fort to watch the rare sport, but John sent them off, reminding them that they, too, were required to adhere to work schedules. Then, with the other members of the council watching him apprehensively, he loaded his pistols and shoved them into his belt.

If he wished, he told the immigrants, he could jail their ringleaders for mutiny. He could go even further, and have those who refused to do their fair share of labor executed. In fact, he had the authority to shoot them all down, here and now, singly or together. But, instead, he chose to show them compassion. They were free to do as they pleased. Those who wanted to search for gold could devote all their time to such an enterprise.

The immigrants started to cheer, but he raised a hand for silence. He wanted no misunderstanding, John said. Jamestown was the King's colony, and existed under a royal patent. The walls that protected its inhabitants were the King's walls, and food supplies were locked away in the King's warehouses. Naturally, those who elected to accept no share of responsibility for the community's burdens were not entitled to the protection of Jamestown's armaments, the shelter of Jamestown's houses, or the life-sustaining qualities of Jamestown's provisions. He told all gold seekers to remove themselves and their personal belongings from the settlement within an hour. Thereafter they would be free to roam wherever they pleased on the North American continent, but would not be welcome in Jamestown.

There was a long silence as the men digested his words. Then the ringleaders went off for rakes, hoes, and spades, and the others quietly followed them. The incipient rebellion was dead, and never again did anyone shirk his duty because of a mistaken idea that he could find gold in the vicinity.

Shortly after dawn on April 20th, the gentleman-adventurer in charge of the sentry shift fired a pistol, a warning that the settlement was in danger, and a few moments later a trumpeter aroused the sleeping colonists. The veterans ran to their assigned posts in the fort, with gunners taking their places at the cannon.

John was one of the first to arrive, and through his glass he saw a large ship in the distance. Ratcliffe, although very ill, looked through the glass, too, as he was supposedly the expert on nautical affairs. It was his opinion that the vessel was a Spanish warship that intended to attack Jamestown.

John, who had probably seen far more Spanish warships than Ratcliffe had ever encountered, declared the ship didn't look like a frigate to him, and instead he believed her to be a merchantman. He could take no chances, however, and the cannon were primed and loaded. Most of the immigrants, whose military training to date had been rudimentary, huddled fearfully at the rear of the fort.

A shout shook the wall of the wooden building when the ship broke out her distinguishing pennant, the British flag. And less than an hour later the *Phoenix,* which appeared to have arisen from a watery grave, dropped her anchor at the new James River wharf that had been built under John's supervision.

Francis Nelson, captain of the *Phoenix,* was a bluff, hearty seaman with "an honest mariner's face," and his arrival was a miracle that saved Jamestown from starvation. The cargo in his hold was intact, as his passengers and crew had lived on food he had obtained by barter and purchase from the natives of the West Indian islands. In fact, the decks of his ship were loaded with "tunny" fish he had caught the previous day when the *Phoenix* had sailed into a school of the huge creatures.

John gave Nelson a warm welcome, and everyone, including the 40 new immigrants who came ashore, went to work salting the tuna. For the first time in Jamestown's brief history, there was now more than enough for everyone to eat, even though the permanent community numbered 158 men and boys.

The weather had become balmy as Jamestown enjoyed its most pleasant season of the year, and a new spirit of optimism pervaded the colony. John put everyone to work on a bone-wearying schedule. Trees were felled and stumps removed to enlarge the settlement's farmlands, new houses were built, and the newcomers spent a minimum of two hours each day drilling, learning to handle firearms, and practicing skirmishing in the wilderness.

Powhatan's Chickahominy and the Chesapeake both caused trouble that spring by stealing tools that careless immigrants left in the open at night. John knew that the savages would become bolder unless he took positive steps to curb the abuses, and he went out with twenty of his veterans to round up the thieves.

Five Chickahominy were caught, and were taken to the *Phoenix,* where John had them lashed to the mainmast. He threatened them with torture, shot off muskets and pistols a few inches from their faces, and terrified them so thoroughly that, after he released them and allowed them to go to their own villages, the Chickahominy caused the colony no more problems.

John spent all his spare time writing his first book, *A True Relation,* and sat up until all hours at a table in the new, larger house into which he had recently moved with Martin and Scrivener. His principal reason for writing the book was to give the English public an accurate idea of conditions in the New World. As an administrator—for all practical purposes, the president of the council—it annoyed him when newcomers arrived with false notions of the gold and gems they would find. The public, John believed, should know the truth, and a class of immigrants better able to withstand the hardships of wilderness living would come to Jamestown.

A True Relation was a factual history of the original colonists from the time they had first set sail from England. John wrote modestly of his own efforts and successes, gave full credit to others for their accomplishments, and was so fiercely loyal to the colony that, unlike Wingfield in his *Discourse of America,* he consistently minimized and made light of the bitter quarrels and feuds between rival leaders and factions. There was virtually no sign of the flamboyance that was to appear in John's later works, and at no time did he exaggerate or stretch the truth. Its accuracy and quiet, dispassionate tone made *A True Relation* one of John's better books, perhaps his best.

He also wrote a number of long reports for Archdeacon Hakluyt, enclosing maps, charts, and sketches he had drawn, and he prepared several maps of the North American coastline for Henry Hudson, basing them on what he had learned from the late Bartholomew Gosnold and on the crude charts that had come into his possession when Gosnold had died.

How John found time for his writing is inexplicable. He was in charge of the day-to-day administration of the colony, supervised the military and civilian training of the immigrants, and kept close watch on the planting of grains and vegetables on which Jamestown's future depended. He also took direct charge of preparing the cargo of prime cedar he intended to send off in the *Phoenix* to the directors in London. He selected the trees to be felled, and inspected every plank before it was stored in the ship's hold.

Far more important than all of his other activities, he designed and supervised the construction of a new three-thousand-ton shallop. It was a clumsy but practical vessel, a barge with sides sturdy enough to withstand bad weather in waters that might become more turbulent than the James River.

John was an administrator because there was no one else at hand to perform necessary executive tasks, but his real love was still exploration. He had made up his mind to search all of Chesapeake Bay, and he prepared for the venture with the same sense of excitement he had felt when, as a boy, he had bravely and foolishly put out to sea in an attempt to emulate Sir Francis Drake.

He completed the manuscript of *A True Relation* late in May, and each day added a few paragraphs in order to keep the record up to date. Finally, on June 2nd, Captain Nelson was ready to sail for England, and John gave the closely written pages to Martin, whose poor health was forcing him to leave Jamestown.

Apparently John was prepared to pay for the publication of the book out of his own pocket, a practice commonly followed by authors of his day, but Martin proved to be a good literary agent after the *Phoenix* reached London, and the Prince of Wales assumed financial responsibility for the publication of *A True Relation,* hoping it would encourage the immigration to Virginia of men willing and able to cope with rough wilderness living.

The shallop sailed with the *Phoenix* on June 2nd, escorting the merchantman as far as Cape Henry and then turning north into the bay. John was accompanied on his voyage by thirteen men, most of them ill-equipped for the mission. Six were gentlemen-adventurers newly arrived in Jamestown who gaily thought they were going on a sight-seeing cruise and had no concept of the hardships they might be forced to endure. One was a blacksmith who had nothing to contribute except his physical prowess, and another was a physician, whose services might prove useful. There were three former soldiers in the party, and if they knew nothing about sailing, at least they were expert marksmen. The other two were veteran colonists who had long been assigned to a fishing detail and hence were familiar with the handling of boats.

This monumental voyage of discovery, combined with a subsequent trip John also made into Chesapeake Bay, enabled him to draw an astonishingly accurate map of the area, which even included the location of all Indian villages—information of vital importance to contemporary and future colonists. This map, together with John's carefully detailed description of the region, was published in 1612, and if he had done nothing else in his life, it assured him of a high place in the ranks of New World explorers. Although he made a few minor errors in pinpointing streams and their headwaters, the task he performed, using no instruments other than a compass, was remarkably efficient. In time it led to the establishment of other English colonies in Virginia, Maryland, Delaware, and Pennsylvania.

The key to his success was the thoroughness of his research. He had the good sense not to rush, and painstakingly sketched every curve and break in the great bay's shoreline. His principal interest was that of finding harbors and sweet-water rivers that could be utilized as the sites of future colonial towns, and his energy, as always, was inexhaustible.

He was aided by the friendly Accowmack Indians, who spoke the language of the Chickahominy and gave him long descriptions of other nations living in the vicinity. Once again, John's ability to speak the tongue of the savages paid dividends. He enjoyed himself enormously, but the gentlemen-adventurers were miserable. The shallop was an open boat, and rainsqualls drenched the men and their bread. Twice, stiff winds cracked one or the other of the masts and forced John to put ashore for repairs.

By June 13th, less than two weeks after leaving Jamestown, the gentlemen had had their fill of wildnerness living and were ready to return to the relative comforts of Jamestown. John refused to listen to their pleas that he abandon the voyage. The party carried a month's supply of food, he told them, and he would be ashamed to "look into the faces of civilized men" if he went back to the settlement before the provisions were exhausted. Rain-soaked bread, he declared, dried quickly in the sun, and even splashes of salty seawater didn't make it inedible.

On June 16th, John discovered the mouth of the Potomac River and immediately decided to sail upstream. Even the most discouraged of his companions were excited by the finding of a major river. The shallop moved slowly for more than thirty miles up the Potomac before several warriors armed with bows and arrows were seen. The savages made threatening gestures, hoping to drive away the strangers, but John ordered several muskets fired, and the braves changed their minds.

John was taken to the sachem of their principal village and quickly established trade relations with the Potomac nation. Always looking toward the future, he found the soil rich, and marveled at the beaver, sable, and otter in the area. There were so many fish in the river that the physician, Walter Russell, tried without success to scoop some of them into the shallop with a frying pan.

A few days later, John developed a new technique of his own for catching fish and speared them on his sword. He caught so many that the little company had more than they could eat, and the next day he tried his luck again. Unfortunately, he plunged his arm into the water and was stung by "a strange sea-monster, nearly as transparent as glass in color, quite vicious, with many tentacles."

Soon his arm was twice its normal size, he suffered excruciating pain, and his panicky companions expected him to die at any moment. But Russell put some "precious oil" on the wound, which lessened his pain, and he promptly assumed command of the expedition again. He seemed indifferent to death, the others later reported in Jamestown, and he showed neither pleasure nor surprise when the swelling in his arm gradually lessened.

A more serious accident incapacitated Anas Todkill, one of the soldiers, when he tripped over a rock while the party was marching along the shore of the bay. After a careful examination of Todkill, Russell said that the man had broken his leg in two places. It was impossible to give the injured Todkill the attention he needed, and John decided to take him back to Jamestown.

The shallop reached the settlement on July 21st, after an absence of seven weeks, and John found affairs there chaotic. Many of the new immigrants were finding it difficult to adjust to the heat of Virginia swamplands in summer, and were ill. Those who were not confined to their beds were in a state of near-mutiny against President Ratcliffe, who had diverted men from other projects to build him a fine house. He was also accused of using more than his own fair share of vitally needed provisions.

Virtually the entire community—members of the council,

other gentlemen-adventurers, and commoners—were unanimous in demanding that Ratcliffe resign his post and that John Smith replace him. John was neither flattered nor pleased. He believed it essential that a president serve his full term, if the community was to develop true respect for his authority, and he thought it wrong for the chief executive of Jamestown to be forced into a position of necessary reliance on the goodwill of a mob.

But he stood alone. The men refused to heed his dispassionate pleas in favor of orderly government and orderly transitions. Ratcliffe, who was suffering from a fever, solved the problem by resigning, so John had no choice. On July 21st, the day of his return to Jamestown, he was unanimously elected to the office he had held in everything but name.

He accepted on two conditions. The first was that he be allowed to appoint his own deputy, who would become acting president whenever he was absent from the colony, and the second was that he be given a free hand in the selection of staff members whom he believed to be honest, competent men. The colonists agreed, the council ratified the suggestions, and John immediately named Matthew Scrivener his deputy.

The new president was thinking far more in terms of his exciting journey of exploration than of the administration of the colony's affairs. Certain that Jamestown would be in good hands under Scrivener's direction, he spent only three days at the settlement, setting out again in the shallop. Five of the six gentlemen-adventurers who had accompanied him on his first voyage were now sufficiently enthusiastic to go with him again, and so were four of the commoners. Volunteer replacements made up the rest of the party.

John immediately sailed to the point north of the mouth of the Potomac which he had reached before being forced to turn back. One evening six of his men became ill after eating a fish "with sweet meat, white as a shirt of fine lawn," and

John decided it would be best to spend the night on board the shallop, which he anchored a short distance from the shore of Chesapeake Bay. It was fortunate that he took the precaution, for the following morning the soldier on sentry duty aroused him to tell him that eight large Indian canoes filled with warriors were approaching the boat.

The braves, John saw, were heavily armed with spears, knives, bows and arrows, and he was afraid they might attack if they became aware of his weakness. So he resorted to a simple but effective trick. The men who had been suffering from indigestion were still weak and at his order concealed themselves beneath tarpaulins. The rest of the company hastily collected all the hats, helmets, and other headgear on board, and stood them on sticks and swords so their tops showed above the sides of the shallop. The warriors, members of the Massawomeke tribe, thought that a large party was on the boat, and discreetly withdrew.

A few days later, the explorer reached the northern end of Chesapeake Bay, where he discovered the mouth of another great river. Friendly Indians warned him that a nation of unusually tall, husky savages called the Susquehannocks lived on the river and permitted no one to travel upstream without their permission. Bribing his informants, John sent them as messengers to tell the Susquehannocks that he came as their friend and was bringing them gifts.

After a wait of two days, a band of sixty warriors appeared. They, too, carried gifts, among them several welcome quarters of venison. Their language was similar to that of the Chickahominy, which enabled John to communicate with them, and he spent a long time trying to determine whether the river led to the Pacific. Even after he had satisfied himself that it did not, he was still so curious that he and his companions spent three days traveling upstream with the warriors. To his other honors he now added that of discovering, exploring, and mapping the Susquehanna River.

At the end of three days, deep in the wilderness of what would later become Pennsylvania, he returned to Chesapeake Bay. He and the Susquehannock exchanged more gifts before parting, and John promised to return the following year to trade with them.

He sailed south along the eastern shore of the Bay, still mapping carefully, and crossed again to the western side in order to make a brief journey up the one river of consequence he had not yet explored—the Patuxent. He soon satisfied himself that it was a small stream, and he started back to the bay. This side trip, however, had tragic consequences. One of the gentlemen-adventurers, Richard Fetherstone, had eaten some strange berries on shore and suddenly became violently ill. An hour later he was dead, in spite of the efforts of John and Anthony Bagnall, the physician now accompanying the party, to save him. He was buried with military honors.

For all practical purposes the voyage had come to an end, but John was not yet satisfied. Before returning to Jamestown he proposed to scour the southern shore of the bay, where the colonists' enemies, the Chesapeake, lived.

He was the first to set foot on the site of the future town of Norfolk, and he sailed about fifteen miles up the Elizabeth River before turning back. This postscript to a voyage of exploration had unexpected results. Relations were established with the small and independent tribe of Nansemond, who presented him with four hundred large baskets filled with corn and "so many bales of dried venison that the shallop sat low in the water."

Not only had John fulfilled the difficult mission he had set for himself, acquiring a vast store of knowledge that was to prove of tremendous value to colonial planners in England, but he was returning to his colony with enough grain and meat to feed everyone in Jamestown for many days. He had not forgotten his obligations as president.

Late in the morning of September 7, 1608, the shallop sailed up the James River, and Matthew Scrivener led a welcoming party that flocked to the wharf to greet the explorers. John was glad to be back in the place he now considered home, and he went ashore to face a host of new problems that he alone had the authority and competence to solve.

XV

The First Citizen of Virginia

Affairs in Jamestown were less chaotic than they had been after John's previous absences, thanks to Scrivener's efficient management. But the deputy president, still new to Virginia, had hesitated to take decisive steps in matters with which he was unfamiliar. Accordingly, John plunged into work with his usual furious energy.

The first matter that required his attention was a personal problem. Former President Ratcliffe had been imprisoned on charges of mutiny, conspiracy, and treason, which had been violently and falsely exaggerated, and only Scrivener's firmness had prevented the colonists from breaking into the fort's cell and lynching him. John reviewed the flimsy evidence, immediately set Ratcliffe free, and informed the colony in a firmly worded proclamation that he would prosecute anyone who harmed a sick man who was still recovering from his accident.

New work schedules were drawn up, and construction began on houses for the next group of immigrants, who were due to arrive at any time. The summer had been so damp that many roofs had rotted, so all were replaced, and building was resumed on Ratcliffe's "palace," which John intended to use as a meeting hall. Military training had been lax during the hot weather, so everyone was ordered to resume drill, musket practice, and skirmishing in the wilderness. Formal drills were held every Sunday, after worship services, in a cleared area outside the town palisades that came to be known as Smith Field.

Every evening John dined in private with Scrivener and a small staff of assistants, reviewing the day's accomplishments and outlining, revising, and refining future plans. The food situation was brighter than it had been at any time since the founding of the colony. Rain had spoiled some of the corn, but planting had been so extensive that the harvest yield was ample, and the storehouse was filled to overflowing, making it necessary to build an addition.

A perfectionist in matters of defense, John was dissatisfied with the fort. Having learned a great deal about the savages' techniques in conducting surprise attacks, he came to the conclusion that a triangular fort was inadequate. After thinking about the matter at length, he decided that a five-pointed, star-shaped fort would afford the best protection, because it would be simple to give musket support to any one point under attack from the flanks adjacent to it.

He drew a sketch for a new fort, and the hard-pressed colonists went to work under Scrivener's watchful eye, enlarging the fort and changing its shape. John's design proved so successful that it was later copied by other settlements and became standard in the American colonies, from New England to Georgia, until the eve of the American Revolution more than a hundred and fifty years later.

When John's other activities of the day were done, he sat down alone to work on his new book, *A Map of Virginia, with a Description of the Country*. He wanted to put his impressions on paper while the details were still fresh in his mind, and he labored diligently, checking his notes and sketches to make certain there were no errors. *A True Relation* had been inspired by a desire to tell the people the truth about Jamestown and clear up current public misconceptions about the New World, but he had posterity in mind when working on *A Map of Virginia.*

His studies under Hakluyt and Plancius, combined with his own experiences as an explorer and traveler, had taught him the value of accurate maps and charts, as well as the advantage of knowing something about a strange, wild land. He hoped his new book would win him a measure of lasting fame, and it did. From the time of its publication in 1612, at Oxford, it was hailed as a cartographical masterpiece.

A Map of Virginia assured John a place in history, and it is unfortunate that his vanity compelled him to draw a pen-and-ink sketch of himself on the major, or overall, map. This act gave his critics an opportunity to attack him, which they did with vigor, to the subsequent injury of his reputation in his own day. In time, however, his egotistical gesture was forgotten and forgiven. Thanks to it, Simon van der Paas, a talented artist who was his contemporary, had a basis from which to work in drawing John's portrait. Like so much in the life of John Smith, the accuracy of that portrait is difficult to determine, as its foundation rests on John's own pen-and-ink concept of himself.

Twenty-eight colonists had died during the summer, most of them newcomers who had succumbed to the heat. John noted in the text of *A Map of Virginia* that the longer a man remained in the New World, the more hardened he became to nature's perils. A little more than a decade later, the Pilgrims, who settled in New England, would make the same discovery. The longer a man lived in America, the greater became the chances of his survival.

In mid-October, five weeks after John's return, the *Susan Constant* arrived at Jamestown for the third time, carrying seventy immigrants. As usual, Captain Newport's hold was filled with provisions and other necessary cargo. Two of the new gentlemen-adventurers arrived with orders from the directors giving them places on the council. Richard Waldo and Peter Winne were both competent, sensible, hard-working men who contributed much to the stability and welfare of Virginia.

Two of the newcomers were women, the first to come to the English New World, and the days of an exclusively male colony were ended for all time. Unfortunately, almost nothing is known of either. One was a Mistress Forest, probably the wife of Thomas Forest, a gentleman-adventurer, or perhaps the wife of George Forest, who may have been related to him. There are no portraits or descriptions of the lady in existence.

The other was her maidservant, one Anne Burrowes, who was about twenty years old. John called her "lively, intelligent and modest." Anne enjoyed the distinction of being the first Englishwoman to marry and rear a family in America. About a year after her arrival she was married, in a ceremony conducted by the Reverend Mr. Hunt, to John Laydon, who had been a member of the original expedition. Laydon had started life in Jamestown as a laborer, and by the time he and Anne married he had become an expert farmer. Their sons owned small plantations, and their grandsons became wealthy tobacco growers.

The arrival of two females changed the whole atmosphere of Jamestown. Gentlemen took care to trim their beards and wear clean linen, and the commoners no longer stripped to the waist in hot weather. John issued orders prohibiting gaming, brawling, and the use of foul language in the streets. The men were directed to use outhouses and stop their practice of relieving themselves in the clearings beyond the palisades.

The greatest significance of the arrival of Mistress Forest and Anne Burrowes was symbolic. Their presence meant that the colony was truly a permanent settlement now, and the men began to think of bringing sweethearts to Virginia. Others urged John to ask the directors to send shiploads of unmarried female immigrants to Virginia. Men who had been struggling to tame the wilderness were able to enjoy the luxury of thinking in terms of owning their own land, building their own houses, and settling down.

Among the newcomers were a number of foreigners, some of them Dutch and a few of them Polish. Overnight Jamestown became a multilingual community. In time, the presence of non-Englishmen almost inevitably created frictions.

For the moment, however, John had no chance to look that far ahead, for Newport carried clear-cut directives from the investors that could not be fulfilled. In brief, some of the directors stubbornly refused to believe what John had written in *A True Relation* or to accept Newport's own description of Virginia. These nobles still dreamed of gold, felt certain that there were rich veins of it in "the mines of the Naturals," and had sternly ordered Newport not to return to England without a "a goodly supply" of gleaming nuggets.

Newport had been angry, but had grown calm and philosophical on the long voyage across the Atlantic. John, however, became furious. It was obvious to him that the wealthy supporters of the colony had literally no idea of the problems the settlers faced, nor any concept of the magnitude of the attempts being made by the president and the council to put Jamestown on a self-sustaining basis.

John lost his temper when Newport showed him the order, and cursed so violently that Scrivener became alarmed. There was worse to come. The president was also directed to crown Powhatan in a coronation ceremony and obtain from him a pledge of allegiance to "his higher monarch," King James.

In addition, the Polish and Dutch immigrants were to work in a "factory" making glass and tar, since there was a demand for these products in England, and the investors saw a chance to increase their profits.

John cursed again in impotent rage. He had seventy more mouths to feed, and his principal concern was that of increasing the production of corn, wheat, and vegetables.

Newport quietly told him they had to go through the motions of obeying London's orders. Therefore, the two men paid a visit to Powhatan, who had no use for the gilded crown they gave him, but enjoyed a scarlet, silk-lined cape. He and his warriors stared in amused wonder at still another of the directors' gifts—a four-poster bed.

John made an attempt to explain to the sachem that the directors expected him to swear obedience to an overlord who lived across the sea, but Powhatan brushed aside such nonsense, pretending not to hear what was being said to him. John and Newport decided they had gone as far as they could without making an implacable enemy of the most powerful Indian chief in the region.

Then, using time and effort needed to help the new immigrants in their attempt to become adjusted to bewildering, primitive living conditions, John and Newport, accompanied by a small group, sailed up the James River to find the gold that the investors demanded. They went eighty miles by water, but had to leave the shallop with several guards when they came to the river's great falls. Still fuming, they marched an additional forty miles on foot.

All they found were several small Indian villages. One member of the party, William Callicut, was a metal refiner, and at one point he claimed he had discovered a small deposit of silver in the ground, but a single glance was enough to convince John and Newport that he held only dirt in his hand.

The expedition returned to Jamestown, and John prepared his own report to the directors, which would augment Newport's. Here the unbridled imagination of the inventive Captain was useful, and his description of the search for gold was a minor masterpiece of fiction. The shallop became a flotilla of ships, the overland hike of a few men was transformed into a gigantic search conducted by intrepid men who, fanning out over a wide area, conducted innumerable tests as they made their way slowly from hill to hill.

The report finished, John went to work with a vengeance to put Jamestown's house in order. Scrivener went off into Indian country to barter for corn, and John sent word to the chiefs of all the tribes of the neighborhood, telling them he would give them gifts of knives, mirrors, and blankets for fur pelts.

Most of the president's efforts were directed toward the indoctrination of the newcomers. His treatment of two newly arrived gentlemen-adventurers was typical. These young men, Gabriel Beadle and John Russell, were hard-drinking, overdressed London playboys who had never done a day's work in their lives, and had no intention of working now. John quickly taught them that in Jamestown everyone who wanted food and shelter earned his way.

Beadle and Russell were put to work chopping down forty- to sixty-foot trees. Their tender hands became blistered, and they cursed unceasingly. John sent a member of his staff to record the number of oaths they had sworn, then hauled the pair before him in the presence of the whole community. In order to wash away sin, he said with a straight face, Russell and Beadle were to have a can of water poured up their sleeves for each oath they had sworn. The two struggling, gasping gentlemen were half-drowned by the time the ceremony ended.

The following day, neither cursed. And a week later, John wrote, they discovered they had started to master the wilderness. Their hands had toughened, and their skill had improved so much that they were able to accomplish more in an hour than they had been able to do, initially, in a day. It became their delight, he said, to hear the thunder of falling trees. Eventually both became sober, conscientious members of the community and, according to John, "learned to look with loathing upon their former noxious pastimes."

Other problems were more difficult to solve. Although the services of the Dutch and Polish immigrants were urgently needed for the tasks that kept the rest of the colony busy, John followed the orders of the directors and put them to work making glass and tar. Scrivener returned from a tour of the Indian villages with small quantities of grain, and John had to take time he couldn't afford to give up in order to visit some of the villages himself. His own efforts were so successful that Ratcliffe, who seemed incapable of controlling his envy, urged Newport to depose the new president.

Newport, of course, had neither the desire to set John aside nor the power to force him out of office. Unfortunately, however, relations between the president and the master mariner became strained, chiefly because Newport was unable to control his own crew. The sailors defied the laws of Jamestown and the strict instructions of the directors in London and went out into Indian country to barter butter, beer, oatmeal, and pickled beef for furs and treated animal skins that would bring high prices in London.

They were ruining the market, forcing the colonists to pay dearly for anything they purchased from the savages, and John complained bitterly to Newport. Unable to halt this illicit trade, Newport made an attempt to defend his men, but John finally lost patience and took matters into his own hands, placing three members of the *Susan Constant*'s crew in jail. Newport lost his temper and demanded their release, but John coldly refused to set them free. Thereafter the two men who, between them, were largely responsible for the success of the colony, rarely spoke. But the other sailors abruptly stopped trading with the natives.

There was a demand in England for "red roots," from which a bitter-tasting powder was made by apothecaries and used for a variety of medicinal purposes. The colonists had discovered that these weed roots were useless and had no curative properties. However, it was John's duty to send the directors what they wanted, so he made a five-day trip to the eastern shore of Chesapeake Bay in order to obtain several baskets of the roots from the Indians.

Early in November, 1608, the hold of the *Susan Constant* was filled with lumber, tar, and glass. Bales of precious furs that might have rotted below were lashed to the main deck and covered with tarpaulins. Enough of the "red roots" to keep the physicians of London happy for a time were also included in the cargo.

But there wasn't one ounce of gold on board, and the realization that the directors would be sorely disappointed caused John and Newport to call off their feud and draw together again. Only by uniting could they stave off the consequences of the directors' wrath.

John had decided the time had come to speak bluntly to the investors, so he sat down and wrote them a frank letter describing the colony's true situation, its problems in making ends meet, and the desperate, never-ending struggle to obtain enough food. He called the directors' longing for gold foolish, and sent along several rock samples, which he said might contain a little iron, but he emphasized that there was no gold in Virginia.

He enclosed copies of the detailed maps he had made of Virginia and Chesapeake Bay. With them he sent full descriptions of the land and its potentials, the navigability of rivers, as well as the disposition and temperaments of the local Indian nations. In a separate packet he sent maps to his friend Henry Hudson, who received the valuable documents just before leaving England for Holland and entering the employ of the Dutch. A few months later, in March, 1609, Hudson would sail with an English and Dutch crew to the New World, and using John's maps as a guide to the North American coastline, would discover the great river that bears his name.

The bulk of John's letter was devoted to a criticism of the immigrants London was sending to Jamestown. Many, he declared, were unsuited for wilderness living, and some died because they were unable to withstand the hardships. Others gradually learned how to survive, but first had to rid themselves of their foolish dreams of finding gold. There were men Jamestown badly needed, John said, and he listed them for the edification of the directors. He wanted: gardeners, "husbandmen," carpenters, fishermen, masons, blacksmiths, and "fellows with strong backs and hands who will dig up the root-stumps of trees."

Courageous men had performed miracles, he said, but the hazards of day-to-day living were increasing. The colony now numbered more than two hundred, and there was friction between the English on the one hand and the Poles and Dutch on the other. In fact, the members of the two minority groups strongly disliked each other. A single crop failure could cause the entire colony to perish, and he urged the directors to protect their investment by sending at least three ships, preferably four, to Jamestown with supplies in the immediate future.

Twenty-four hours before the *Susan Constant* sailed, President Smith summoned his council to a meeting and strongly urged that Captain Ratcliffe, the perennial troublemaker, be sent back to England. The council unanimously passed a resolution to that effect, but Ratcliffe refused to cooperate and insisted he would remain in Jamestown. John remained firm, however, so the next day the protesting Ratcliffe was escorted onto the ship at pistol point, and guards were stationed on shore to prevent him from landing again at the last moment. The members of the *Susan Constant*'s crew would have enjoyed evening the score with the strong-minded president, but his musketmen made sure no tricks were played.

Once the ship had sailed, John devoted all of his attention to the food problem. The Nansemond had promised to set up permanent trade relations with him and provide him with a regular supply of corn from their overflowing warehouses, so he sent Scrivener with a small party of gentlemen-adventurers to them for the food. The men returned crestfallen, Scrivener reporting that the savages had changed their minds.

John refused to accept the answer of the Nansemond, and sent Scrivener back to them under orders to make a show of force. Scrivener and his men fired their muskets in the air, frightening the savages so badly that the Nansemond traded them enough corn to fill three boats.

Percy, Waldo, and Winne went out on small food-gathering expeditions, too, and enjoyed only a mediocre success. In spite of John's urging, other colonists shortsightedly refused to learn the native languages that would have enabled them to deal more easily with the Indians.

By late December, 1608, the warehouses at Jamestown were emptying rapidly, so John opened negotiations with the ever-reliable Powhatan. By now the sachem had discovered he could set a high price for grain, and he acted accordingly. He demanded that the settlers build him a house similar to the largest building in Jamestown—Ratcliffe's "palace"—in return for one hundred and fifty hogsheads of corn. John was forced to accept his terms.

A party of forty men went to Paspahegh to build the house, with John himself in charge of the expedition. Scrivener remained behind, and John expected him to do his usual competent job of taking charge as deputy president. Unfortunately,

Scrivener had become infected with the disease to which so many others before him had succumbed. He had been given just enough power and responsibility to believe that he should become the sole head of the community, and he began to conspire behind John's back. The veterans would have no part of his schemes, but he found willing listeners in the ranks of the recently arrived gentlemen-adventurers who were irked by the regulations that compelled everyone, regardless of rank, to work.

The weather was raw, and the men building Powhatan's house were hampered by frost and snow, but John set an example by laboring for twelve hours each day with saw, hammer, and nails. On Christmas Eve he went off into the forest and shot two wild boars, which the workmen roasted for their Christmas dinner. They also ate oysters, "wildfowl in plenty," and baked fish, so their meal was a pleasant one, and they spent the whole day at their ease.

The next day they returned to their labors. Unfortunately, John drove them so hard they became disgruntled. Several Dutch carpenters conceived the idea of murdering him, and others fell in with the plot. Eventually the colonists decided they would avoid future repercussions if the savages did their dirty work for them.

Men who had been members of the original Jamestown colony refused to have any part in the scheme. One of them went to John with word of what was happening behind his back. Contemptuously—and a trifle too carelessly—he brushed aside the warning. Work on the house continued, and on the surface everything remained serene.

The warriors who had been bribed by a handful of the disaffected settlers continued to make their preparations for the murder, however. Powhatan certainly knew of the plot, even if he had no active part in it. John was never able to determine just what role the sachem played in the scheme, if any. One fact is outstanding, however. On the day the attempt was to be made, Powhatan discreetly withdrew into the forest with his entire family.

The day seemed like any other. Some of the settlers felled trees, others cut them into boards, and the carpenters, who were now working on the second story of the house, were busily sawing and hammering. Some of the colonists knew nothing of the scheme; others, although refusing to participate, had been told by the plotters to keep their distance or risk losing their own lives.

It was the custom for everyone to halt work late in the morning for a relatively light meal of cold meat, fish, and corn bread. At the usual hour John, who had been supervising construction of the second story, climbed down to the ground. Accompanied by John Russell, he started toward the party's campsite, but halted when a score of screaming warriors ran toward him from all sides, brandishing spears and knives.

He and Russell immediately placed themselves back to back and went to work. John had always been at his best in hand-to-hand combat, and a lack of practice hadn't dulled his skill or his relish for such fighting. He drew both his pistols, took careful aim, and fired one pistol. It blew off the head of a senior warrior who was one of Powhatan's closest friends and advisers. His second shot killed another brave.

Russell, also firing at close range, killed one warrior and wounded another.

Of the thirty-eight remaining colonists working on the house, not one came to the assistance of the pair. Several of the gentlemen-adventurers tried, as did a number of the commoners, but the Dutch plotters drew their own pistols and held them off.

John, completely in his element, began to hack at the warriors with the scimitar he always carried, and Russell used his own sword advantageously. Neither had an opportunity to reload his pistols, so both knew they had to depend on their blades, and both fought furiously. John cut down a brave who was foolish enough to leap at him, then slashed at another raising a spear over his head. The savage lost his arm, and fell to the ground.

Russell was enjoying a more limited success, but managed to hold the savages at bay. John, as witnesses later testified, seemed to go berserk. He suddenly dashed forward, the scimitar whirling in the air over his head, and lunged at a group of warriors. His blade moved too rapidly for others to see precisely what was happening, but within a few seconds he had killed one warrior and severely wounded a second.

The others lost their appetite for battle and fled. The ground, littered with corpses, belonged to the two Englishmen.

This was not a moment for recriminations against the unfaithful, much less for delay. Hundreds of warriors lived in the village, and if they decided to avenge their fallen comrades, all the settlers would be slaughtered. John formed his men into military ranks and marched them to the Chickahominy storehouses, where he ordered them to take as much corn and smoked venison as they could carry.

He, Russell, and four others stood guard with loaded, primed muskets as the others made repeated trips between the warehouses and the two shallops, which rode at anchor in the James River a short distance away. A number of Chickahominy watched them from a safe distance, but made no attempt to halt them, and the loading operation continued until both boats sat low in the water.

Then all the settlers' tools were collected, and the party sailed the short distance down the river from Paspahegh to Jamestown. John considered the deal with Powhatan broken because the warriors had attacked him, and he ruthlessly carted away as much food as he could. Neither then nor at any later date was the work on the sachem's house completed. In fact, John and Powhatan never met face to face again.

John was silent on the short voyage downstream, but was quick enough to act when the shallops reached Jamestown. The food was carried to the safety of the colony's own warehouses, and then John ordered three Dutchmen and two Englishmen arrested for plotting against him. At the trial held several weeks later, one of the Englishmen was cleared of the charges against him. The four schemers were convicted and given sentences of fifty strokes with a whip—a severe penalty. More urgent matters made it necessary to postpone the actual beatings.

The most immediate problem was the possibility that the Chickahominy, having lost so much food, might retaliate. An alert was sounded, the gates of Jamestown were closed, and a watch was established at the fort. But Powhatan neither sought reprisals nor tried to recover the provisions. Apparently he thought John had been within his rights to take the supplies, and the Chickahominy kept their distance.

Normal intercourse with Powhatan's people was not resumed until sometime in the spring, when Chickahominy warriors again appeared at Jamestown with furs to barter. Until then the colonists and the Chickahominy scrupulously avoided each other, neither seeking a fight and neither wanting to ignite the spark that might cause a major war. Curiously, the Indians were concerned with saving face and with little else, when they did approach the settlement again. No mention was made of the attempt to murder John, and the braves behaved as though nothing out of the ordinary had taken place.

The attempted killing and its violent aftermath had unexpectedly beneficial results. Word of the terrible wrath displayed by John Smith when he was provoked spread through the wilderness and, in all probability, the story grew as it was carried from tribe to tribe. The other Indian nations of the area were anxious to appease the ferocious leader of the foreigners, and warriors appeared from every part of the region with corn, native wheat, venison, and smoked fish, which they offered at reasonable barter rates. The colonists ate heartily all winter, and when spring came the warehouses were still full. For the first time in its brief history, Jamestown was free of the fear of impending famine.

Even though the Indians caused no troubles in the early months of 1609, John and his council had their hands full. They were appalled by the incident at Paspahegh and thought it disgraceful that a handful of traitors could have kept more than thirty men from coming to the aid of a pair of fellow colonists being attacked by savages. Military training was intensified, which made no one happy, and the settlers grumbled.

John had grown callous to their complaints, but the situation had become more serious than he realized. Percy came to him privately with word that Scrivener was scheming against him, trying to persuade individual members of the council to depose him. John could not believe that the man in whom he had placed full trust would betray him. John Russell, now the most loyal of his followers, came to him with the same story, and so did Peter Winne, one of the new council members, who told him that Richard Waldo, the other new member, was in league with Scrivener.

John felt he had to take up the matter with Scrivener but postponed the showdown until Scrivener returned from a fishing trip that he, Waldo, Anthony, Gosnold, and five of the commoners were making in the gig from the *Discovery*.

A fierce gale swept in from the west about thirty-six hours after the fishing party sailed, and fears mounted when the men failed to return. Four or five days later, a small party of Indians arrived at Jamestown with the news that the gig, unmanned, had been driven ashore on the eastern banks of Chesapeake Bay. Subsequently, the bodies of two of the men were recovered; the others were lost at sea.

It was John's duty to examine and make a list of the personal effects of the storm's victims, but he insisted that Winne and Percy accompany him. His worst fears were confirmed when he came across a diary Scrivener had kept. In it the deputy president had written at length about his plot to get rid of John and have himself elected chief executive of the colony. It was shocking to read that Scrivener had been disappointed by the failure of the Chickahominy attack. John merely recorded the facts and expressed no personal reaction. It was small wonder, however, that for the rest of his life he remained skeptical of the value of human friendship.

There was relatively little work to be done during the winter, so the hours of labor were reduced. The additional leisure time unhappily led to boredom and periods of brooding. The colonists' complaints became louder, and one group, which had among its other tasks the raising of a herd of pigs, planned to kill two of the animals and roast them in the forest some miles from the settlement. Learning about the scheme before it could be carried out, John realized that strong, immediate steps were needed to preserve order and discipline.

He called a meeting of all the men in the community and delivered an address that he took care to preserve on paper. He pulled no punches, saying, "Countrymen, the long experience of our late miseries, I hope, is sufficient to persuade everyone to a present correction of himself, and think not that either my pains, nor the Directors' purses, will ever maintain you in idleness and sloth. You must be more industrious, or starve, how ever you have been heretofore tolerated by the authority of the Council, from that I have often commanded you.

"He that will not work shall not eat, except by sickness be he disabled. There are forty in this company who are honest and industrious. The fruits of their labor shall not be consumed by one hundred and fifty who are idle.

"And though you presume the authority here in Jamestown is but a shadow, and that I dare not touch the lives of any but my own, here is my answer. The Letters patent on which this colony is founded shall each week be read to you, whose contents will tell you the contrary. I hold all needful authority in these, my hands, and will use it for the good of all.

"Therefore he that offendeth, let him assuredly expect his due punishment."

The whipping of the three Dutchmen and the one Englishman who had conspired with the Chickahominy against him took place the following day, in the presence of all male members of the colony. John and the other members of the council wore full armor and battle swords. They watched the execution of the sentence from a platform that had been erected at one end of Smith Field for the purpose, and in front of them were stationed thirty of Jamestown's most experienced soldiers, all of them carrying loaded muskets.

The prisoners were led out from the fort blindfolded and manacled, and the crowd stirred uncomfortably. The last to appear was a man—never identified—who wore a black hood over his face. Anyone who had ever served a prison term or had watched a hanging on London's Tyburn Hill instantly realized that a royal hangman, endowed with the full authority of the Crown, was at work in the New World.

The first of the prisoners endured his punishment in silence for a time, but began to moan after he had received thirty strokes. He was screaming by the time the lash had been laid across his bare back for the last time.

One of the Dutchmen and the young Englishman wept and begged to be given another chance. But they, too, were tied to stakes and beaten. The third Dutchman began to shriek before he felt a single blow, and fell unconscious after receiving fourteen strokes. A bucket of water was poured over his head to revive him, and the whipping continued. Twice more he lost consciousness, and each time he was awakened in the same, brutal manner.

No one except the prisoners made a sound. Then soldiers carried the bleeding, bruised conspirators back to their jail cells, where a physician put "healing oil" on their backs. The troops formed into line, the masked hangman behind them, and John brought up the rear, the council members walking ahead of him. No one stirred until those taking part in the procession vanished into the fort.

After only a muttered exchange of words, men hurried off to their own houses. The communal noon meal was served soon thereafter. No one was hungry, however, and soon every man was going off to his appointed tasks quietly, without complaint.

"The settlers," Percy wrote, "learned well their lessons that day."

John adopted one more disciplinary aid. He posted a chart in the common room of the fort, listing on it the name of every man, his duties for the week, and his accomplishments in fulfilling his obligations. Each member of the council was given supervision of a group and made the necessary notations on the weekly chart. Almost overnight the problem of indolence vanished.

Various improvements were made during the latter part of the winter. Three "sweet water" wells were dug, to the relief of the whole community, men having complained since the first days of the colony that the waters of the James had a bitter, metallic taste. Twenty-two new houses were built, the church was given a sturdier roof, and when the weather was bad, everyone went to work making fishnets of vines, similar to those used by the savages.

John also improved the settlement's defenses by erecting a

blockhouse at the narrow point that connected the peninsula with the mainland behind it. Two small cannon were emplaced there, and sentries were assigned to watchtower duty around the clock. Men could now work in the fields outside the palisades of the main town without fear of a surprise attack.

A smaller blockhouse was built and manned down the river on what came to be known as Hogs' Island, so a warning could be given in time should the Spaniards launch an assault by sea. The president was prepared for any emergency that might develop.

By spring there was a marked improvement in the food situation, too. Captain Newport, on one of his voyages, had brought three sows and about twenty-five chickens and roosters to Jamestown. According to John's latest count, the pig population now exceeded seventy and was growing rapidly. There were more than six hundred chickens in the coops, and their numbers were still multiplying, too. Hard-boiled eggs, once considered the rarest of delicacies, had become commonplace.

Rats were stealing the corn from the warehouses, however, and various measures of rodent control were tried without success. A few common house cats could have solved the problem, and John made a notation to himself to ask the next ship's captain who put into Jamestown to leave a few cats behind. Every merchantman that sailed the Atlantic carried a complement of cats.

John well knew that the success or failure of the colony ultimately depended on the settlers' relations with the savages, and by the spring of 1609 he had put Jamestown's own house in order and was able to concentrate on improving his friendship with the Indians. He sent invitations to the chiefs and sub-chiefs of numerous tribes, asking them to visit him at feasts given in their honor. The leaders of the various nations were delighted to accept. John treated them with exaggerated courtesy, gave them the best food available, and dispensed gifts lavishly.

Only Powhatan absented himself. His sons appeared in his stead, and John not only was the perfect host, but sent a gift of two hammers, a saw, and a small keg of nails to their father, delicately suggesting that the sachem might want to put his own subjects to work completing the house on which construction had been halted because of Chickahominy perfidy.

The policy of openhanded generosity and kindness to the savages paid off handsomely. Permanent trade relations were established with every nation of the area. The natives brought so much corn, venison, and other provisions to Jamestown that it soon became possible to barter for furs and other articles of value. After a long, hard struggle, Jamestown had at last become virtually self-sufficient.

The most unpleasant incident of the spring was caused by a Dutch settler whose name was variously spelled as Francis, France, or Fraunce. This ambitious but shortsighted man knew the savages were eager to obtain fireams and would pay a fortune in fur pelts for muskets, gunpowder, and ammunition. So he began to steal munitions from the arsenal in the fort, burying them in the forest until he acquired enough to make a trade that would enable him to return to Europe a wealthy man.

John Russell was in charge of keeping the inventory at the arsenal, and soon discovered the loss of significant quantities of powder. He reported immediately to John, who lost no time in seeking the culprit. All members of the community were called into the president's office in the fort, one by one, and subjected to close questioning.

Francis broke down under John's interrogation and admitted his theft. The stolen munitions were recovered, and Francis was sentenced to a public whipping, a jail term, and deportation on the next ship that came to Jamestown.

Perhaps the most encouraging aspect of colonial living was the remarkable improvement in Jamestown's health record. Peter Winne died of a fever, as did another gentleman-adventurer named Leigh, but the fever that carried them away did not spread. The settlers, now adequately housed, fed, and dressed, had developed a resistance to disease. John, who was preparing a report of his stewardship for the directors, wrote that he had reason to hope there would be no more epidemics.

Nature was exceptionally kind to Jamestown in the spring of 1609, too. Berries of five or six varieties were so plentiful that it became possible to make jams, which were stored away for future use. The forest seemed filled with bears and deer, and some of the more venturesome of the colonists shot buffalo a few miles into the interior. Huge flocks of wildfowl, flying north, rested on the lakes and ponds and were snared by the hundreds. Vast schools of sturgeon and shad appeared in the James River; the latter were eaten fresh, and the former were smoked, then mixed with some native herbs that helped to preserve the meat in a semi-paste form for some months.

In one way or another, John had accomplished the seemingly impossible. Even though he had not discovered any of the gold the directors craved, he had transformed the colony into a safe, healthy, and comfortable place in which to live. He was proud of his achievements and believed the directors would recognize them. Certainly he had no idea of the cruel and unjust blow being planned in London—a blow that would shatter even the strongest of men.

XVI

Farewell to Virginia

On July 10, 1609, the small cannon in the blockhouse on Pigs' Island boomed three times, a signal that a friendly ship was approaching up the James River. A short time later a merchantman commanded by Captain Samuel Argal cast anchor. Her master stepped ashore, bringing the good news that his hold was filled with provisions, tools, bolts of cloth, and hundreds of other articles the Jamestown settlers wanted.

Argal, a burly man with a red beard and small, almost hypnotic eyes, was blunt and completely lacking in tact. He carried with him a letter to Captain John Smith from the Company's directors, and he was a messenger who was so candid that his manner was brutal. Before delivering the letter, he laughed and told John to prepare himself for a shock. Then he sat back to watch the reaction of the Jamestown president as he read the communication.

The directors began their long letter by criticizing John severely for his alleged mistreatment of the Indians. Their charges were unsubstantiated and, as John later learned, several of the investors had been influenced against him by his old enemies, Gabriel Archer and John Ratcliffe.

The directors also expressed their disappointment in the quality of the cargoes he had been sending to England. They grudgingly accepted the furs, but called the cedar, herb roots, tar, and glass inadequate. They even hinted that they considered him guilty of mismanagement and wondered whether he was making a personal profit at their expense. In all, they showed no understanding of the colony's problems. John was understandably furious.

But the most crushing blow was contained in the latter portion of the letter. The nature of the Jamestown experiment was going to be changed in the immediate future, the directors said. They had finally succeeded in interesting King James himself in the colony. Crown funds were being made available for a vast expansion project. Therefore, a fleet of nine ships was being prepared for a voyage to the New World. They would bring between five hundred and six hundred new colonists, both men and women, to Virginia.

A colony of this size would require a new type of administration, and the directors had decided to send one of their own number to Virginia. Thomas West, Baron De La Warr, would become the first royal Governor of the colony. Lord De La Warr was a competent soldier and strict disciplinarian, and John had no objection to serving under him.

But the rest of the directors' news was unbearable to a man of pride. A large staff would assist the Governor, and each of its members had a resounding title. Sir Thomas Gates, baronet, would become Lieutenant Governor. Sir George Somers, knight, an officer in the Royal Navy, would become Admiral of the New World fleet. Sir Thomas Dale, baronet, a part-time soldier with family influence at court, would become High Marshal, a post combining the duties of military commander and chief of police. Sir Ferdinando Wainman, knight, would hold the title of General of Horse, although no mention was made in the letter of sending mounts for cavalry. And Captain Newport would return permanently to Jamestown as Vice Admiral of the fleet.

The present council was being disbanded, and all its members—President Smith included—were being dismissed from office and relieved of all responsibility. If they wished to remain in Virginia, they would become private citizens. The directors, displaying no sense of gratitude for work well done and, inexcusably, making enemies when a few words might have helped soothe ruffled feelings, refrained from thanking John and his council for their efforts.

A postscript added the last bitter drop of gall to the noxious brew. Troublemakers Gabriel Archer and John Ratcliffe were returning to Virginia, as was John Martin, who had recovered his health and claimed he knew the location of "secret" gold deposits. The directors, in their ignorance, were guaranteeing that the new rulers of Virginia would encounter virtually insurmountable difficulties.

An ordinary man would have sailed for home at the first opportunity, but John stubbornly refused to see his years of hard labor nullified. He was president until relieved by Lord De La Warr, and was determined to do his duty. He could have filled the hold of Argal's ship with furs and timber and sent the mariner off on his return voyage, but instead he ordered the port closed, freezing all shipping.

Percy and other gentlemen-adventurers were threatening to rebel against the latest directives from London, and John wanted Argal to remain in Jamestown for the present. In this way he was able to assure the disgruntled that, if conditions became unbearable, a ship was at hand to take them back to England.

The colony's luck had changed, a fact that soon made itself evident. A hurricane struck the ships of the squadron sailing for the New World, scattering them somewhere in the vicinity of Bermuda. All suffered heavy damage as they limped toward Jamestown. Passengers had been lost overboard in the storm; a mysterious illness took the lives of many immigrants; and even the crews of the vessels were ill.

On the morning of August 3, 1609, a battered ship, ironically named the *Blessing,* slowly made her way up the James River to her anchorage. In the next eight days she was followed by the *Lion,* the *Falcon,* and the *Unity,* which was virtually a ghost ship. All of her seventy living passengers were ill, and no members of her crew were able to stand on their own feet except her master and two sailors.

A few days later the *Diamond* arrived, with Archer and Ratcliffe on board, both seeking vengeance against the man they considered responsible for their past disgrace—John Smith.

The arrival of several hundred sick, helpless men and women strained the facilities of Jamestown and threatened to empty the warehouses within a few weeks. Under the best of circumstances the situation would have been difficult, but it quickly became intolerable when Archer and Ratcliffe, both in excellent health, began undermining John's authority. On the very day they landed, they insisted that John was no longer president and demanded that a young gentleman-adventurer named West, who was Lord De La Warr's brother, act as temporary governor.

It might have been possible to avert tragedy had De La Warr and the other newly appointed officials reached the colony, too. But their flagship, the *Sea Venture,* had been blown far off her course by the hurricane. Many months would pass before the duly appointed Governor, Lieutenant-Governor, Generals, and Admirals reached their destination.

The directors had paid no attention to John's advice regarding the types of settlers best suited to New World living, and most of the newcomers were greedy gold-seekers anxious to find fortunes and disinclined to subject themselves to discipline of any kind. John knew he had to move swiftly in order to prevent the complete disintegration of the colony.

Acting under the authority still vested in him as president, and supported by all the veteran gentlemen-adventurers and commoners in the community, he placed Archer and Ratcliffe under house arrest. Unwilling to grant them parole, he stationed troops at the door of their hut to make certain they remained isolated. Then he gave living quarters to married couples and established guards at one end of the compound, which he assigned to eighteen unmarried women, whom he urged not to venture out alone.

Hoping to render the raucous, undisciplined newcomers harmless, he sent one hundred and twenty of them to the great falls of the James River, with a few veterans as guides. There, under his instructions, they were to establish a new plantation. More than one hundred of the gold-seekers were still in Jamestown, so he dispatched them to the land of the Nansemond to clear the forest and start still another plantation.

If John was disgusted and discouraged, he neither admitted it to anyone nor put his thoughts on paper. He had so many more mouths to feed that food was his most pressing concern. He sent Percy and Russell into the interior to barter with the Indians for corn, venison, and any other grains, vegetables, and meat available.

Meanwhile, discouraging reports began to filter back to Jamestown from the wilderness. The men who had gone off to the great falls had spent a night near a Chickahominy village. Borrowing a leaf from the natives' book of tricks, they had stolen weapons, clothing, and cooking utensils from the savages, who naturally became incensed. The Chickahominy retaliated by threatening a major war, and John realized he had to make a personal trip into the interior to reestablish cordial relations with the Indians.

But so many urgent domestic matters demanded attention that he had to leave someone responsible in charge. Therefore, he called a meeting of the council and explained that, since his own term of office was drawing to a close, a successor should be chosen to hold office until the new Governor arrived. At his suggestion, John Martin was chosen by unanimous vote and took charge during his absence as president-elect. Meanwhile, everyone in the settlement was working frantically, clearing land, building new houses, and going off on daily hunting, fishing, and berry-gathering expeditions.

John traveled up the James by shallop, halting at every Chickahominy town and village to distribute gifts. Knowing the Indians, he asked nothing in return, and they, appreciating his gesture, were mollified.

When John reached the falls, he found conditions chaotic. The colonists had chosen an indefensible site for their plantation, so he moved them to higher ground. He put them on regular, strict work schedules, and remained with them long enough to make certain they stopped floundering. Under his direction they cleared two hundred acres for the planting of crops, built themselves houses, a small fort, and a palisade, and worked out a reasonable barter arrangement with the savages who lived nearby, to guarantee they wouldn't starve during the winter.

It was late September when John started back to Jamestown with a few companions in the shallop. Many of the colonists had adopted the Indians' habit of tobacco smoking, and one night, while John was asleep on the open deck, one of the men accidentally set fire to the President's gunpowder bag while lighting his pipe with a tinderbox and flint.

There was a sudden flash, and a moment later John's entire body was enveloped in a sheet of flame.

Quick thinking saved his life. Realizing it would be impossible to put out the fire, he jumped into the deep waters of the James River, only to discover he had been so severely injured that he could not swim. The colonists on the boat threw him a line, to which he clung. Eventually they were able to haul him out of the water. He had suffered serious burns on his thighs and stomach, and was in agony during the rest of the voyage back to Jamestown. A physician treated him with "healing oil," but for several days the entire community expected to be notified that he had died.

His will to live was so great, however, that even though invalided and still suffering excruciating pain, he insisted on supervising the affairs of the colony from his sickbed. Ignoring the advice of the physicians, who had told him that rest was essential, he conferred several times each day with President-elect Martin and the other members of the council.

Ratcliffe and Archer, who were to face a new trial on charges of conspiracy, were in despair. They knew they would be convicted if John lived, and they realized that if they were deported to England a second time, their careers would be terminated. Therefore, when it seemed that John would survive, they hired two men named Dyer and Coe to shoot the helpless invalid late at night. At the last moment, however, the would-be killers lost their courage and were arrested. The following day they made a full confession to Martin, who ordered them to stand trial.

It soon became obvious that John needed medical attention unavailable in the New World, and he was persuaded by Martin, Percy, and others to return to England. Because his pain was great, and because he realized that, with the *Sea Venture* expected at any time, there was little more he could do for Virginia, he agreed to their proposal. He had grown tired of the efforts of his enemies to harm him, he was discouraged by the Company's failure to recognize all he had done for Jamestown, and the thought of going home suddenly appealed to him.

Three of the ships had been made seaworthy again and were sailing for London with cargoes of furs, herbs, and timber accumulated during John's presidency. On October 4th he was carried on board the *Unity,* while most of the settlers wept. But his foes rejoiced, and before the little squadron sailed they prepared a long list of false charges against him, which they sent to the directors.

The ships sailed in mid-October, and John was so ill that he was asleep when the *Unity* glided down the James and moved out into the open Atlantic. Never again did he see the land to which he had given so much of his time and talents and energy.

His contributions to the stability and welfare of Jamestown are best illustrated by the fate of the colony after he left. Martin was unable to establish order and was succeeded by Percy, who wrote in disgust that so many men were conniving against him that "there are now twenty Presidents." Food disappeared from the warehouses, and the thieves were never caught. Relations with the Indians deteriorated so rapidly that the Chickahominy went to war against the settlers, and scores of English men, women, and children were killed or injured.

The winter of 1609–10 was known in Jamestown as "the starving time." Gentlemen-adventurers scheming against each other for places on the council took the pigs and chickens for their own use and left the commoners to their own devices. People were reduced to searching the windswept beaches for oysters and clams. When they dared to venture into the forest to find nuts and berries, they were slain by savages. On the day John sailed for England, there was a total of 573 colonists in Virginia. By the middle of the following May, their number had been reduced to 61.

John, discussing the situation candidly in his *Generall Historie of Virginia,* which was published a decade and a half later, says that the frenzied survivors were reduced to cannibalism. Percy and several other writers freely admit the charge.

It was during this winter that the name of Pocahontas first appears in the works of authors other than John Smith. Percy says that a teen-age boy named Henry Spelman, the youngest son of Sir Henry Spelman, a noted scholar, wandered into the wilderness and was taken prisoner by the Chickahominy. But, Percy writes, Pocahontas intervened with her father on the boy's behalf, and his life was spared. Spelman, who survived and returned to England himself in 1614, told of his adventure in a little pamphlet, *An Account of the Starving Time in Virginia,* which was published in London late in 1614, but received little attention.

The similarity between Spelman's experience and the story John later told of his own relations with Pocahontas is marked. It is possible, although it cannot be proved, that John "borrowed" the idea and enlarged on it.

In any event, Lord De La Warr, Sir Thomas Gates, and Sir George Somers finally reached Jamestown in late May, 1610, with a company of one hundred and fifty settlers on board two ships. They arrived just as the emaciated survivors were about to abandon Jamestown and set out for England in the dilapidated *Discovery* after enduring a nightmare existence for seven months.

De La Warr was a competent administrator, and under his direction order was restored. The directors of the London Company and the Crown poured new money into the enterprise, and eventually Virginia regained her strength. However, several years of hard, unremitting labor were needed before the colony again became as secure and comfortable as it had been when John Smith had been in command.

John himself cared little about Jamestown or anything else on his eight-week voyage to London. Autumn storms rocked the *Unity,* making it impossible for the invalid to rest, and his burns continued to torture him. He was delirious for about ten days, and thereafter remained so ill that he was unable to take any nourishment other than "a few biscuits and a little barley water."

When the battered vessel finally sailed up the Thames and anchored at the London wharves in time for Christmas, 1609, John tottered ashore in shabby armor, patched breeches, and worn boots. He was still suffering from his burns, and was so heavily bandaged that he walked with great difficulty. Although he was not yet thirty years of age, his hair was graying, and he moved with the halting, uncertain steps of an old man.

All of his belongings were packed in two old sea chests. One contained his clothing, which was almost without value, and his weapons. The other was precious to him. It was filled with charts, maps, and detailed notes—papers he had accumulated from the start of his voyage to the New World three years earlier—and he knew that the data he had gleaned were priceless.

No one in England yet recognized the worth of his many contributions to the Jamestown colony, and there was a distinct possibility that if the directors of the London Company seriously considered the claims of his enemies, criminal charges would be preferred against him. He had spent long years in a far distant wilderness creating a civilized community, but not one person was on hand to greet him.

Too tired to walk, he engaged a sedan chair and hired two men to carry his sea chests. Then, feeling lonely as well as ill, he went off to the Strand in search of lodgings. A cold, bone-penetrating rain was falling, and London seemed unchanged. But John, in spite of his disappointments and physical pain, would never be the same man who had gone off in search of fresh adventures. He had fallen in love with the New World, and America would continue to enthrall him as long as he lived.

XVII

The Rehabilitation of a Hero

JOHN SMITH'S RECOVERY WAS a long, slow, painful process. Injured in body and bruised in spirit, he took inexpensive lodgings in a house on a small lane near the Thames and for about three months saw no one but the physician who visited him daily. A boy, whom he hired for the purpose, brought him his meals from a nearby tavern, but he enjoyed neither the good English beef nor the rich English beer for which he had longed during his years in the New World. The burns on his thighs and stomach healed slowly, leaving permanent scars, but he gradually regained his health and vitality.

His mental state, however, remained depressed. Jamestown, he wrote, had been an expensive experiment. He had spent "near five years in work, and more than five hundred pounds of my own estate, for which there is no recompense; beside all the dangers, miseries, and encumbrances and loss of other employment I endured gratis." It was a source of satisfaction to him, however, that he had left more than five hundred English men and women well provided. Not until later did he learn what had happened to them after his own departure.

The lack of confidence in him shown by the directors of the London Company, combined with their seeming inability to understand the problems of the New World, disturbed him so much that he had no intention of explaining the true situation or trying to clear his own name.

He sent brief letters to his sister and brother, informing them of his return to England. But he made no attempt to get in touch with his friends or the printer of *A True Relation,* even though he had learned from Captain Argal that the book was enjoying a brisk sale. It was difficult, however, to live the life of a hermit in the heart of London. Inevitably he began to think of women. He had been celibate for years, difficult for any man in the prime of life, and sheer torture for someone as virile as John Smith.

So he got in touch with Frances, Duchess of Richmond, and they resumed their affair. Frances, however, was not content to be a mere mistress. She was appalled by John's drab lodgings and manner of living and took immediate steps to force him to assume a more active role in the world. First, with the help of her husband, who may or may not have known of her affair, she secured better lodgings for John on the Strand. When he told her he had insufficient furniture for a grand suite of rooms, she moved some of her own chairs and tables into the place for him.

It was Frances who gave him the good news that *A True Relation* was the most popular book in England. Thereafter, he needed no prodding to visit his printer, George Hall of Fleet Street. To his astonishment, John learned that the book had already earned him more than one thousand pounds and was continuing to sell at a rapid rate. Even though the directors of the London Company had rebuked him unjustly, the people of England were enjoying his book.

Whether he expected an apology or some other form of vindication before sitting down with the directors is still something of a mystery. John never explained his motives, apparently taking it for granted in his later books that his readers would understand his feelings in the matter. In any event, Frances took the initiative and arranged a private supper party at the Richmond town palace. The only guests were John and Richard Hakluyt, and at the end of the meal Frances and her husband discreetly withdrew.

Nothing is known of what was said that night in the great hall of the Richmond palace where John and the Archdeacon talked until dawn. Hakluyt had not been in complete sympathy with the stand taken by some of the wealthy and powerful nobles who were his fellow directors, so he listened with an open mind to John's account of affairs in the colony. He had always been somewhat skeptical of finding gold in America. His chief concern now, as always, was that of finding a sea passage to the Pacific.

He accepted John's opinion that in Virginia and the region directly to the north of it, at least, there were no such rivers. The Archdeacon's friendliness was the first sign of a thaw, and John met him again the next day, this time armed with the many maps and charts of Virginia, Chesapeake Bay, and the land of the Susquehannocks that he had made. Poring over them together, the two men forgot the coolness that had separated them.

Hakluyt was a scientist who had only a limited interest in human relations, but the things John told him about the disruptive influences of men like Archer and Ratcliffe distressed him, and he felt that Prince Henry should know the true state of affairs in Virginia. John was reluctant to meet the Prince of Wales, believing that Henry had insulted him. But he could not refuse a summons to an interview at Henry's quarters in Fleet Street, and he grudgingly accompanied Hakluyt there.

The Prince of Wales was flanked by two of the London Company's new directors, the Earl of Southampton and Sir Ferdinando George, who had Anglicized the original spelling of his family's name, Gorges. Both of these wealthy patrons were strongly interested in the discovery and exploration of new territories, and they were at least partly convinced that it would be wiser to emulate the Dutch, who were making themselves wealthy in trade with hitherto unknown peoples, than to copy the gold-seeking Spaniards who sometimes went bankrupt.

John Smith shrewdly saw and grasped an opportunity to do more than vindicate his good name. The Prince of Wales was, after his father, the most powerful man in the realm. The Earl was enormously wealthy, and so was Sir Ferdinando, who also happened to be one of the few men close to King James. The trio, if they chose, could finance any future expeditions he might want to undertake, and he was already thinking in terms of the future.

He delivered an impassioned address, substantiating everything he said with the copious notes he had made during his stay in turbulent Jamestown. Never had he given a better performance, never had he been more persuasive or charming.

It was beneath the dignity of the Prince of Wales to offer an apology to a mere gentleman, but Henry did the next best thing. His own relations with his father had improved considerably in recent years, and he found it easy to arrange an audience for John with the King.

A few days later, John was called to Whitehall. He had made such a good impression on the Earl of Southampton and Sir Ferdinando that they accompanied him, thereby serving notice on their fellow directors of the London Company that they accepted and supported John's position.

The audience itself was no more and no less successful than most of the King's interviews. James was an enigma to most men. Certainly his interest in the New World was limited. He had made royal funds available to the London Company only because his elder son and heir had given him no peace until he had opened the Treasury vaults. He asked polite questions and seemed bored by John's replies.

The cold, suffocatingly majestic atmosphere of James Stuart's throne room was not conducive to a display of John's brand of histrionics. When first summoned to the audience, he had planned to make a strong plea for sensible colonization of the sort he believed would succeed in the New World, but Frances convinced him that the King would not appreciate a speech. It may be that Prince Henry added a private word on the subject, too.

In any event, few men found themselves able to speak freely in James's presence. It had been the King's misfortune to follow the enormously popular Elizabeth I to the throne, and he was always conscious of his predecessor's luster. He moved his audience chamber to a hall she had seldom frequented, and soon found why she had chosen not to use it. No matter how many great fires blazed in its hearths, it was always chilly. Even the luxurious tapestries that lined the stone walls did not prevent dampness from seeping into men's bones.

It was so cold in the throne room, in fact, that courtiers were permitted to wear hats as well as wigs, and the ladies of the court, who usually wore very low-cut gowns, went to great lengths to avoid royal audiences in the throne room. Only the King and a few of his flamboyant noble favorites like the Duke of Buckingham were permitted to sit. Thrones for the King and Queen stood at one end of the hall, although Queen Anne rarely availed herself of the privilege of using her chair. There were smaller, less comfortable thrones for Prince Henry and Prince Charles, but the King's sons found innumerable excuses to absent themselves from their father's audiences.

Servants appeared with chairs for Buckingham and a handful of other fortunates, and it was common knowledge that when James asked someone to sit during an audience, he was pleased. John Smith stood.

The King looked down his long nose at the man who had done so much to enlarge his realm, asked perfunctory questions, and paid scant heed to the answers. He yawned, scratched his prominent chin, and occasionally gestured to a page, who brought him a silver dish filled with the hard sugar candy he enjoyed and that did so much to ruin his skin.

John spoke soberly and took care to say nothing beyond replying directly and succinctly to each question. Unlike many who came to the throne room, however, he was not overawed by James, nor did he speak softly, having been warned by Frances that there was an acoustical problem in the hall. The tapestries muffled sounds, and ordinarily it was impossible for anyone standing more than ten or fifteen feet from the dais to hear a word exchanged by the King and his guests.

John knew that several of the London Company's directors were present in the hall, and he took care to insure that they heard everything he said. He spoke in the voice he ordinarily reserved for the drill field, and even the men huddling near the hearths were able to hear him.

The audience lasted no more than thirty or forty minutes. When the King signified that it had come to an end by doffing his hat, John bowed deeply and backed out of the hall. He was joined in an anteroom by Southampton and Sir Ferdinando. They conducted him to the apartments that Henry was now using again. There a buffet meal was served, "together with many fine and rare wines." Many of the London Company's directors were present, among them the Chief Justice, Sir John Popham, an indefatigable gold-seeker.

In this informal atmosphere John was able to express himself with less restraint, and undoubtedly he accomplished some educational missionary work. In all probability Prince Henry, the host, was responsible for creating a golden opportunity. John had a chance to meet privately with men who had been critical of his conduct at Jamestown, and he could say what he pleased at Whitehall, where no notes were taken and no records kept of conversations.

Virtually nothing is known about what went on at the party. Neither John nor anyone else ever revealed the guest list, which would have been an insult to royal hospitality. The party lasted far into the evening, however, and at its end John accompanied the Prince of Wales and Sir Ferdinando to the austere lodgings of Archdeacon Hakluyt. The geographer was too busy to attend even royal parties and rarely appeared at audiences before the King.

By now John had been able to explain the facts of life at Jamestown to a majority of the London Company's stockholders, and the formal meeting of the directors to which he was invited in May, 1610, was anticlimactic. Apparently the investors had reached a sensible conclusion and had sheathed their knives. Not one word of censure appeared in the minutes of the meeting, and John, who was present in the role of an adviser, was treated with great courtesy.

When the directors told him they were thinking in terms of sending to Virginia still more men and supplies, John advised them that the future of the colony lay in her limitless resources of timber and furs. He knew of no gold or silver anywhere in the area, nor did the Indians wear any jewelry or other items made of precious metals.

Again he made a plea for honest artisans and husbandmen, and emphasized that conniving adventure seekers like Archer and Ratcliffe could destroy Virginia. It was ironic that, at approximately the same time the meeting was being held, Lord De La Warr was landing in the New World and was discovering to his own astonished horror just how much damage men of the caliber of Ratcliffe and Archer actually could do.

The directors neither rebuked John again nor withdrew their former complaints against him. It is obvious that the majority gleaned no clear concept of all he had accomplished, for he was not voted praise or thanks for his efforts. In all, he was treated far more casually than he deserved. Years would pass before the English people gained any real idea of how much he had done for the cause of colonization in the New World.

His position now was strictly that of an outsider. His own modest investment in the Company did not entitle him to a seat on the new directorate, whose members had given vast sums. If the Company showed a profit, which it could not for many years, he would earn financial dividends. Until then, however, he was regarded by the nobles as a useful, rather well-informed former employee.

In the next few years John was asked, from time to time, to attend meetings of the directors. On these occasions his advice was sought, but not always accepted. His loyalty to Jamestown and his hard work were taken for granted. But his realistic views were often at odds with the romantic notions of high-born gentlemen who spent their entire lives in London and rarely traveled more than one hundred miles from the King's court.

In spite of the cavalier treatment he received, John was always blunt and honest when questioned. On one occasion, he was asked to reduce some of his opinions to paper. He did, and appended a personal note to his report. "If I speak too plain," he said, "I humbly crave your pardon. But you requested me, therefore I do but my duty."

It was the ultimate frustration for a man who loved praise to be denied the recognition he deserved. It wasn't enough for John that the heir to the throne and several other men of enormous influence knew what he had done in Jamestown and appreciated his worth. He believed, with justification, that he had accomplished more in the field of colonization than any other Englishman of his time, and he wanted fame as great as Sir Walter Raleigh's or Sir Francis Drake's.

It may be that he privately hoped he would be knighted for his work in the New World. If so, he was too diplomatic to confide his wishes to Prince Henry, who would have believed himself being used. The Duchess of Richmond, John's confidante, hints at his secret desires in a letter to Elizabeth, Countess of Southampton, in which she writes, "My friend amuses himself by devising a new coat of arms, in which the new town at Virginia will be prominent."

But the Crown granted John no honors. He had to be content with the title of former president of the Jamestown council. This resounding name meant nothing to most people, and when his next book was published, in 1612, he called himself the former Governor of Virginia. In spirit, at least, he was being accurate.

During the summer of 1610, John appeared confident that his services to the cause of colonization would soon win him the fame he craved. He appeared in public with the Prince of Wales on a number of occasions, was often seen with the Earl and Countess of Southampton, and spent at least one week at Sir Ferdinando's estate in the west of England. Then he visited the city of Plymouth, of which Sir Ferdinando was governor, but in September disappeared from the public view.

No record can be found of his activities during the better part of the next year. He continued to see Frances from time to time, her correspondence indicates, and once, in the early winter months of 1611, she appears to have been annoyed with him because of his interest in another woman. His fancy or infatuation, whatever it may have been, was passing, and he formed no noteworthy liaison.

The most mysterious aspect of this period is that he vanished from London, after giving up his lodgings. Apparently he did not visit his boyhood home, because his sister and brother continued to write to him thereafter that they hoped to see him in the near future after being separated from him for so long.

It is possible that he went off for a long period of rest and recuperation at one of Southampton's estates, or at a farm belonging to Sir Ferdinando on the outskirts of Plymouth. In any event, no one appears to have been alarmed or upset by his absence from London.

Early in the summer of 1611, John returned to the city, his health and vigor restored. He immediately took new, relatively modest rooms in a house on the Strand, and went to his printer, George Hall, for an accounting. He must have been pleased to learn that *A True Relation* was still selling and that it had earned him an additional seven hundred and eighty pounds.

He had news of his own that delighted Hall. He was in the last stages of composition on his new book, *A Map of Virginia with a Description of the Country*, to which he intended to append the observations of others who had been in Jamestown and shared his ideas on colonization. This section he planned to call *The Proceedings of the English Colony in Virginia*. Percy, who had now returned to England, had written his own history of Jamestown for this section, John Martin had added some tart, pertinent comments, and John Russell had prepared a short essay. Other men who had been members of the "Smith faction" in Jamestown had also prepared letters and critiques for the book.

John's material was ready for the printer by the autumn of 1611, but he found Hall strangely reluctant to accept his business, an attitude that seemed particularly puzzling in view of the continuing success of *A True Relation*. John pressed for a decision, and Hall eventually told him he could not publish the book.

It was not too difficult for John to guess that one or more people in high places opposed the publication of a book that treated colonial living and its problems with blunt candor. The directors of the London Company were disinclined to discuss the subject with him, and only after a long investigation was he able to discover that his enemy was a young man of great physical charm and no discernible talents who stood very high in the King's favor at the moment.

Robert Carr, the younger son of a Scottish noble, had accompanied King James to England as a page boy, had fallen from royal grace, and recently had become the King's favorite again. He was so handsome, arrogant yet effeminate, and dressed with such elegance that it was commonly believed he had become James's homosexual lover. Only a few months earlier, he had been made a viscount and was now known as Lord Rochester. Within a short time he would become a member of the Privy Council and private secretary to the King; in less than two years he was destined to climb still higher in the peerage as Earl of Somerset.

Unfortunately for John Smith, Lord Rochester had been persuaded to invest a large sum of money in the London Company. A romantic dreamer, he was convinced the New World colonists would line his purse with gold and fill it with diamonds. He was horrified by John's realistic discussion of affairs in Virginia and believed that *A Map of Virginia* would discourage colonization and deprive him of a fortune. He found it easy to persuade several fellow directors to accept his view.

Printer Hall had been called to Rochester's sumptuous suite at Whitehall and had been told that if he published John's book he would receive no more printing orders from the Crown. Like everyone else in the field of publishing, Hall depended on royal business for his living, so he had to reject the request to publish *A Map of Virginia*.

John never gave up without a fight, but he discovered that the friends to whom he appealed for help had no desire to become embroiled in a dispute with the King's favorite. Sir Ferdinando had earned James's displeasure several years earlier, and had to tread carefully. Southampton was endowed with a belligerent disposition, but was persuaded by his Countess to do nothing that might incur the wrath of the King.

Prince Henry could have swept aside all opposition. Unfortunately, he had fallen ill, was seeing no visitors and, within a few months, would be dead. John sent two letters to the Prince of Wales, but neither was answered. It is possible that Henry, confined to his rooms at the palace and surrounded by his father's courtiers, might not have received either communication.

The odds against John were overwhelming, but he continued his struggle. Not only was his book worthy of publication, but the cause of English colonization in the New World would suffer if prospective settlers were hoodwinked. Only the truth would impel colonists of the type needed to establish permanent communities in the wilderness to cross the Atlantic.

Suddenly and unexpectedly, *A Map of Virginia* was published in Oxford in the spring of 1612, the edition bearing the name of no printer. It was obvious that one of several men who printed books for the students at the great university there had done the job and had discreetly chosen to remain anonymous. It was also apparent that influence had been used on John's behalf to insure the publication of the book.

Suspicion fell on Richard Hakluyt, who feared no man, including James or his favorite of the moment, and who had intimate and enduring relations with the academic community. If the Archdeacon was indeed responsible, he kept his mouth shut, and so did John. No correspondence between the two men on the subject has ever come to light, so it can only be surmised that it was Hakluyt who made certain that *A Map of Virginia,* which would be of enormous value to colonial planners and almost countless thousands of settlers, saw the light of print.

Rochester and his friends were furious and tried to persuade the King, acting through his Privy Council, to direct the Lord Chamberlain to have the book withdrawn. But James hesitated. In spite of his many faults, he tried to be a fair man and rule for the good of all his subjects. Elizabeth, Countess of Southampton, wrote to her good friend, Frances, Duchess of Richmond, that the King had glanced through *A Map of Virginia* and actually may have read portions of it.

In any event, he decided it contained nothing seditious, and refused to have it banned. John Smith may have been an impertinent fellow who was jeopardizing some large colonial investments, but not even the King could deny that he had spent several years in Virginia and that, according to the scrupulously detailed reports written from the colony by Lord De La Warr, many of his ideas were sound. James could see no valid reason why John should be denied the right of any literate Englishman to express his opinions in print.

Rochester made another mistake and foolishly tried to intimidate London booksellers, threatening them with a removal of his very limited patronage if they offered the book to their customers. Word of his rash conduct spread quickly through the circles of those who were able to read. The net effect was to stimulate interest in *A Map of Virginia*. Men who otherwise would have been indifferent to it were now anxious to read it.

The book was an immediate, resounding success. The modest initial printing disappeared from the shelves of booksellers within a few days, and two much larger printings sold out within six months. It made such a stir, in fact, that sales of *A True Relation* picked up again, and George Hall was placed in the financially pleasant but personally embarrassing position of having to bring out a new edition of that work.

By the autumn of 1612, John found himself enjoying the respect and admiration he had craved. Prince Henry, his sometime patron, had died, and Lord Rochester made certain that he would neither be rewarded by the Crown nor be received at court. But in spite of the royal snubs he was being forced to endure, he had become a personage of consequence.

Nobles thinking of investing in the new companies being formed for purposes of exploration and trade not only sought his advice, but paid him handsomely for it. Prosperous merchants of the growing middle class eagerly asked his opinion of conditions in the New World and wanted his guidance as they groped for ways to capitalize on the opening of new markets. The whole country was thinking and talking of discovery and colonization, and the flames of excitement were fanned by Henry Hudson's exploits. It did no harm when Hudson, who returned to England after finding the site of what would become New York, publicly praised his friend and thanked him for his assistance.

It no longer mattered to John that men whispered about him and nudged each other when he walked into a tavern, or that total strangers sought a few words with him on the streets. He had grown more mature and had learned that the substance of stature was far more important than its surface manifestations. While still wanting recognition, his principal concern was the establishment of colonies that would survive and flourish.

In several ways, however, he was unchanged. When prospective emigrants wrote or came to him in person, he told them the unvarnished truth about conditions in the New World. Sir Walter Raleigh, who was trying to win release from the Tower by promising the King he would find a rich gold mine for the Crown in Central America, told John, who still visited him occasionally, that he was a fool, and that he would end his days in prison, too, unless he told people what the King wanted them to hear.

But Jamestown had left its permanent mark on John Smith's character, just as the powder burns he had sustained on the James River had left ineradicable scars on his body. America, he insisted, had no need for idle adventure seekers, but there would always be a place for the honest man willing to earn his living by hard labor.

John's integrity did not extend to his relations with the opposite sex. His increased renown made him more attractive to women, and he had two brief affairs in 1612, one with a young woman about whom literally nothing is known. The other was Margaret Wriothesley, a cousin of the Earl of Southampton, whose blonde beauty was praised by some of the poets whom the Earl so generously patronized.

Margaret had flax-colored hair, deep-blue eyes, and a ravishing figure. She was only seventeen years old, and had not yet been formally presented to the King and Queen at Whitehall, where, it was expected, an appropriate noble marriage would be contracted on her behalf.

Like so many others who preceded and followed her, Margaret found John's charms irresistible and succumbed to them, thereby damaging her chances of finding a suitable husband. She also was responsible for a sudden chilling of the friendship between the Duchess of Richmond and the Countess of Southampton, the former holding the quaint theory that the latter might have encouraged the affair and could have prevented it.

Frances was also wildly angry with John. The spirit of the age being what it was, she knew better than to hope that her husband would be faithful to her, but believed the least she could expect from her lover was fidelity. How and when she conveyed her emphatic views to John is not known, but she managed to communicate them to him, and he hastily terminated the brief liaison with the lovely Margaret.

The tempest quickly subsided. Margaret returned to the home of her parents in Sussex. According to the rules considered inviolable in such matters, she was expected to remain there for a year or two, until gossip about her affair died away. Then she would be considered an eligible near-maiden and would be permitted to return to court for purposes of husband-hunting.

John's situation was far more complicated. Frances had been his friend as well as his mistress, and had been of great help to him when he had needed aid. Now she closed the doors of her town palace to him, making no reply to two flowery letters of apology he sent to her. He was so upset that, in a gesture similar to those found in French bedroom farces, he asked her husband to intervene on his behalf. There is no record of whether the Duke obliged him. If he did, the attempt failed. Frances remained outraged and adamant.

For the first—and last—time in his life, John found himself in the humiliating position of begging in vain for a lady's forgiveness. But Frances, who had looked the other way when he had indulged in brief, meaningless affairs with lower-class women, could not tolerate the insult of being displaced by another blue-blood.

Eventually, however, he found the key to Frances' bedchamber. He bought her a ruby ring set in gold. It must have been a consolation, and perhaps even a source of satisfaction, for him to realize he was sufficiently prosperous to mollify a jealous mistress with an expensive bauble far beyond an ordinary man's means.

XVIII

New England

By 1613 it was clear to everyone interested in colonization that the English experiment in Virginia had succeeded. Lord De La Warr, applying John Smith's principles of self-support and discipline, had restored order, guaranteed the directors of the London Company a modest but steady return on their investment, and made certain that England would not be left behind in the European race to acquire territory in the New World.

Captain John Smith followed developments in Virginia with the eager anxiety of a proud parent, but like a father whose son had outgrown him, found he had no place in the colony's future. In both conversation and correspondence with some of his former superiors he made it plain that he was willing to forget past slights and return to Jamestown if useful work could be found for him there. Unfortunately, his insistence on speaking the truth, no matter how painful it might be, combined with his attitude of fierce independence, had made him too many enemies in high places, and by early 1613 he realized there was no future for him in Virginia.

Nevertheless, he continued to feel a desperate longing for the wilderness he had partly accepted, partly conquered. His experience and knowledge made him uniquely qualified to lead expeditions of exploration, discovery, and settlement, and he could not tolerate the thought that other men might eclipse his achievements in America.

The New World, he believed, was his personal domain. He knew more about its people, their languages, and their customs than any other man in England. He had sailed up unknown rivers and marched across hundreds of miles of forest that no other civilized human being had ever seen. He could not remain in London, sleeping in a comfortable bed and eating in taverns that served the best in food and drink, while others, sacrificing a few personal comforts, made history.

Fortunately, the interests of England were not confined to Virginia, and John was superbly equipped to take the lead on behalf of his country elsewhere. Specifically, his thoughts turned to that portion of the North American continent that he himself would soon name New England.

In the past eleven years a few snippets of information had been gleaned about that territory. The first Englishman to visit a portion of it had been Captain Bartholomew Gosnold, John's good friend and companion at Jamestown. Gosnold had spent about two months, from May to July, 1602, in a "paradise" he had called Martha's Vineyard. John still had in his possession all of the late Captain Gosnold's maps, charts, and notes, which were woefully incomplete.

Gosnold's discoveries had so aroused the interest of Richard Hakluyt that the Archdeacon had persuaded the wealthy citizens of the city of Bristol to send out an expedition in 1603. It had accomplished very little, other than to report that the waters off the coast of North America were teeming with fish. Two years later, in 1605, Captain George Waymouth had sailed to the area and had come home with charts that, in hundreds of details, contradicted Gosnold's. He, too, had reported the presence of fish and valuable whales.

In 1606 King James had taken an important step, primarily intended to eliminate domestic rivalries. London-based investors were granted primary rights in those sections of North America that extended from what would become Maryland to present-day Georgia. The vast, virtually unknown, and ill-defined area to the north was reserved for financiers from Plymouth, Bristol, Exeter, Newport, and other cities of southwestern England.

The men who had proprietary rights in this part of North America were John's closest friends and supporters, among them Sir Ferdinando and the Earl of Southampton. The Earl had dispatched a private expedition to the area in 1607, but its achievements had not been worth the tremendous expense involved. Southampton's ship had returned with word that the area eventually named Cape Cod was part of the North American mainland, rather than an island, as had been believed. In addition, several Indians had been carried back to England, cruelly and against their will. People had flocked to see them as though they were strange and exotic animals, but little information of value had been obtained from them.

Another expedition, financed by Sir John Popham, had been even more of a failure. The Lord Chief Justice had hoped to establish a permanent colony somewhere on the northern coast, but his pioneers had been badly led and poorly equipped and had returned to England after spending a few miserable weeks in the wilderness.

John Smith conceived the idea of making a voyage for the specific purpose of obtaining accurate information about the area north of Henry Hudson's river. In a letter he sent to the Earl of Southampton, he proposed that he make an accurate map of the coastline and explore "such portions of the interior as may seem worthy of discovery."

Southampton encouraged him, as did Sir Ferdinando, and he acquired all the data that Archdeacon Hakluyt had gleaned. Then he went to Plymouth, where he settled down in one of Sir Ferdinando's houses to make a quiet, thorough survey of the situation.

One fact above all others struck him as significant. Henry Hudson, prior to his first monumental voyage to the west, had twice sought an Arctic outlet to the Pacific on behalf of investors calling themselves the Muscovy Company. At an island to become known as Spitsbergen he had found a huge colony of whales and had set off a wild race between fishermen from England, France, Holland, Spain, and other countries. Whale oil had an enormous commercial value, and a small portion of the mammal called ambergris, which was used as the base in making perfume, was precious. Boomtowns were mushrooming at Spitsbergen, and the governments of various nations, England included, were giving their fishermen financial aid and naval protection.

It seemed strange to John that although every expedition sent across the North Atlantic had reported the presence of whales in large numbers off the American coast, no similar commercial race had developed there. He knew, too, from Gosnold's notes and the logs of Waymouth, which he borrowed from Archdeacon Hakluyt, that there were vast schools of cod and tuna there. And he could not forget the lucky tuna catch that had, at one point, saved Jamestown from starvation.

A simple idea occurred to him, one so basic he marveled that no one else had thought of it. An expedition equipped with harpoons and other weapons for catching whales, heavy nets for the landing of cod and tuna, and empty kegs and salt for the preservation of fish and oil, could more than earn its own way. There was no need for investors to spend large sums of money with little hope of an immediate return. He conceived of a voyage that would show a profit the very day the investors' ships returned to England.

Enlarging on his theme, it seemed logical to him that a man who understood the savages of North America—and he certainly was such a man—would be able to barter with the savages for valuable furs. He declared, politely and rather unconvincingly, that he intended to search for gold and copper, but if such attempts failed, "Fish and Furs will be my refuge."

Leaving as little as possible to chance, he sought out the Indians who had been brought to England by Southampton's previous expedition. The English climate had proved too much for three of the savages, but two were still alive, and John spent many days with them. His familiarity with Chickahominy and other Virginia dialects enabled him to pick up the language of these northern braves with relative ease, and he made orderly, extensive notes on all they told him about their homeland. Astonishingly, perhaps because of the language barrier, no one had obtained such data from them since their arrival in England.

John well knew the value of guides in the North American wilderness, and he made an offer to the two Indians. If his voyage materialized, as he hoped, he would give them transportation to their homes if they, in turn, would act as guides for him in the New World. Both leaped at the opportunity.

The warriors were shorter than the men of the Chickahominy, and of slighter build, with dark, copper-colored skins. Both were in their late twenties or early thirties, and John's offer was the prelude to one of the most astonishing incidents in American history. He kept his word and transported the two Indians to New England, leaving them near the site he marked on his master map of the area as New Plymouth.

One of the warriors died soon thereafter, but the other survived. Thus it was that, in 1620, six years later, when a small band of Englishmen who crossed the Atlantic in the

Mayflower came ashore near New Plymouth, they were greeted by a brave wearing a tattered English hat and shirt and speaking their own tongue in the accents of London's lower classes. Thanks to John, the Indian known as Squanto, who served the Pilgrims so faithfully, had an opportunity to win his own niche in history.

In any event, John made his plans with great care. Borrowing from the experiences of Hudson, he decided to make his voyage with small crews in order to hold expenses to a minimum. He wanted two ships, each of about one hundred tons, with holds large enough to store the oil, fish, and furs that would pay for the expedition.

John won Archdeacon Hakluyt's immediate, enthusiastic support and obtained overnight financing. Three men supplied all the funds for his expedition. One was the Duke of Richmond. This enabled John, rather indiscreetly, to name his flagship the *Frances*. Southampton and Sir Ferdinando supplied the rest of the money he needed and guaranteed him a free hand in obtaining personnel and in outfitting and directing his expedition.

His first act was to hire two expert seamen. Captain George Langam had sailed with Waymouth and was a ruddy-faced, silent man of impeccable personal character. Captain Marmaduke Royden, who had been second mate under the noted explorer, John Davys, on a voyage to Greenland—and therefore a shipmate of Hudson's—was more of an extrovert. He had red hair and a booming voice, a beard almost as full as John's, and a jolly manner. John, who had made no mistakes in his judgment of men other than that of placing his trust in Matthew Scrivener, was confident that Royden was the type of master mariner he wanted.

Langam and Royden selected their own crews, but John sat in with them, retaining for himself a veto power, which he exercised prudently. Remembering from his Jamestown experience that reliable gentlemen-adventurers could be valuable assistants on shore, he also hired two former professional soldiers, William Skelton and John Buley. Little is known about either, other than that they were expert swordsmen, superior marksmen, and fearless enough to follow wherever John led.

The pace of preparations increased in late 1613. John bought a ship of one hundred and five tons, which he renamed the *Frances,* and gave her to Langam. Shortly thereafter he acquired a ship of eighty-two tons, which he diplomatically called the *Queen Anne*. Royden insisted that his was the better vessel, and events proved that the *Queen Anne* was indeed easier to handle in stormy weather.

The captains, assisted by the two gentlemen-adventurers, bought the provisions and equipment for the voyage, and John personally examined every keg of meat and fish, every barrel of flour. He had already learned through bitter experience that merchants were anxious to unload inferior merchandise on the unwary. Accordingly, he made certain that no spoiled food, lumpy gunpowder, or weevil-infested biscuits went into the holds of his ships.

The ships were outfitted at Southampton, where the Earl owned extensive wharves and warehouses, and early in February the crews went on board. For about ten days John continued to live in a town house the Earl had made available to him; then he transferred his gear to the *Frances,* on which Skelton, Buley, and the two Indians were also sailing. As admiral of the expedition, John enjoyed the luxury of a private cabin, in which there was a bunk and a ledge that, when lowered from a bulkhead, could be used as a desk or table. A sea chest served as his chair.

Foul weather, as usual, delayed the sailing. But on the morning of March 3, 1614, the sun came out, the sea became calm, and the two little square-rigged ships nosed out into the English Channel. The entire company, including John, his gentlemen-adventurers, the Indians, and a physician assigned to each ship, was made up of forty-five persons. Of this number, two were cabin boys.

John's planning had been so thorough and his subordinates knew their business so well that the voyage across the North Atlantic was made without incident. A storm separated the ships for three days, but they found each other again. They saw an iceberg they mistakenly assumed to be an island. And John, in his book entitled *A Description of New England,* solemnly declared that he and several members of the *Frances*'s crew saw a mermaid perched on the iceberg. Such delusions were common in the seventeenth century; Hudson, among many others, also claimed he saw a mermaid on one of his voyages.

In mid-April the two ships arrived off the Grand Banks of Newfoundland, where fish were so plentiful that the men lined the decks of the vessels and gaped at them in wonder. John ordered his captains to sail down the coast, and two days later whales were sighted. Here was an opportunity to earn a fortune, and all hands went to work with a vengeance.

But John quickly discovered that sighting a whale and killing one were two very different matters. Harpoons glanced off the tough hides of the huge mammals, which showed remarkable speed and agility as they escaped. Royden decided the whales were not of the breed that carried ambergris or made oil that could be used in lamps. John refused to admit defeat for another twenty-four hours, until the elusive whales finally convinced him that he was incapable of catching them. Then, with his usual sound common sense, he decided to concentrate on fishing.

By this time the ships were standing off the coast of what would become known as Nova Scotia, and John developed a technique he utilized for the rest of his stay in the New World. Seven small boats that had been built in sections were lashed to the decks of the *Frances* and the *Queen Anne*. These craft were put together by the carpenters, and six of them were used thereafter for purposes of fishing. John, accompanied by the gentlemen-adventurers, the Indians, and three others, rowed close to the shore in the remaining boat and began to draw the first of his careful maps and charts of the entire coastline.

The fishermen enjoyed extraordinarily good luck. Their catches were so bountiful that the entire company ate heartily, and the empty barrels and kegs in the hold were filled with oil, salted cod, and dried tuna. In all, John estimated, approximately fifty thousand fish were caught from the time the ships first moved in close to the North American mainland in mid-April until they began their voyage back to England in mid-July.

John enjoyed an even more resounding success. He drew remarkably accurate maps of the coastline from Nova Scotia and New Brunswick to Rhode Island. He carefully charted the estuaries of Maine's great rivers, the Penobscot and Kennebec, and first went ashore at the site of the future city of Portsmouth, New Hampshire. There, with the aid of his two Indian passengers, he obtained several bales of fine furs from the local Indians in exchange for mirrors, beads, and other trinkets.

Thereafter, beginning on April 30th, he spent most of his time ashore. He discovered the Merrimack River in Massachusetts and traveled a short distance inland on its swift-moving waters. He spent two days with the Massachusetts Indians at the site of what would become the great city of Boston. There he obtained more furs and named the Charles River in honor of King James's surviving son, who would succeed his father as Charles I.

He put his two Indians ashore, as he had promised, near the spot he named Plymouth, and found many fish in the waters of the horn-like peninsula to the south called Cape

Cod, a region that Bartholomew Gosnold discovered in 1602. He probed the waters of Rhode Island's Narragansett Bay and finally satisfied himself that it was not the estuary of what he at first believed to be the greatest river he had yet found.

Everywhere he traded with the Indians, obtaining superb pelts and skins, and everywhere he continued to make his careful maps.

He later declared, "I carried with me six large charts of these localities, each so unlike another and most so differing from any true proportion or resemblance of the Country, that they did me no more good than so much waste paper, though they cost me more."

He spoke modestly of his own efforts, saying, "I have drawn a Map from Point to Point, Isle to Isle and Harbor to Harbor, with the soundings, sands, rocks, and landmarks as I passed close aboard the shore in a little boat, although there be many things to be observed which the haste of other affairs did cause me to omit. For being sent more to get present commodities than knowledge by discoveries for future good, I had not power to search as I would. Thus you may see, of this two thousand miles of New World coastal lands, more than half is unknown to any purpose."

In spite of his self-deprecation, which he could well afford to express in view of all he accomplished, he made the first complete map of the area. It was, like all his efforts, remarkably accurate. He also knew his voyage had been a resounding financial success: the holds and decks of his ships were almost literally overflowing with barrels of oil, kegs of salted fish, and huge bundles of the finest furs anyone had ever acquired in the New World.

His mission accomplished, John sailed for home on July 18th. After a calm, pleasant voyage, he reached England at the end of August. The entire voyage, from beginning to end, had lasted less than six months, and within twenty-four hours after his arrival in England the entire cargo had been sold. After the payment of all expenses, including the cost of purchasing the ships themselves, the investors made the astonishing profit of eight thousand pounds. They gratefully gave John fifteen hundred pounds, enough to let him live in great comfort for several years.

His success opened the eyes of noblemen and merchants interested in the New World. Precisely as he himself had preached since first going to Jamestown, there were huge profits to be drawn from New World sources other than gold, silver, and diamonds. Only now, more than seven years after the beginning of the Jamestown experiment, did it dawn on the wealthy that the natural resources of the New World available to anyone were as valuable as precious metals and gems.

John ignored the stir he had created in financial circles and retired to a farm outside Plymouth that belonged to Sir Ferdinando. There he went to work filling in the details and completing the maps he had made while in American waters. He presented the original of his master map to the new Prince of Wales, and politely asked Charles to change any of the names he had given to various places.

The young Prince made two major changes. He called Cape Cod by the name of Cape James, after his father, but men preferred John's name, and through common usage Charles's wishes were ignored. International romantic sentiment suffered a more permanent blow, however. Cape Tragabigzanda, which John had named after his Turkish mistress, was too clumsy for a Prince of Wales and his future subjects to swallow, so the Prince changed its name to Cape Ann, after his mother. As a gesture to John he did not alter the name, Smith's Isles, which the explorer had given some shoals lying off the coast of New Hampshire.

Archdeacon Hakluyt was delighted with John's map, as

were the geographers on the faculties of Oxford and Cambridge Universities. John was eager to receive academic honors, but his thirst for glory gave the dons second thoughts. His map completed, he made a triumphal return to London. There he made the rounds of his favorite taverns wearing a great cape of fox fur over his suit of light armor.

Men eager to invest in his future projects wined and dined him, made a fuss over him, and competed with each other for the honor of taking him to dinner or escorting him to the theater. Attractive young women showed a lively interest in him, too. There are hints in his correspondence with Sir Ferdinando that he enjoyed the favors of several belles, but he conducted his affairs with discretion. Frances was in London, openly enjoying his company, and he had no intention of arousing her jealous wrath again.

Starved for praise, John made such a spectacle of himself in the autumn of 1614 that the academicians canceled their tentative offers asking him to deliver lectures or meet with the faculty members of various Oxford and Cambridge colleges. John may have become a gentleman, but he wasn't conducting himself in a manner that won the approval of the conservative dons. Regardless of his accomplishments, and in spite of the fact that academicians were quick to adopt his name, New England, the universities pretended he didn't exist.

Profit-hungry nobles and merchants were less inhibited. Lord Rochester, who had just been made Earl of Somerset, went out of his way to treat John with great consideration. Men may have laughed behind the vanity-stricken explorer's back when he wore his fox cape, but at the same time they well knew those furs would bring a tidy sum if offered for sale in the open markets of London.

John was enjoying an experience new to him. Scores of potential investors begged for the opportunity to become partners in his next expedition and were so eager to enlist his services that they offered to sign him on any terms that pleased him. He found their interest flattering, but in business matters he remained completely honest and ethical. Richmond, Southampton, and Sir Ferdinando had given him their support when no one else had been willing to advance him a farthing, and he remained loyal to them. He would make voyages of discovery, exploration, and trade for no other investors, he said.

His new "friends" promptly lost interest in him, and he was able to devote himself to planning a new expedition. This venture was the most ambitious of all his projects. He intended to establish a colony in New England and support it with the profits made from fish and furs. A very few settlers would make the initial trip to the New World and would prepare the colony for those who would follow.

As John envisaged the operation, his investors would be required to spend very little money, for profits from fishing and fur trading would be pumped back into the colony from the outset. By means of judicious management, he believed, the New England settlement could become self-supporting almost immediately.

Several new investors joined the ranks of those who had supported the previous voyage to New England, among them the Dean of Exeter and others who lived in the west of England. As their number increased, so did their friction with John. His primary interest was the establishment of a colony; theirs was the profit to be earned from fishing. He adamantly —and somewhat arrogantly—insisted on making his plans in his own way.

By March, 1615, he was ready to start out on the new voyage. His supporters had bought him two ships, the larger of them a splendid vessel of two hundred tons, the smaller a somewhat battered brig of only fifty tons. The entire company numbered ninety-four persons, fifty of them sailors and fishermen. The forty-four settlers had been hand-picked by

John himself from hundreds of applicants, and he considered all of them trustworthy, earnest men.

Again he took care to insure that he received unspoiled food, properly ground gunpowder, and sharp axes. The former president of Jamestown was going to be the first governor of New England, and he wanted no slovenly inattention to detail to ruin a glowing future.

The departure from Plymouth was quiet and completely lacking in drama. John had been too busy to visit London in the weeks prior to sailing and had calmly, almost casually, written to the Duchess of Richmond that he planned to be absent from England "for a half-decade, mayhap, or a trifle longer."

Nature intervened to upset John's plans. A fierce gale howled across the Atlantic from the west and struck the two ships when they were only three hundred and fifty miles from England. The larger vessel lost her masts and began to leak so badly that half the crew were put to work pumping out water. She was jury-rigged with great difficulty, and John was forced to make a decision that broke his heart.

Aware that his splendid ship had been reduced to a near-derelict incapable of reaching the New World, he gave the order to turn back. The two ships limped into Plymouth after a voyage that had lasted only three and a half weeks. Most of the would-be colonists had been so ill at sea they changed their minds about going to America; the two-hundred-ton ship was a wreck that could not be repaired; and the investors began clamoring for a return on their money.

John was beset by calamity on every side, and struggled valiantly to salvage what he could and start again.

XIX

The Last Voyage

CAPTAIN JOHN SMITH'S DREAM of establishing a colony in New England crumbled swiftly. His flagship was a worthless hulk, his settlers decided to remain in England, and his financial supporters refused to give him any more money until their investment began to pay off. John soon realized he had to make drastic revisions in his plans. No large vessels were available to replace his two-hundred-ton flagship, and he needed time to recruit new settlers. He made up his mind to buy that time.

First he sent off his fifty-ton ship on a fishing expedition in New World waters, knowing that, if the voyage were successful, at least part of his deficit would be repaid. Then he sold the hulk and all of the equipment he had intended to use in establishing his New England colony. His muskets brought a good price, and so did the two cannon he had planned to use in his fort.

With the funds he accumulated from these sales, he bought the best ship he could find, a sixty-ton merchantman, which he stocked with the provisions he had kept for the purpose. Then, hiring twenty-three of the best seamen from the crew of his flagship, he started out for New England. His sole purpose now was to bring back a large haul of fish, and he was so anxious to hold down expenses that, for the first and only time in his career, he acted as his own ship's master.

When he was about ten days out of Plymouth, England, after sailing late in June, he was sighted by a much larger vessel, which chased him for forty-eight hours. He gave a convincing demonstration of his seamanship, but the larger vessel carried several cannon, and her gunners, obviously experts, placed two well-aimed shots across his bow. John had the good sense to realize he would be sent to the bottom if he didn't give up his escape attempt.

The privateer drew alongside, and John was dumfounded by one of those fantastic coincidences that sometimes make history stranger than fiction. The master of the pirate ship, a man named Fry, and his first mate, one Chambers, had both served with John as officers of his battalion in Transylvania. Some of the gunners had been his subordinates, too.

The upshot of the encounter was that he persuaded Fry to accompany him to New England, and the two ships sailed westward together!

Less than a week later, in mid-Atlantic, the Englishmen met four ships, the largest of them a trim sloop of about one hundred and sixty tons. John hoisted the British pennant, and Fry did the same, but the strangers, still bearing in on them, opened fire so abruptly that two of Fry's cannon were put out of action before he could reply. Only then did the strangers hoist the gold-and-white lily banners of France. Inasmuch as England and France were not at war with each other, it was obvious that the Frenchmen were also pirates.

The two English ships were virtually helpless, but John hoped to talk his way out of a difficult situation. Accordingly, he had himself rowed across the water to the French flagship, the *Sauvage*. There he was conducted to the cabin of the commodore, a man named d'Elbert, an elegant ruffian with black hair and the face of a weasel. While the two men talked, d'Elbert sent prize crews onto the two English ships and kept John a prisoner on the *Sauvage*.

Desperate but impotent, John's one desire was to win freedom for himself, his ship, and his crew so he could sail to New England for the cod, tuna, and furs he had to sell in London if he hoped to establish his colony. He tried to persuade d'Elbert to release him, but the Frenchman was enjoying success greater than he had ever known and laughed at his prisoner's vague promises of future rewards in return for immediate release.

The squadron, now comprising its own four ships and the two English vessels, moved southward into the lanes used by the Spaniards in their traffic with South America. John was forced to spend his nights in the gunroom of the *Sauvage*, but had to be allowed on deck during the daytime because ammunition was stored in his prison.

Still hoping to win the confidence of d'Elbert, he helped devise tactics that enabled the Frenchman to capture three Spanish ships in the next two weeks. The net result of his effort was that he convinced d'Elbert he knew a great deal about battle tactics at sea. Nevertheless, his often repeated requests to be allowed to return to his own ship were refused.

The French crews were spread over a squadron now numbering nine ships, and one night the English seamen on John's and Fry's vessels overwhelmed their captors and managed to sail off in the dark. Their absence was not discovered until the following morning. Both ships, it might be noted, successfully made their way to England, where a full report of their capture and escape was made to a Royal Admiralty commission. John Smith was presumed dead, and his loss was mourned by his friends.

But John still had the luck of a cat with nine lives. The French privateers roamed the Atlantic, at one point capturing and sinking a Scottish ship bound for Bristol and carrying a load of sugar from the West Indies.

A courageous Portuguese sloop-of-war put up a brief, hard fight and was taken as a prize. In this encounter d'Elbert, the only Frenchman hurt, was mortally wounded. His place as commodore was taken by the master of the *Sauvage,* a tow-headed giant named Poyrune. Captain Poyrune was ruthless, where d'Elbert had been crafty, and so greedy that he transferred large quantities of nonperishable loot from other vessels to his own.

As a result, the other ships deserted him, one by one. He still continued to raid, burn, and sink wherever he found merchantmen on the high seas. John's lot improved somewhat after Poyrune took command. The Frenchman was reluctant to release someone who had learned so much about his operations, but saw nothing to be gained by keeping his prisoner under guard. Therefore John was allowed to move his mattress to the "great cabin" of the *Sauvage.* When the ship was not actually attacking a helpless merchantman, he was allowed to wander where he pleased.

From August until October, 1615, John remained on the privateer, cruising the Atlantic as the involuntary guest of the pirates. He was restless, bored, and dispirited. Finally, for want of something better to do, he started to work on a new book. *A Description of New England* was the result of these labors, and in it John wrote in detail about his voyage of the previous year. The book enjoyed an enormous sale in England and aroused so much interest in other European countries that it was translated into Dutch, French, and German. Perhaps its most remarkable feature is its smooth, calm, narrative flow, which in no way reflected the emotional turmoil John was suffering.

The crew of the *Sauvage,* some of whom were manning newly captured prize ships, had been at sea for a long time, and Poyrune had an increasingly difficult time keeping his men under control. By late October they became so unruly he was forced to sail for France.

His situation was difficult, as was that of his men. As for John Smith, he knew he would be treated as a pirate by the French authorities if captured in their company. Ever since the days of Drake and Hawkins, whose banditry on the high seas had greatly enriched the treasury of Queen Elizabeth, the British Admiralty courts had been lenient in their treatment of sea robbers, provided they hadn't molested fellow Englishmen. The attitude of the French government was infinitely more severe. A pirate was considered a pirate, regardless of his nationality, and was hanged if caught.

Therefore Poyrune had to make his plans with great care. He finally decided to sail to the seaport fortress town of La Rochelle, about one hundred miles southeast of Nantes. Sailors from La Rochelle were active in Newfoundland fishing and, if necessary, Poyrune hoped to pass off his ships as fishing vessels newly returned from the New World. However, he had reason to hope it wouldn't be necessary to rely on the thin disguise. Two bleak islands, Oléron and Ré, stand at the entrance to La Rochelle's bay, and the latter had become the headquarters of go-betweens who bought merchandise from privateers, asking no embarrassing questions. Poyrune was carrying loot valued at more than one hundred thousand pounds, and he intended to sell his booty to the smugglers of the Île de Ré.

The pirate ships reached France safely, but a howling November gale forced Poyrune to seek shelter in a cove at one end of the Île de Ré, about fifteen miles from the larger harbor used by the smugglers. There he intended to ride out the storm.

John had become so desperate that he was willing to take any risk in order to dissociate himself from the pirates. While everyone else aboard the *Sauvage* went below for the night, he stuffed the almost completed manuscript of *A Description of New England* under his shirt and went up onto the rain-drenched deck. With the greatest of difficulty, he managed to lower himself into the water in the ship's smallest boat and cut himself adrift with the small knife that was the only weapon his captors had allowed him to keep. Then, buffeted by the wind, he started to row toward La Rochelle.

A vicious crosscurrent threatened to carry the boat out into the open Atlantic, and only a sharp change in the wind saved John's life. He rowed until his arms ached, pausing when necessary to bail out the boat. Although he saw lights burning dimly in the three great fortress towers that guarded the port, they remained remote and seemingly unattainable.

John's nightmare lasted the better part of the night, and he was fortunate that the incoming tide swept him into the harbor. Half-drowned and so tired that he could scarcely force himself to row the boat, he was seen soon after dawn by a sentry stationed in the Tower of St. Nicholas, and a party of customs officers came out to meet him in a longboat.

An hour later, as he revived in the great hall of the tower, eating a breakfast of beef, cheese, and wine, he told the Lord Lieutenant of the port his story, relying on his escape from the *Sauvage* as proof that he was not one of the pirates. An alarm was sounded, and every available ship in the harbor was sent to capture the privateers and their loot.

The storm had been expensive. Two of Poyrune's ships had sunk during the night, and the other two had been badly battered. The pirates on the vessels still afloat fled in boats when they saw the government ships approaching, and suffered still higher casualties. Some were shot, and others, Poyrune himself among them, were drowned when one of the boats capsized.

About forty thousand pounds' worth of booty was recovered, and John became the hero of the hour in La Rochelle, at that time a community of about fifteen thousand people. The Lord Lieutenant of the port officially requested him to remain in the city to appear before an Admiralty court, so he was forced to stay, although his personal situation was embarrassing.

He had no clothes except the boots, cloak, shirt, and breeches he was wearing when he had escaped from the *Sauvage,* but even these garments had been ruined by salt water. And he carried not one penny in his purse.

The citizens of La Rochelle offered him the hospitality of their homes, and it is unlikely that he needed much persuasion to accept the kindness of Madame Adrienne Chanoyes, a widow who lived in a snug Gothic house that faced the harbor. Adrienne was a handsome woman in her early thirties, with the fair, freckled skin and green eyes so common in that part of France. She was, of course, a blonde.

John spent five weeks under the Chanoyes roof as Adrienne's houseguest. Though he was too much of a gentleman to hint, when writing of his adventures, that he had enjoyed an affair with her, their intimacy was common knowledge. In fact, the English Commercial Agent at Bordeaux, an official holding a post similar to that of a consul-general in later times, paid a visit to John at Adrienne's house. In his report to London, Commercial Agent Charles Bridges flatly stated that Adrienne and John were lovers.

Like so many of John's mistresses, Adrienne was good to him. The clothes of her late husband, a sea captain, fitted him reasonably well, and she went each day to the market herself in order to buy the most tender cuts of beef, the most appetizing vegetables, and the most appealingly plump fowl for the visitor who had been literally washed up on her doorstep.

As John later admitted, it was Adrienne, thoroughly familiar with the Admiralty laws of her country, who advised John that he had a right to share in the booty from the pirate ships seized by the French Crown. At her instigation, he entered a claim for "a fair portion" of the prize money.

The hearing was held in late December. Commercial Agent Bridges was there to observe the proceedings, insure that justice was administered to a British subject, and make a full report in writing to the Privy Council in London. The hearing lasted only two days, and John received his just share. Pirates who had been captured and were on their way to the gallows corroborated his story of his capture and involuntary presence on board the *Sauvage*.

The court absolved him, cleared his good name, and extended to him the thanks of the French government for his vital role in the recovery of stolen property. He was also awarded the staggering sum of three thousand, six hundred gold crowns, the equivalent of more than two thousand English pounds.

John immediately celebrated by traveling to Paris with Adrienne, and he remained there with her for several days. He bought himself a handsome wardrobe, including a helmet and corselet of steel and silver, that cost him more than two hundred pounds. Then, after reserving another hundred pounds for purposes of travel, he made the courtliest of all possible gestures to Adrienne by presenting her with the rest of the prize money, a princely gift. In return she gave him a portrait in miniature of herself, which eventually was owned by one of his great-great-grandnephews.

Suitably clad and with a comfortable sum of money clinking in his new purse, John left Paris alone for the last stage of his return journey to England. He traveled to Cherbourg, a sleepy, medieval port town that had become something of an Anglo-French trade center and was used by merchants of both nations in traffic with the cities of western England. After a wait of several days, he was finally able to engage passage on a merchantman bound for Bristol and paid its master to drop him off at Plymouth, which he still considered the headquarters of his operations.

The midwinter weather was blustery, the Channel was rough, and the voyage from Cherbourg to Plymouth lasted the better part of a week. John was anxious to reach England, and the most he could say for the trip was that, after having spent so long a time at sea, he was one of a very few persons on board the small, cramped ship who did not become sick.

When he was rowed ashore at Plymouth on January 12, 1616, after spending his thirty-seventh birthday on board the merchantman, he had no way of knowing that his life of adventure had come to an end and that he would spend the rest of his days in England. Living in an age when the rudiments of sanitation were unknown and superstitious practices were still common in the medical profession, he was already far advanced into middle age.

He did not think of himself as old, however, and his one desire was to organize a new colonizing expedition to New England. The misfortunes that had plagued his last venture were ordinary hazards of the trade, in his opinion, and he shrugged them off. The New World had become his home, and he was eager to establish a new settlement there as soon as he could raise the necessary funds and organize a company.

To his astonishment, he found that his investors' enthusiasm had cooled. His first surprise was the calm that greeted him. Word of his landing at La Rochelle had preceded him to England, and everyone who knew him had recovered from the initial sense of amazement that he had returned from the dead.

In fact, Sir Ferdinando Gorges, or George, received him so casually that he felt hurt.

Sir Ferdinando had an abiding faith in the future of British colonization in the New World, but his confidence in John Smith had become somewhat shaky. He had lost a large sum on John's unfortunate expedition of 1615 and was no longer willing to give him unqualified support.

The Duke of Richmond, thanks to the intervention of his Duchess, refused to give John a ha'penny for a new expedition. Unfortunately for John, the Richmonds had friends in the highest places, and someone on the Privy Council had told them of the wanderer's pleasant interlude in La Rochelle with Mme. Chanoyes. Frances was angry and obtained her revenge by closing her husband's purse.

Temporarily blocked, John returned to London and immediately went to work putting the finishing touches on *A Description of New England*. If the many men who had been clamoring for the chance to offer him financial support had chilled, he intended to reawaken their enthusiasm with his new book. Hall, who was still making money from John's first effort, agreed to publish *A Description of New England,* which was registered at Stationers' Hall on June 3rd. The printing was completed two weeks later and the book created an immediate stir. Nevertheless, the nobles and wealthy merchants were slow to open their wallets to someone who had suffered a miserable failure.

It was during this critical period that Pocahontas and her husband, John Rolfe, were enjoying their unprecedented social triumph in London. Lord De La Warr had returned to England from Virginia, and the young couple were his guests during their stay in the city. Lady De La Warr escorted the Indian girl everywhere; Queen Anne was enchanted; and even King James unbent. After he granted the royal savage a private audience that lasted for the better part of an afternoon, every door in London was flung open for the charming Mistress Rolfe.

At this particular time, however, John Smith was regarded with contempt by every hostess in London. He had chosen to complicate his life immeasurably, when Frances refused to see him, by plunging into an affair with one of the most notorious young women in the country, a girl whom women of standing could not tolerate, no matter what their own sexual escapades.

Barbara Courtenay was blonde and buxom, painted her eyelids to emphasize her violet eyes, and wore the lowest-cut gowns in London to call attention to other features men found agreeable. At one time she had been the mistress of the late Prince Henry. Since his death, she had been free with her favors elsewhere. Inasmuch as she had no visible means of support, her lovers arranged to meet her privately, and under no circumstances were seen with her in public. Barbara had not sunk to the level of the professional strumpets who paraded the streets, but she was not considered the social equal of the ladies whose financial security enabled them to accept no money from their lovers.

Disturbed because he was finding it difficult to obtain support for his new expedition and, perhaps, annoyed because Frances would have nothing more to do with him, John had elected to defy convention by living openly with the notorious Barbara in his Strand lodgings. Unfortunately, he was neither powerful enough nor wealthy enough to thumb his nose at the aristocracy, and even the lords who had known Barbara intimately in the past were inclined to give him a wide berth. Their outraged wives found it convenient to pretend John no longer existed.

The net result of his gesture was that he compounded his already difficult problems. It must have been a blow to his pride as well as his hopes for his New England colony when the Earl and Countess of Southampton, paying a visit to London, refused to receive him at their house. His middle-aged fling was proving far more expensive than he had realized, and he grew desperate.

Others were talking of settling in New England, and a representative of a religious sect known as the Separatists, whom King James had sent into exile, had sent a representative to London to explore the possibility that these English men and women might find a permanent home for themselves on English soil in the New World.

It began to appear as if John might be left behind in the race, and so he redoubled his frenzied efforts to find financial support.

XX

Admiral of New England

JOHN SMITH'S LODGINGS ON THE Strand consisted of a parlor, a bedchamber, a dressing room, and a study, in which he worked. The study was the only place he could call his own. Nowhere else could he find privacy. Barbara Courtenay appropriated the rest of the apartment, but was not satisfied with the situation, either. Even though she was squeezing him out of house and home, and he found her gowns, shifts, and shoes everywhere, she complained incessantly because he had forbidden her to set foot in his study.

Her letters to her sister, Lady Endicott, are filled with self-pity. In one she writes, "How I wish I were with you in Sussex. I long ago learned that all men are filled only with their own wants, but Captain Smith is worse than most. Some five or more of my clothing boxes have not been opened since I came to this house, but he will not grant me leave to put my few miserable gowns in his working-room, which is empty save for some scimitars and shields, some Indian trinkets and the pages of books he is writing spilled onto the floor. I would never marry so selfish a man."

Perhaps the real reason Barbara didn't marry John was his failure to propose to her. "If I leave him today," she says in another indignant letter to her sister, "he will scarce know I have gone."

Obviously she was only a stopgap mistress, a woman who filled his sexual needs, but offered him no companionship. It is also plain that John had far more important matters on his mind. Perceiving the great success of Pocahontas, he decided to cash in on it for his own purposes. It was at this critical period in his life that he wrote the footnotes regarding his alleged experience with her for *A True Relation.* Hall was willing to bring out such a printing, and the book was published in haste.

John also began to show the good sense to appear in public on occasion without the buxom Barbara. This fact, combined with the interest that *A Description of New England* aroused everywhere, may have been responsible for a partial social thaw that set in. The blue-bloods held no grudge against him, and as long as he didn't make them uncomfortable and upset their wives' sense of propriety by appearing with Barbara on his arm, no one had any real reason to snub him.

The Earl and Countess of Southampton relented. So did the Earl of Somerset, whose vast palace was directly across the Strand from John's lodgings. In fact, Somerset was no longer as intimate with the King as he had been, and he may have felt a twinge of sympathy for a fellow social exile. John is known to have dined at his palace—without Barbara—on several occasions in 1616.

At some time during the year, John and Pocahontas are believed to have met face to face on one occasion. The Duchess of Richmond, who was not present, says the meeting took place at Somerset's palace. According to a tradition that has refused to die, the daughter of Powhatan and the man who established English relations with the sachem saw each other at the town house of Lord and Lady De La Warr. Apparently Barbara Courtenay was not present.

Everyone who has written about the meeting agrees on one point: Pocahontas did not know John when he was presented to her. Perhaps he had changed over the years, and in justice it must be admitted that she did not look like a wilderness savage. Her hair was piled high on her head in the latest style, the necklace of amethysts that Queen Anne had given her probably sparkled at her throat, and her slender body was undoubtedly encased in one of the many silk gowns that now made up her wardrobe.

Strangely, no portrait of Pocahontas survived her own time —if such a portrait was actually painted. She died in childbirth shortly before she and Rolfe were scheduled to depart for Virginia. Her widower returned to the colony with their child after burying her in a churchyard at Gravesend. In death, as in life, she remained a shadowy figure, which may be a factor in the perpetuation of the legend about her.

The only known portrait of Pocahontas appears in John's own book, *The Generall Historie of Virginia, New England, and the Summer Isles,* which was published in 1624. Inasmuch as the original painting from which the engraving was supposedly taken was never found, later generations were inclined to doubt that any such portrait had ever existed.

It was in that book, too, that John retold the story of his own experience with Pocahontas, including it in his main text and enlarging it. There, too, he describes his meeting with her in London. After admitting that she did not know him when he first came up to her, he goes on to say that she recognized him a moment later and was delighted to renew their friendship.

No other source indicates any such moment of recognition.

Regardless of the authenticity of the Pocahontas story, the new edition of *A True Relation* also helped to increase interest in the New World. Gradually the climate changed in John's favor. In the autumn of 1616, he terminated his affair with Barbara Courtenay and went to visit Sir Ferdinando in Plymouth. This time his quest for financial support was successful. Sir Ferdinando, who was more interested in exploration and colonization than in moneymaking, made a contribution of about two thousand pounds.

That broke the ice. The Earl of Southampton invested a larger sum, and other wealthy men in Plymouth, Bristol, and Exeter, who had read *A Description of New England* with avid interest, followed suit. John worked frantically outfitting a new expedition, bought three ships, and hired his crews.

But he ran into two difficulties. His description of the obstacles to be overcome in the American wilderness had been too realistically accurate, and prospective colonists were slow in agreeing to risk their lives in the New World. John was not interested in the aggressive adventurers willing to take chances if they could become wealthy overnight. On the other hand, the better type of citizen remained wary.

John's second problem was an outgrowth of the first. Winter came to England early in December, 1616, and it was the most severe weather the country had suffered in years. Fierce gales kept shipping port-bound. Men who had agreed to settle in New England looked at the ice and snow on the decks of the three ships and changed their minds.

Rather than force his investors to wait too long for a return on their money, John decided to send all three vessels to the Newfoundland fishing banks as soon as the weather improved in early spring. He was becoming more cunning and was playing a long-range game now, hoping that profits would whet the investors' appetites for still bigger ventures. And the respite would give him the opportunity to scour the country more thoroughly for the type of emigrant he was seeking.

Therefore the ships sailed without him in March, 1617. He

himself set out on a tour of those communities in the west of England whose nobles and merchants qualified, under the terms of the King's charter, for the right to invest in a New England settlement. Displaying the same restless energy that had driven him all his life, he traveled as far north as Shrewsbury. He went to Worcester and Hereford, Gloucester and Cheltenham, and he spent six weeks in Bristol, where he was the guest of Sir Edward Eames, a baronet who had become one of his most enthusiastic advocates.

The three ships returned from their fishing trip with a rich haul, arriving in Plymouth late in August, 1617. John was able to pay each of his supporters two pounds, five shillings for each pound invested, and his prospects improved considerably. Sir Ferdinando called a meeting of interested parties in Plymouth, and the men of substance assembled there in late September.

John addressed the gathering at length in the Citadel, a stone fort that had been built by Henry VIII at the head of one of the port's inlets. The meeting was strictly unofficial, but Sir Ferdinando, as Governor of Plymouth, had the right to use it as he pleased. And John was at his persuasive best as he stood in the great hall of the gloomy fort, lecturing and cajoling, exhorting and inspiring the wealthiest men of western England.

He used his atmosphere to its best advantage, reminding his audience that Sir John Hawkins had used this building as his headquarters when he was Admiral of the Fort, and that Sir Francis Drake had slept in this very room before setting out, in 1577, on his voyage around the world. Sir Humphrey Gilbert had spent several days there, too, before leaving on his second voyage of discovery to the New World. Now the nobles and merchants had their opportunity to win immortality, to have their names linked for all time with those of England's greatest sailors.

The effects of John's spellbinding oratory were electrifying.

Vast amounts of money were pledged, on the spot. Even John was dazed when he added the sums and discovered there would be enough to send a fleet of twenty ships, carrying one thousand settlers, to the New World.

He so impressed his audience that he was given a grand new title, issued under the royal patent for New England. Sir Ferdinando solemnly presented him with an inscribed, sealed parchment testifying that he was now Admiral of New England and would hold his rank for the rest of his life.

Why John continued to call himself Captain Smith rather than Admiral Smith is an unsolved mystery. Perhaps, in time, he became disgusted when the investors started to quibble and quarrel among themselves and the great plan collapsed. As he later wrote, "Nothing but a voluntary fishing expedition was effected, for all this air."

He began to suspect that all was not well before the wealthy gentlemen began to depart for their homes. It was his fond hope that the expedition could set out in 1618. His new scheme was both complicated and ambitious. He planned to go to New England himself with a small company of hard-working men who could build a fort and a town, clear fields, and plant grain. Then, eight or ten months later, the other immigrants would begin to arrive, and the colony would be prepared for them. His supporters paid lip service to his ideas before going off to their own homes, but few of them produced the hard cash he needed.

As a result, after spending a whole year on the project, John realized he needed someone of greater stature than Sir Ferdinando or Southampton to act as the head of the company's directorate. Telling no one his thoughts, for fear of offending his principal supporters, he returned to London for a survey of the political climate. Using his lodgings on the Strand as his base, he made frequent trips to the taverns frequented by the mighty, where he listened to the gossip.

Charles, the Prince of Wales, was still a boy and had no

power. The most influential man in the country was George Villiers, a dashing, energetic young man in his mid-twenties who was the recipient of every honor the King could heap on him. Already Earl of Buckingham, he was made a Marquess on New Year's Day, 1618, and five years later would be made Duke. Already one of the wealthiest nobles in the realm, he supervised the education of Prince Charles, had been given a sweeping mandate to reorganize the Army, and had taken command of the Navy.

John first thought of applying direct to Buckingham for aid, but soon realized he would be wasting his time. The great lord had his own court, and applicants for favors inundated him with their requests. Equally important, Buckingham showed no interest in the New World, but was preoccupied with the balance of power in Europe. In effect, he had already become Great Britain's foreign secretary, and was busy playing off the nations of the Continent against each other.

John knew he had to look elsewhere. His obvious target was Buckingham's tutor, Francis Bacon, who was almost universally regarded as the greatest scholar of the age. Richard Hakluyt had died in 1616; only Bacon had his zeal for scientific research—and the power to authorize the expenditure of royal funds on scientific projects. Bacon, now in his late fifties, was a genius of many talents, a philosopher and dramatist, an attorney and essayist, a statesman, and a scientist with an unquenchable thirst for knowledge.

His own star had risen swiftly in recent years. In 1613 King James had made him Attorney General. Early in 1617, helped by Buckingham, he became Lord Keeper of the Great Seal. That title meant little, but it was a step toward his next promotion, and in January, 1618, he became Lord Chancellor and a member of the Privy Council. It was common knowledge that he would soon be given a place in the peerage. In fact, a few months later James made him Baron Verulam.

Bacon, then, seemed the obvious man to whom John felt he should apply for patronage. Perhaps the greatest of the obstacles in his path was the unfortunate fact that he had never met the brilliant Lord Chancellor. Another, almost as great, was that he needed some sort of intellectual prod to titillate Bacon's interest in the New World.

After considerable thought, John sat down to write a new book for a readership of one. He closeted himself in his workroom, had his meals brought in to him and, writing with concentrated fury, turned out the manuscript of *New England's Trials* in about three months. The sole purpose—and the theme—of the book was to demonstrate the enormous potential of establishing one or more colonies in that part of the New World.

The book completed, John arranged with George Hall to print it for him. The expense was so great that he decided, after conferring with Hall, to order an edition of two thousand copies. If they sold, the proceeds would pay for his expenses.

He sent a copy of the book to Bacon, enclosing a long letter that he found even more difficult to prepare. He was forced to humble his pride in order to plead for favors and was blunt enough to admit the truth in so many words. Having decided that candor was the best approach, he held back nothing. The French, the Dutch, and the Spaniards were so active in American colonization, he declared, that he felt certain they would show an interest in his plan if he went to them. But he refused to seek help abroad. Instead, he wrote, "nature doth bind me to beg at home."

He carefully listed his own qualifications for leading an expedition to New England, and cited his nineteen years of experience in hazardous pursuits. He was careful, too, to say that he was anxious to serve Bacon at home, in England, in any capacity desired.

John's actual request seemed modest, on the surface. He

asked Bacon to provide him with a small warship from the Royal Navy, which could be loaned him on some form of detached service. Of course, the Admiralty undoubtedly would want it manned by Royal Navy personnel. It would be helpful, too, if expert soldiers, men of stable character, accompanied his advance party that would build a town for the settlers who would follow.

Bacon must have seen through the scheme at once. A Navy ship manned by seamen in Crown service and a colony staffed with Army troops would openly commit King James himself to the project. The dignity of the Crown would be at stake, and neither James nor his Privy Council could allow such a colony to fail. John asked for the relatively modest sum of five thousand pounds, carefully emphasizing that more than one hundred thousand pounds had already been spent in Virginia without much effect. But it was obvious to the new Lord Chancellor that, once committed, the Crown would be forced to dip repeatedly into the Treasury in order to insure the success of the New England settlement that John envisaged.

Unfortuntely for John Smith, the Crown, and posterity, Francis Bacon was too busy and had assumed too many new responsibilities to add a new, hazardous undertaking to his many burdens. He sent a brief, courteous reply to the explorer-colonizer, saying he was not in a position to act on the requests.

John took his bitter disappointment in stride. He had dedicated the presentation capy of *New England's Trials* to Bacon, but having failed to obtain the patronage of a single powerful sponsor, he decided to try the broadside approach to fund-raising.

The fishing industry had benefited greatly from the expeditions to Newfoundland, so he ordered some new flyleafs printed and dedicated other copies of the book to "the right worshipful, the Master, the Wardens and the Company of the

Fish-mongers." Other copies were dedicated to gentlemen in Devonshire and Cornwall, the aldermen of Barnstaple, and the Lord Mayor of Exeter. He labored furiously and zealously, and never had he been so active. He had copies of his maps of New England printed by the hundreds and gave them away to anyone who might be a potential investor in his enterprise. But the harder he pressed, the less he accomplished.

It was his misfortune that England was plunged into a financial recession in 1618, and even the Crown was forced to curtail its expenses. The staff of gentlemen-in-waiting at the court was cut, and James asked the Privy Council to plan a new system of taxation in order to increase revenues. Moneylenders charged higher interest rates, and in small country towns citizens quietly hoarded gold coins. Not even the very wealthy felt they could afford to risk an investment in a potential New England colony.

Ironically, the group most interested in the idea was a band of near-paupers, the exiled Separatists who were living in Leyden and Amsterdam. They had been fascinated by *A Description of New England,* and members of their sect, living underground in England, had obtained and sent them two copies of John's new book. A study of *New England's Trials* convinced them they should cross the Atlantic and establish a colony of their own in that part of the New World.

William Brewster, one of the leaders of the sect and its chief propagandist, who spent most of his time writing tracts that the British Crown considered seditious, decided to pay a personal visit to England in order to pursue the matter.

This journey was typical of the courage of the man later known as Elder Brewster, the religious leader of the Pilgrim colony. Robust and hearty, with a strong, lined face, he was middle-aged, and like John Smith, refused to shrink from danger. He knew that if the Crown learned he was in England, every bailiff in the country would search for him. If they caught him he would be tried, found guilty of treason, and hanged.

Therefore every precaution was taken by his friends in England to conceal his identity while he was in the country. He lived under an assumed name, rarely spent more than a few nights under the same roof, and saw only those people whose discretion could be trusted. The thick blanket of secrecy surrounding his visit deprived later generations of an accurate account of his dealings with John Smith.

The known facts are few. At some time in 1618 a member of the Separatist sect communicated with John and, presumably, obtained from him a solemn pledge that he would not give Brewster away to the authorities. Thereafter these two stubborn, strong-minded men met on a number of occasions.

Their aims as well as their personalities clashed. John wanted to establish a royal colony that would grow each year in size and influence, a province that could become self-supporting through sending the much-needed products of the New World to England. Brewster, on the other hand, sought only a safe asylum for the Separatists, a refuge where the band of Pilgrims could worship as they pleased.

The Separatists acknowledged their debt to John, but refused to become citizens of a community in which they would be deprived of their religious freedom. They insisted on setting up their own colony and planned to elect a governor and council from their own number.

They respected John, however, and wanted to take advantage of his experience in the New World. He understood the savages, and had learned how to deal with them. Above all, he had succeeded in putting Jamestown on its feet. They, of all Englishmen, appreciated to the full what he had achieved in America.

So Brewster offered him the position of military leader of the Separatist colony. Everyone in the band would be responsible to him for the defense of their colony, but he, in turn, would have to report to their governor and council.

John was tempted by the idea, even though he found the terms repugnant. So great was the lure of the New World wilderness that he contemplated giving up his own ambitious plans in order to accompany the small, poverty-stricken company to New England. He and Brewster continued their sporadic negotiations until some time in 1619, with each presenting terms and rejecting counter-demands.

The Separatists' ultimate refusal to consider any basis for an agreement other than their own finally caused John to break off the negotiations. As a man of honor, however, he kept his word and did not turn Brewster over to the Crown bailiffs.

This conflict of wills prevented John from becoming a member of the first permanent colony in New England. The Separatists hired a former Army officer, Captain Miles Standish, as their military leader. After overcoming tremendous obstacles, they crossed the Atlantic in 1620 to the place John had named New Plymouth.

In the years that followed, John nursed a continuing grievance against the Separatists. They had taken advantage of his knowledge and experience, while rejecting him as their leader. On more than one occasion he ridiculed their frugality, castigated their "singularity," and spoke with lofty disdain of their "contempt of authority."

Even while dealing with Brewster, he continued his other efforts to raise funds for his own enterprise, but as he writes some years later, "all availed no more than to hew rocks with oyster shells."

New England was his great love. He showed no desire to return to Virginia, where the establishment of tobacco plantations was at last bringing the investors a respectable return on their money. A man obsessed, he wrote and traveled, talked incessantly, and badgered virtually every man of stature and wealth in England.

Little is known of his personal life from 1618 to 1622. The Admiral of New England had neither ships nor sailors. The self-elected governor of a royal colony had no citizens to rule, no New World towns, no provisions or armaments. He continued to make his headquarters in the apartment on the Strand, but appears to have had few friends and, perhaps, no mistresses. His single-minded devotion to his cause left him with little time or energy for social life.

In 1621, as an aid to his efforts, he brought out another small edition of *New England's Trials*. He was spending his own money freely as he tried to raise funds, and his purse felt the pinch. Accordingly, in 1622 he published a public edition of the book, and its sale enabled him to live in the comfortable style to which he had become accustomed.

It was during the latter part of this period that he finally abandoned the dream of leading an expedition to New England in person. He was now forty-two years old, and for the first time in his life he was plagued by physical ailments. The dampness of England caused him to suffer from aches in his bones, and he developed an uncomfortable, dry cough that persisted to the end of his days. There was no single incident that caused him to give up his obsession. The process of erosion had been as slow as it had been painful.

Gradually he had been compelled to recognize facts. In spite of his own enthusiasm for colonization, others were not yet ready to invest large sums of money in his project or in any other. Virginia had been a constant headache to the men who had poured money into it, and even though they were now earning a steady but modest profit, they had lost their eagerness to set up English outposts in the New World.

Other nations, meanwhile, recognized the benefits of colonization. The Dutch, the French, and the Spaniards were engaged in a feverish race, but the British were awakening at a snail's pace to an expansionist policy. This lethargy was galling to a pioneer who had spent more than fifteen years trying to arouse his fellow countrymen.

But John was not ready to give up the struggle. Even though he was beginning to accept the fact that his own days of great adventure were ended, he believed it his solemn duty to continue ringing the alarm bells. His motives were not completely unselfish, of course. His vanity was unappeased and unappeasable, and he wanted the recognition from Englishmen that he was being accorded in France, Holland, and the German states.

It angered him that his friend Henry Hudson, who had been left by a mutinous crew to die of cold and starvation on the shores of the great bay that now bore his name, had been unknown and unsung during his lifetime. Only now, after his untimely death, was he being hailed as a great patriot and hero.

John Smith was determined not to meet the same fate. But he was caught in a cruel trap from which there seemed to be no escape. Forces beyond his control had prevented his returning to New England and setting up the colony that, he knew, would flourish and win enduring fame for its leaders. In time to come, new accomplishments would dwarf his own efforts, and he would be forgotten. The New World had been his principal concern for the better part of his adult life, yet no one thought of him as a Hawkins, a Drake, or a Raleigh—or even a Henry Hudson. Aware that his strength was ebbing, he searched for a means to achieve a double purpose—aid the cause of colonization and win for himself a permanent niche in English history.

XXI

The Author

In the winter of 1621–22, John Smith stopped seeking unattainable goals, and his life became quiet, orderly, and realistically purposeful. It could not have been accidental that during this period he and the Duchess of Richmond became reconciled. Frances, like John, was older, wiser, and tired of the eternal chase. She was bored by her brief, meaningless affairs, and the chronic illness of her husband, who would receive his duchy in the English peerage in 1623 and die a year later, saddened her.

She and John were ripe for the resumption of a relationship that was more than sexual. Neither had known many real friends of the opposite sex, and when they started seeing each other again, both were pleased to discover that their friendship had survived their separation. Frances Stuart was neither a virtuous woman nor an intellectual, and her enemies were right when they called her a flighty hedonist. She was, nevertheless, a good influence on John.

He was able to confide in her and, for all his cunning, she

had a common-sense approach to life that he lacked. It was only after they started seeing each other again that he finally decided to give up his dream of establishing a settlement in the New World.

Instead, and perhaps influenced by Frances, he decided to devote his full time to a new project. In the spring of 1621 he had conceived the idea of writing a general history of the New World to date. He had sought the support of various noble patrons for what he had envisaged as another vigorous propaganda tract that might win him nationwide support for the colony he wanted to build. Now he enlarged his horizons and decided to write an exhaustive book. It would be the masterwork on the subject of British colonization in the New World.

Patiently encouraged by Frances, he spent more than three years working on what he finally called *The Generall Historie of Virginia, New England and the Summer Isles*. He spent months on research before committing a word to paper, and worked more carefully than ever before. If he could not live in the memories of other men as a great colonizer, he intended to win recognition as a great historian. In the process, he would make certain that his own achievements were not slighted.

Most of the book was written at his Strand lodgings, but during the final weeks of Ludovic Stuart's illness he moved into Richmond Palace in order to offer what comfort he could to the dying man and Frances. It was at this time, if not earlier, that his friendship with the Duchess became platonic. She was horrified some months later when she learned that some members of the nobility had placed a false but obvious misinterpretation on John's move into the palace. She immediately lashed out at her critics in indignation so fierce that it probably could not have been feigned.

The book was completed early in the summer of 1624 and was registered for publication on July 12th of that year.

George Hall had died, and it was printed by his sons, who had inherited his business. Through coincidence, the book was published only a few days after the London Virginia Company suffered a complete financial collapse, due in large part to the continuing insistence of its shortsighted directors that there were precious metals and diamonds in the colony, and that the settlers should devote all their time to seeking these riches. Ironically, the scandal of the Company's failure enhanced public interest in John's book and virtually guaranteed it a large sale.

John had redrawn and refined his maps of Virginia, Chesapeake Bay, and New England, and he included one, based on the originals of other men, of Bermuda, then known as the Summer Isles. It also contained the engraving made by Simon van der Paas that was drawn from John's pen-and-ink self-sketch.

The first edition was dedicated to Frances, Duchess of Richmond. This public acknowledgment of their friendship was a sure sign they were no longer sleeping together. A gentleman—and John certainly liked to think of himself as one—did not dedicate books to a current mistress.

The Generall Historie consisted of six volumes, much of it material John had previously published. Volume One was a history of the attempts to colonize Virginia prior to 1605. John courageously paid handsome tribute to Sir Walter Raleigh, whose final expedition into the Caribbean in 1617 had been a miserable failure, and who had been executed the following year on Crown orders. Only a very brave man dared, even indirectly, to reproach James I.

Volume II and Volume III were revised accounts of John's previously published work on the establishment of Jamestown. In them he gave a prominent place to Pocahontas, expanded the story of his encounter with her, and sprinkled the account of his journeys into the interior of Virginia with frequent reference to her. The Pocahontas–John Smith legend is based in its entirety on what John himself writes in these pages.

Volume Four was a history of Virginia from the time of John's own departure to the early months of 1624. Pulling no punches, he blamed the greedy investors for most of the colony's problems, but remained enthusiastic about the country's future.

Volume Five was the story of the discovery, settlement, and development of the Bermudas. The first to find the islands had been Juan Bermudez, a Spaniard, who had been sailing to Cuba with a cargo of hogs early in the sixteenth century. Some of the animals had escaped, and consequently vast numbers of wild hogs roamed Great Bermuda, or Main Island, which solved the basic food problem. In 1609 Sir George Somers had been shipwrecked there while voyaging to Jamestown, and the British subsequently called the islands by his name, but public usage corrupted the name to the Summer Islands.

The Virginia Company had taken possession of the Bermudas in 1612, and a small colony had been established there in the same year under the vigorous leadership of Henry More. John's history was inaccurate, through no fault of his own; he had been forced to rely on the Virginia Company for his material and had been given misleading information which he had accepted in good faith.

Volume Six, John's history of New England, was in part a revised version of *A Description of New England* and *New England's Trials,* and in part a collection of recent essays written by others who had visited the New World. This volume was openly propagandistic in tone and approach. John could not find enough superlatives to describe the future in store for this land, and he repeatedly urged Britons of every class to migrate there.

Although John's modesty in describing his own exploits is feigned, *The Generall Historie* must be regarded as his best book. It is a long labor of love, dignified in the main, and enlivened with charm and wit. Above all, it is an enthusiastic tribute to the New World of Captain John Smith, and it survives as a monument to the man himself.

John paid for the publication out of his own pocket, and the exceptionally large first printing of seven thousand copies strained his resources. Like everything else he had written, the book was an immediate success. All copies were sold within two years, and a second large printing was published in 1626. It sold even more rapidly, and a third appeared in the next year. The book remained popular for a long time. Two more editions were printed after John's death, one in 1632 and another in 1635.

Eventually *The Generall Historie* showed a substantial profit, but the principal beneficiaries were John's sister and brother. A six-volume book was expensive to publish in quantity, and for the rest of his life John was forced to live in reduced circumstances. The trickle of royalties into the author's pocket was slow and, paradoxically, the more successful the book, the greater became the sums that John had to pay his printer.

As a consequence, he was forced to give up one of the rooms in his suite on the Strand, buy less expensive clothes, and eat in taverns that charged modest prices. He made no complaint, however, and enjoyed a sense of well-being that had always eluded him in earlier life. There could be no doubt that, as a result of his efforts, all England had at last awakened to the potentials of New World colonization.

Although he virtually ignored the Separatists at New Plymouth in his volume on New England, he continued to follow the establishment of their tiny colony with interest. Finally, in 1629, his work bore real fruit. As he himself writes, "Now this year a great company of good rank, zeal, means, and quality have made a great stock, and with six good ships in the months of April and May, they set sail from the Thames for the Bay of Massachusetts, otherwise called Charles River." He had good reason to believe that his propagandizing efforts had resulted in the establishment of the Massachusetts Bay Colony and the city of Boston by the settlers who called themselves Puritans.

The publication of *The Generall Historie* also gave John the social stature he had always sought. He was no longer regarded as a onetime explorer, a fading celebrity of dubious standing. He was now able to take his place among the intellectuals of London. Men thought of him as the authority on the New World, and many who had made their own mark in the world rightly considered him their equal.

He was now totally committed to the life of an author, and in 1626 he wrote the shortest and most unusual of his books. Various friends had been curious about life at sea and had listened spellbound as John had described the day-to-day existence of sailors. Sir Samuel Saltonstall, one of John's friends, persuaded him to write a handbook for young men anxious to seek their fortunes at sea.

The result was a small book that bore the strange title, *An Accidence; or, the Pathway to Experience*. In effect, it was a seventeenth-century volume of advice to adventure seekers, and because of the ever-increasing interest of young Englishmen in a nautical career, it enjoyed the most durable success of all John's books. The first printing appeared in 1626, and the following year another edition was published under the more explicit title, *The Seaman's Grammar*.

In one of the most extraordinary freaks in the history of publishing, the book prospered under both titles. New editions under the name *An Accidence* were published in 1627 and 1636. As *The Seaman's Grammar,* the book had an even longer life. Expanded versions written by others were published in 1653 and again in 1691 and 1692.

John was very proud of the book. He believed, as did most of his contemporaries, that it was the first ever written on the profession of the sailor. Other books had appeared as early as the last quarter of the preceding century, but had enjoyed no popularity, and even erudite scholars were unaware of their existence.

For all practical purposes, John's claim was accurate. He was, indeed, the first to describe a life at sea and instruct a young man who wanted to become a sailor in such matters as navigation, naval gunnery, how to evade pirate ships, and how to handle a vessel in a storm. He also discussed such personal, practical topics as the wardrobe a seaman needed and the foodstuffs it might be wise to carry in order to vary the monotony of shipboard diet. John must have been aware of a booklet written some thirty years earlier by a fellow explorer, John Davys, called *The Seaman's Secrets,* which had enjoyed a great success, but which had dealt with only a small fraction of the subjects treated in *An Accidence.*

The prestige John acquired as an author after giving up plans to lead an expedition to New England was offset by his choice of feminine companions during these years. He and the Duchess of Richmond drifted apart again, although they remained on friendly terms. Frances had grown tired of court intrigues and sexual liaisons, and had retired to the country, spending most of her time at one or another of the Richmond estates far from London.

John was at loose ends and resumed some of the habits of his younger days. He lived with an ever-changing succession of mistresses about whom little is known other than that they were young, blonde, and by no stretch of the imagination socially acceptable.

In 1628 John's nephew and namesake paid a visit to London and wrote to his parents, "My uncle's housekeeper is a doxie with yellow hair, who is as bold as you please. When I last visited him, on Tuesday, he was elsewhere, and she asked me to tumble her, which kind invitation I refused out of respect for him and that fear of the French disease which the bawds of this city do inspire."

Apparently John's lower-class mistresses did not accompany him when he dined with friends. Therefore they did no harm to his social standing. He had reached a high point in his life, and although never invited to Whitehall or the universities, was recognized as an authority on the New World. He alone was responsible for an abrupt change for the worse in his status.

At some time during the 1620s he became acquainted with one of the most curious men of the period, the Reverend Samuel Purchas. This short, slender clergyman, once described as a man with "the features of a fox, the manners of an archbishop and the soul of a cutpurse," was consumed by an ambition to succeed the late Archdeacon Hakluyt as the driving force and spiritual leader of discoverers and explorers. Although sincerely interested in far-distant, previously unknown places, he lacked Hakluyt's discernment, judgment, and scientific background. Consequently, the books he wrote on the subject contained much that was misleading, in large part because he himself was incapable of distinguishing between the accurate and the false.

Purchas made it his business to meet everyone in England who had traveled extensively, and so was acquainted with John. They saw each other infrequently, and it must be stressed that their relationship was casual. The clergyman was the rector of St. Martin's Church in London. However, he paid scant attention to the needs of his parishioners, and was known principally for two books he had published on the subject of exploration, the first in 1616 and the second in 1619.

In the early 1620s he was planning a new edition of his book, called *Pilgrimes*. In 1623 or 1624 he obtained a copy of a book that had been written, in Italian, by one Francisco Farnese, who had long been the personal secretary to Prince Sigismund Báthory—John's commander-in-chief in the war against the Turks. Farnese had dealt at some length with John's exploits in that campaign, and Purchas, who translated the book into English, printed these passages verbatim.

The new edition of *Pilgrimes* appeared in 1625, and some of John's friends, who had known nothing of his early life, were surprised to learn of his gaudy exploits in central Europe.

They were inclined to consider some of his more fantastic adventures distortions of the truth, but no one blamed him for them. After all, the stories had been written by Farnese and translated by Purchas, who died in debtors' prison in 1626, thoroughly discredited.

Occasionally someone asked John about his life as a mercenary soldier, and eventually it occurred to him that there might be a demand for a book on the subject. In 1628 he began work on *The True Travels, Adventures and Observations of Captaine John Smith,* an autobiography covering the years prior to the Jamestown expedition. The last section was a series of essays, some very brief and some long, dealing with his views on everything under the sun down to the time he completed the book.

The True Travels was registered on August 29, 1629, but John was obliged to act as his own publisher. Unfortunately, his funds were insufficient to defray the cost of the book, and he didn't acquire enough capital for the purpose until the following year. *The True Travels* first appeared in two volumes and was dedicated to the Earl of Lindsey, Lord Chamberlain of England, who was his boyhood friend Lord Willoughby.

Most of the questions regarding the veracity of John Smith's work arise from the inability of scholars, either in his own time or later, to accept many of the stories he tells. His basic facts are truthful, but he embroiders them, enlarging on theme after theme, incident after incident, in order to tell a more exciting and romantic story. Repeatedly he enlarges, magnifies, and exaggerates, and goes far beyond the dry truth related by Farnese.

Although the core of *The True Travels* is accurate, this work destroyed John's reputation as a historian. Serious scholars and friends who knew the truth were unable to accept his many adventures as real, and were irritated by his purple prose, so different from the elegant style he had employed in his previous books. The bare truth regarding his exploits was difficult enough to swallow; told in exaggerated form, his story was indigestible.

The True Travels was financially successful, but many men who had been proud to list John among their friends now laughed behind his back. Those who openly teased him were challenged to duels, which they refused to fight, and he was mortally offended when some men actually snubbed him.

It may be that, writing in retrospect after so many years, he was no longer able to distinguish truth from fiction. His conduct during these trying days indicates that he himself believed he had written an accurate autobiography.

A few friends continued to stand by him, among them Sir Samuel Saltonstall. In addition, he received a gracious letter from the Earl of Lindsey which indicated that the Lord Chamberlain, at least, accepted *The True Travels* as an authentic account.

For a time John was gloomy and changed mistresses even more rapidly. His health was failing, the attitude of Londoners distressed him, and he was glad to accept the invitation of Sir Humphrey Mildmay, a former colonel of a royal household regiment, to spend several months at the small Mildmay estate in Essex.

There, in the autumn of 1630, he wrote his last book, *Advertisements for the Unexperienced Planters of New England*. Similar to *An Accidence* in format, it was a handbook of advice to those interested in migrating to the New World.

It was published the following spring, shortly before his death, and was the least successful of all his books, perhaps because it contained little material that had not appeared in his previous works.

He was preoccupied with his health, and there were several veiled references in the book to his impending death. It is quite possible that he was thinking of his soul when he dedicated *Advertisements for the Unexperienced Planter* to the Archbishop of Canterbury, whom he did not know.

He also took the opportunity to air several grievances, returning again to a favorite theme—the ignorance of the investors who had done so much harm to Jamestown. He stated without equivocation that he considered Separatists incapable of establishing a successful colony in New England or elsewhere, stubbornly blinding himself to the fact that the Plymouth settlement was thriving after some lean and tragic years.

He had not forgotten old enemies like Captain Gabriel Archer, either, and he made fun of gentlemen-adventurers "that can neither shift Sun nor Moon, nor read their Compass, nor walk through a forest without leaving behind them a trail that the most stupid of Naturals could follow with ease."

Advertisements for the Unexperienced Planter also contained several poems. These efforts, like the occasional poem he had included in earlier books, were undistinguished jingles in which he preached little homilies.

Above all, he once again expressed his complete confidence in the future of New England and Virginia, and urged all his fellow countrymen to migrate to "this glorious land, which will prosper more than any other Country I have known." None of his contemporaries realized that he was a remarkably accurate prophet.

Early in 1631 he left Essex and returned to his lodgings in London, where he took another coarse blonde strumpet as his mistress-of-the-moment. His health had seemingly improved somewhat, and he began work on what he planned as a companion book to his *Generall Historie*. It was to be equally sweeping, and he intended to call it *History of the Sea*.

He had never forgotten his boyhood admiration of Drake and Hawkins, and his notes indicate that he hoped to dedicate it to their memories. This book was to have been a complete history of all voyages of discovery made by both Englishmen and Continentals. Material on the Cabots and later explorers who sailed under the English flag was relatively easy to assimilate and classify, but it was far more difficult to acquire what he needed from other lands. He paid several visits to the Dutch and Spanish ambassadors in England and opened a correspondence with men in Paris, Amsterdam, and Lisbon.

Had he lived, *History of the Sea* well might have become the definitive classic he wanted to write. But his enthusiasm was greater than his physical strength. In May, 1631, he had so much difficulty breathing that he was forced to suspend work on the book and retire to his bed.

John continued to enjoy a steady but modest income from the sale of his books, which had not yet earned back his investment in them. Consequently his resources were still limited. In one of the last letters he wrote, to his brother, he complains of the fees charged by physicians, "who do nought but shake their heads and prescribe for me elixirs that worsen my ague."

His mistress was his only nurse, and sickbed duty bored her so much that she frequently went out on the town for hours at a time, leaving the sick man alone. Only a few of John's friends called on him, and he fought his last battle in solitude. When he knew he would live only a short time longer, he called in an attorney and wrote his will.

He named Sir Samuel Saltonstall as his executor, and left most of his cash assets to his friend, together with most of his personal papers. Incidentally, the Saltonstall family was so strongly influenced by John's enthusiasm for the New World that Sir Samuel's descendants migrated to Massachusetts Bay, where they became prominent leaders.

John's property in Lincolnshire and the rights to his literary estate were left to his sister, his brother, and their children. His mementos of his travels, Turkish shields and scimitars, Indian knives and other personal treasures he considered precious, were to be distributed to a small handful of friends who had remained loyal to him.

One day in June the Duchess of Richmond paid a brief visit to him. She had arrived in London some weeks earlier, but had just learned of his illness. She hurried at once to his bedside. Both John and Frances found the meeting so painful that she remained with him for only a brief time, promising to return in a few days. She did not see him alive again.

On the morning of June 21, 1631, John signed his will in the presence of the attorney, Sir Samuel, and three other witnesses. His mistress was not present. He was feeling miserable, and the company left him when he expressed a desire to sleep. When his mistress returned to the rooms later in the day, she found that he had died peacefully in his sleep. He was fifty-one years old.

Only a few people attended his funeral at the Church of St. Sepulchre, among them the Duchess of Bedford, the Earl of Lindsey, and Sir Samuel, all of whom ignored the blonde strumpet who was present because she hoped he had named her a beneficiary in his will, and was furiously angry when she discovered he had left her nothing.

John was buried beneath the choir vault of the church. Over his tomb was erected a modest monument bearing the coat of arms he had won, the proof that he was a gentleman. Thirty-five years later, the church and all it contained were destroyed in London's devastating Great Fire. Only Captain John Smith's great achievements, his books, and his dubious reputation survived him.

SELECTED BIBLIOGRAPHY

THE WORKS OF CAPTAIN JOHN SMITH

A True Relation of such occurrences and accidents of noate as hath hapned in Virginia Since the First Planting of That Collony, London, 1608

A Map of Virginia, with a Description of the Countrey, Oxford, 1612

A Description of New England, London, 1616

New England's Trials, London, 1618-22

The Generall Historie of Virginia, New England and the Summer Isles, London, 1624

An Accidence; or, the Pathway to Experience, London, 1626

The True Travels, Adventures, and Observations of Captaine John Smith, London, 1630

Advertisements for the Unexperienced Planters of New England, London, 1631

OTHER SOURCES

Arber, Edward, *Captain John Smith, a Critical Survey,* Birmingham, 1886

Boyd, E., *The Story of Pocahontas and Captain John Smith,* London, 1905

Bradley, A. G., *Captain John Smith,* London, 1905

Breton, Nicholas, *The Courtier and the Countryman,* London, 1618

Brown, Alexander, *The Genesis of the United States,* Boston, 1890

Brown, John Carter, *New England's Trials,* London, 1867

Campbell, Mildred, *The English Yeoman Under Elizabeth and the Early Stuarts,* New Haven, 1942

Chatterton, E. Kemble, *John Smith,* London, 1927

Coates, Mary, *Social Life in Stuart England,* London, 1924

Davies, G., *The Early Stuarts, 1603-1660,* London, 1937

Deane, Charles, *Notes on Wingfield's Discourse on America,* Boston, 1859

Dole, Christina, *The English Housewife in the Seventeenth Century,* London, 1953

Doyle, J. A., *English in America,* London, 1882

Drummond, J. C., and Wilbraham, Anne, *The Englishman's Food,* London, 1940

Dyer, Frederick R., *The Pocahontas Myth,* Boston, 1901

Fiske, John, *Old Virginia and Her Neighbors,* New York, 1897

Forerunners and Competitors of the Pilgrims and Puritans, ed. by Charles Herbert Livermore, New York, 1912

Fuller, Thomas, *Worthies of England,* ed. by John Freeman, London, 1952

Green, John Richard, *A Short History of the English People,* London, 1915

Hart, Albert Bushnell, "American Historical Liars," *Harper's Magazine,* 1915

Haydon, A. L., *Captain John Smith,* London, 1907

Heydin, Peter, *Examen Historical, or a Discovery and Examination of the Mistakes, Falsities, and Defects in Some Modern Histories,* London, 1659

Hillard, George S., *The Life and Adventures of Captain John Smith,* Boston, 1834.

Johnson, Rossiter, *Captain John Smith,* London, 1915

Neill, Edward Duffield, *English Colonization of America,* London, 1871

———, *Virginia Company in London,* London, 1869

Palfrey, J. G., *History of New England,* Boston, 1858

Peacham, Henry, *The Compleat Gentleman,* London, 1622

Pirenne, Henri, *A History of Europe,* New York, 1938

Poindexter, John, *Captain John Smith and His Critics,* London, 1893

Purchas, Samuel, *Hakluytus Posthumas or Purchas and His Pilgrimes, contayning a History of the World in Sea Voyages and Lande Travells, by Englishmen and Others,* London, 1625

Roberts, E. P., *The Adventures of Captain John Smith,* London, 1902

Scones, W. Baptiste, *Four Centuries of English Letters,* London, 1880

Smith, Bradford, *Captain John Smith,* Philadelphia, 1953

Szerb, Anthony, "Captain John Smith in Transylvania," *Hungarian Quarterly,* VI, 1940

Tyler, Coit, *History of American Literature,* London, 1879

Warner, Charles Dudley, *Study of the Life and Writings of John Smith,* New York, 1881

Wharton, Henry, *The Life of John Smith* (translated from the Latin with an essay by Laura Polanyi Striker), Chapel Hill, N.C., 1957

Woods, K. P., *The True Story of Captain John Smith,* London, 1901

Wyler, Edith Emerson, *Facts Relating to the Turkish Captivity of Captain John Smith,* London, 1913 [illegible] History of Europe, New York, 192[illegible]

[illegible] Captain John Smith and His Critics, London, [illegible]

[illegible]

[illegible] Biographies of Captain John Smith, London, [illegible]

[illegible] of English Letters, London, [illegible]

Smith, [illegible] Captain John Smith, Philadelphia, 1953

[illegible] Captain John Smith in Pennsylvania," Pennsylvania Magazine [illegible]

Tyler, [illegible] of American Literature, London, 1879

Warner, C[illegible] Study of the Life and Writings of John Smith, [illegible]

Wharton, [illegible] The Life of John Smith (translated from the Latin [illegible] by Laura Polanyi Striker), Chapel Hill, [illegible]

Woods, [illegible] The True Story of Captain John Smith, London, 1901

Wyatt, [illegible] Facts Relating to the [illegible] Captivity of Captain John Smith, London, 1913

Index

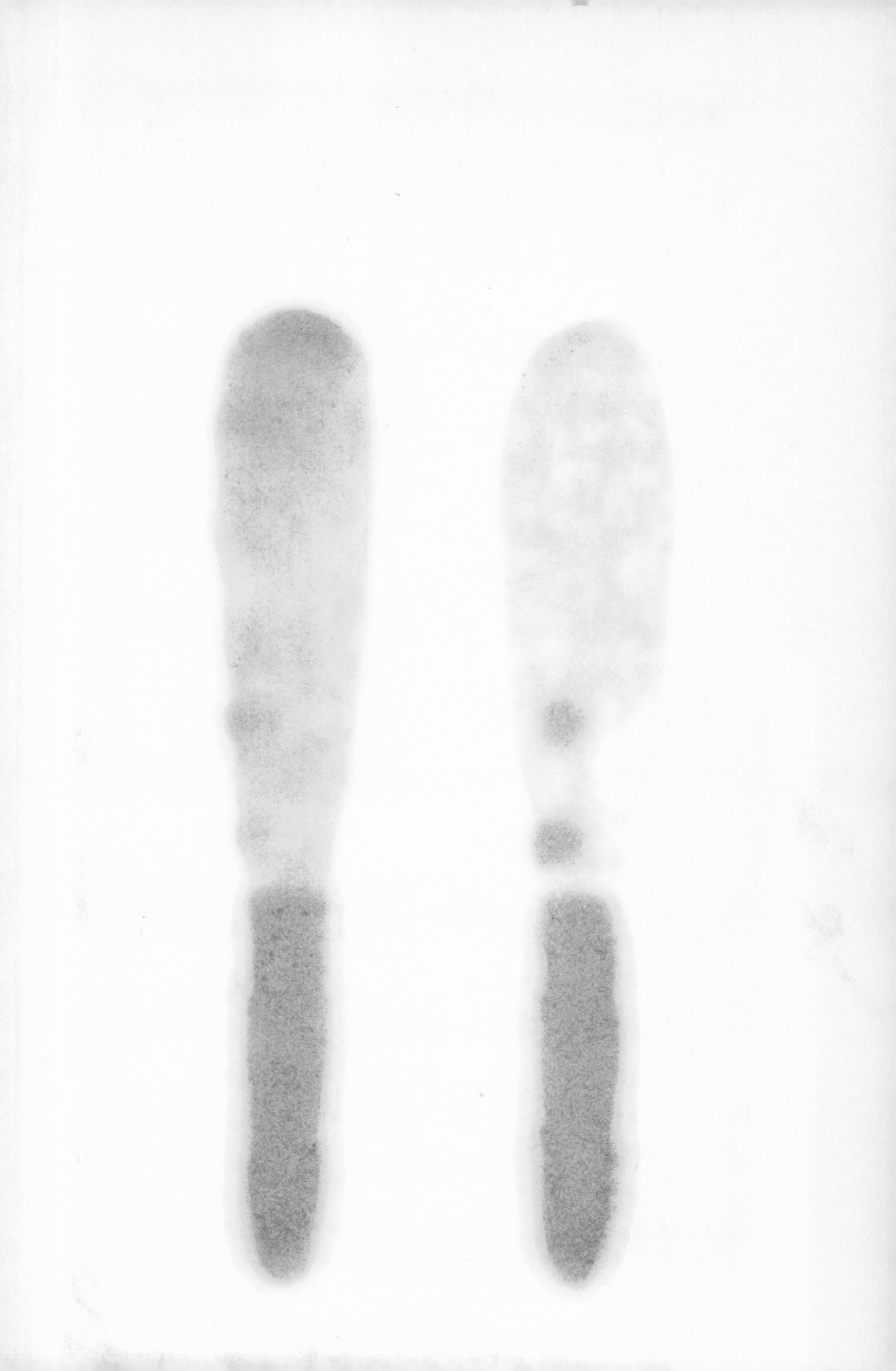

1/14/07

DATE DUE

NOV 01 2006	
OCT 21 2021	